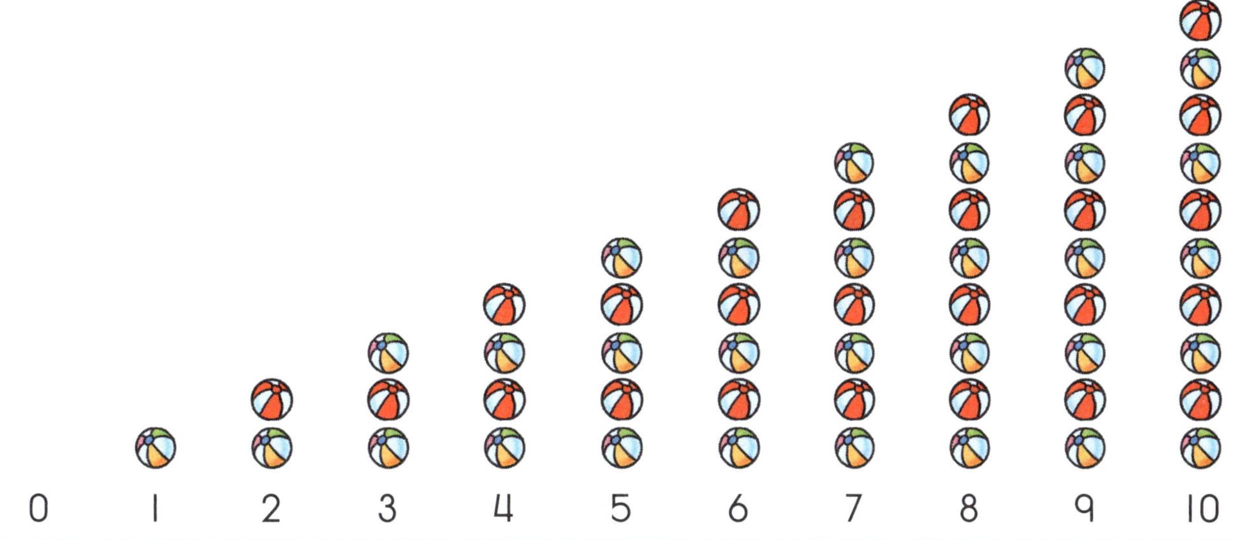

Circle the number that tells how many there are.

MATCHING NUMBERS WITH OBJECTS

How many are there in each group?
Draw a line from the group to the number.

1
2
3
4
5
6
7
8
9
10

DRAWING OBJECTS FOR NUMBERS

Draw the correct number of objects.

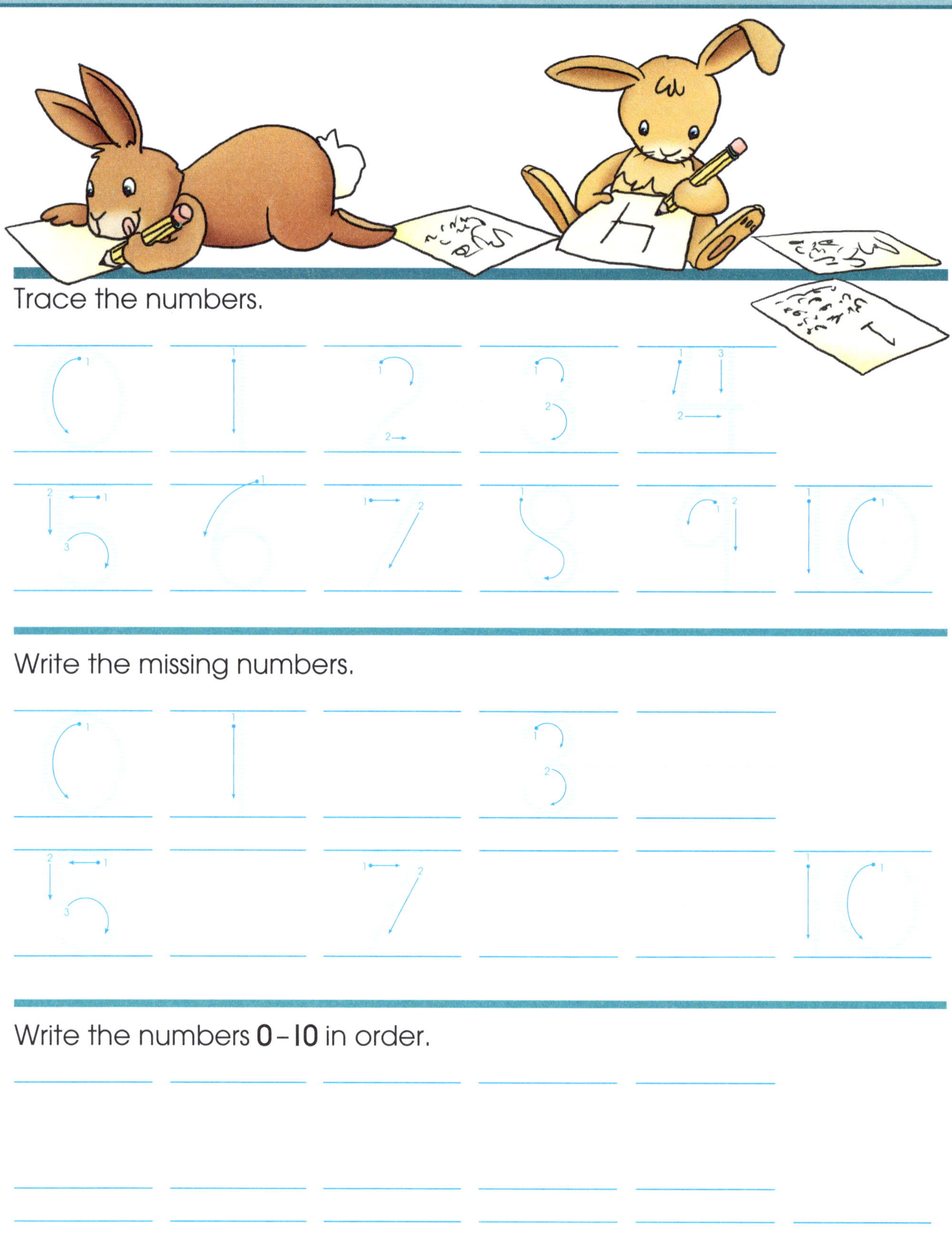

Trace the numbers.

0 1 2 3 4

5 6 7 8 9 10

Write the missing numbers.

0 1 3

5 7 10

Write the numbers **0 – 10** in order.

Write how many animals there are.

1. ______

2. ______

3. ______

4. ______

5. ______

6. ______

7. ______

8. ______

Circle the group that has **more** animals.

1.

2.

3.

4.

5.

6.
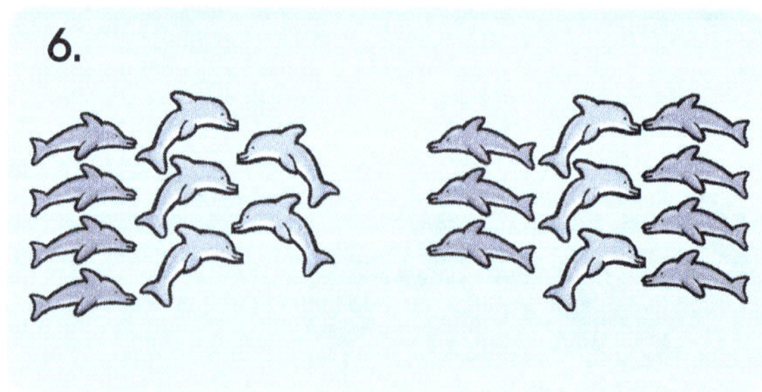

7. Draw a group of 🐟 to show **1 more** than **3**.

How many 🐟 are there? ________

WHICH NUMBER IS GREATER?

Greater means **more than.**
5 is greater than **3**.

Write how many there are in each group. Circle the **greater** number.

1.

______ ______

2.

______ ______

3.

______ ______

4.

______ ______

5.

______ ______

6.

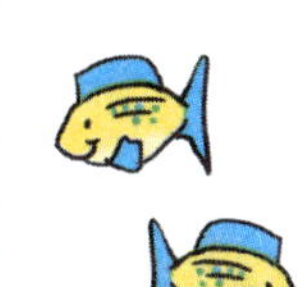

______ ______

Circle the group that has **fewer** animals.

1.

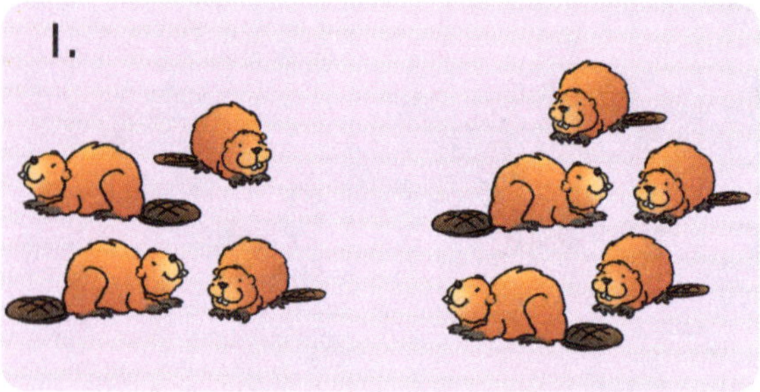

2.

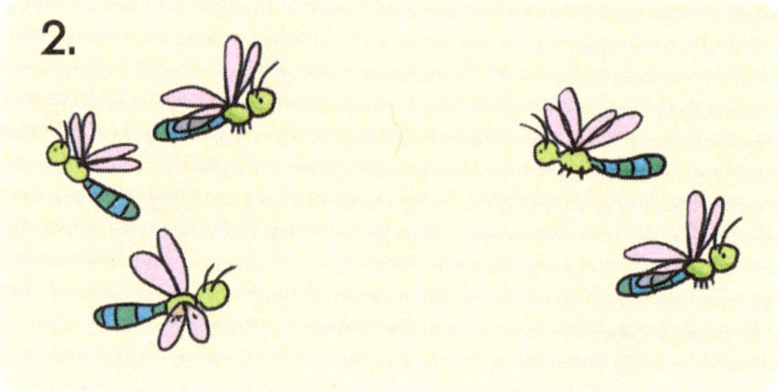

3.

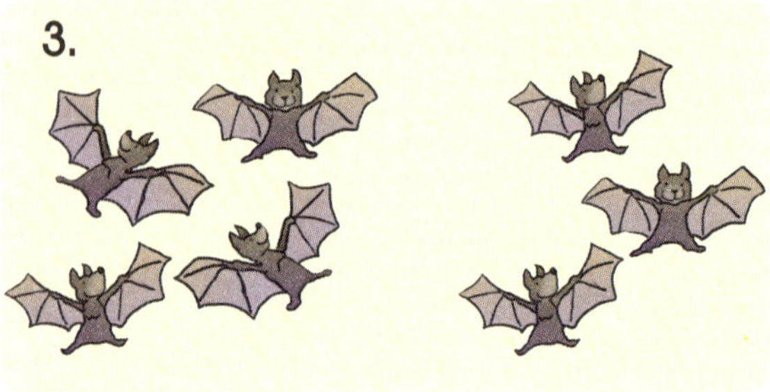

4.

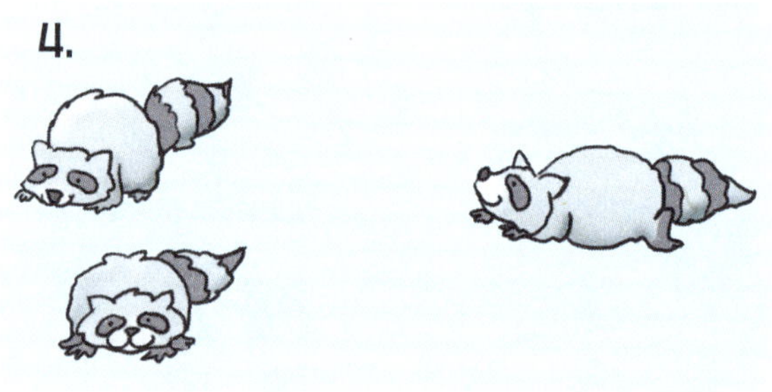

5.

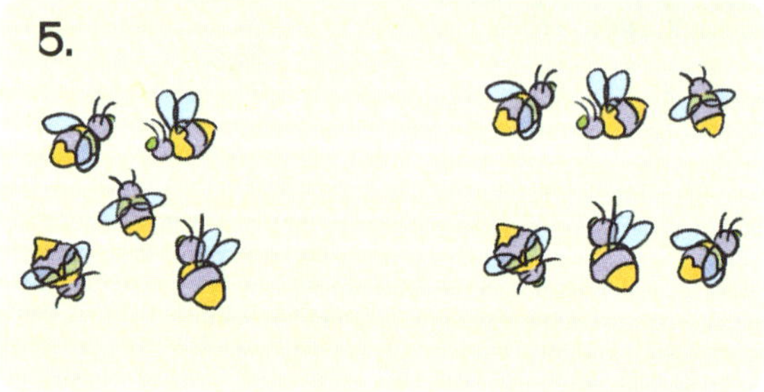

6.

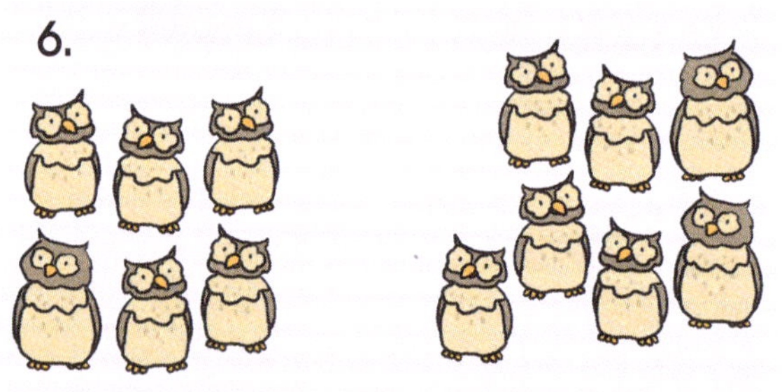

7. Draw a group of [butterfly] to show 1 **fewer** than 10.

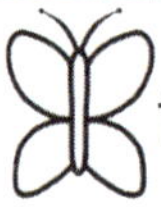

How many [butterfly] are there ? ________

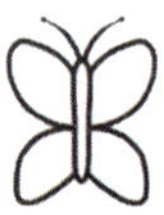

WHICH NUMBER IS LESS?

Less means **fewer** or not as many.
9 is **less** than **10**.

Write how many there are in each group. Circle the number that is **less**.

1.

2.

3.

4.
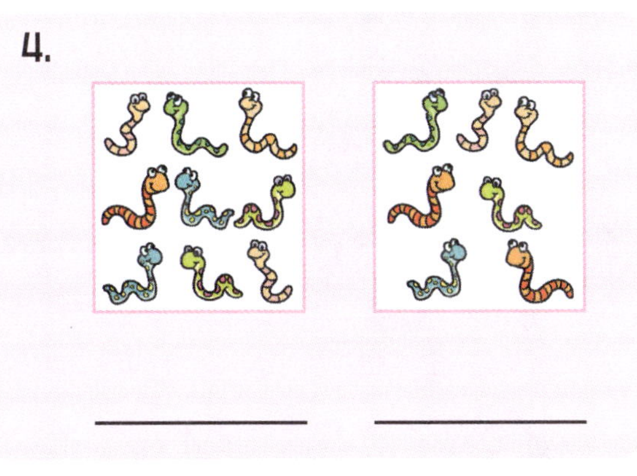

5.

6.

The answer to an addition problem is called the **sum**.
You can write an addition **number sentence** like this: **1 + 2 = 3**.

1 + 2 = 3

Look at the picture. Read the number sentence. Write the **sum**.

1.

1 + 1 = ____

2.

1 + 2 = ____

3.

1 + 3 = ____

4.

1 + 4 = ____

5.

2 + 1 = ____

6.

2 + 2 = ____

7.

2 + 3 = ____

8.

4 + 1 = ____

MORE ADDING

$$\begin{array}{r} 1 \\ +\ 2 \\ \hline 3 \end{array}$$ ← sum

Look at the picture. Read the problem. Write the **sum**.

1.   

$$\begin{array}{r} 2 \\ +\ 1 \\ \hline \_\_\_ \end{array}$$

2.     

$$\begin{array}{r} 1 \\ +\ 4 \\ \hline \_\_\_ \end{array}$$

3.     

$$\begin{array}{r} 3 \\ +\ 2 \\ \hline \_\_\_ \end{array}$$

4.    

$$\begin{array}{r} 1 \\ +\ 3 \\ \hline \_\_\_ \end{array}$$

5.     

$$\begin{array}{r} 2 \\ +\ 3 \\ \hline \_\_\_ \end{array}$$

6.  

$$\begin{array}{r} 1 \\ +\ 1 \\ \hline \_\_\_ \end{array}$$

7.   

$$\begin{array}{r} 2 \\ +\ 2 \\ \hline \_\_\_ \end{array}$$

8.   

$$\begin{array}{r} 4 \\ +\ 1 \\ \hline \_\_\_ \end{array}$$

SUBTRACTING TO FIND THE DIFFERENCE

The answer to a subtraction problem is called the **difference**.
You can write a subtraction **number sentence** like this: **5 – 2 = 3**.

5 – 2 = 3

Look at the picture. Read the number sentence. Write the **difference**.

1.

3 – 1 = _____

2.

4 – 1 = _____

3.

4 – 2 = _____

4.

5 – 4 = _____

5.

4 – 3 = _____

6.

5 – 3 = _____

7.

3 – 2 = _____

8.

2 – 1 = _____

Look at the picture. Read the problem. Write the **difference**.

Fill in the addition facts table by finding the **sums**. Color your answers. Do you see a pattern?

+	0	1	2	3	4	5
0	0					
1						
2				5		
3		4				
4						
5						

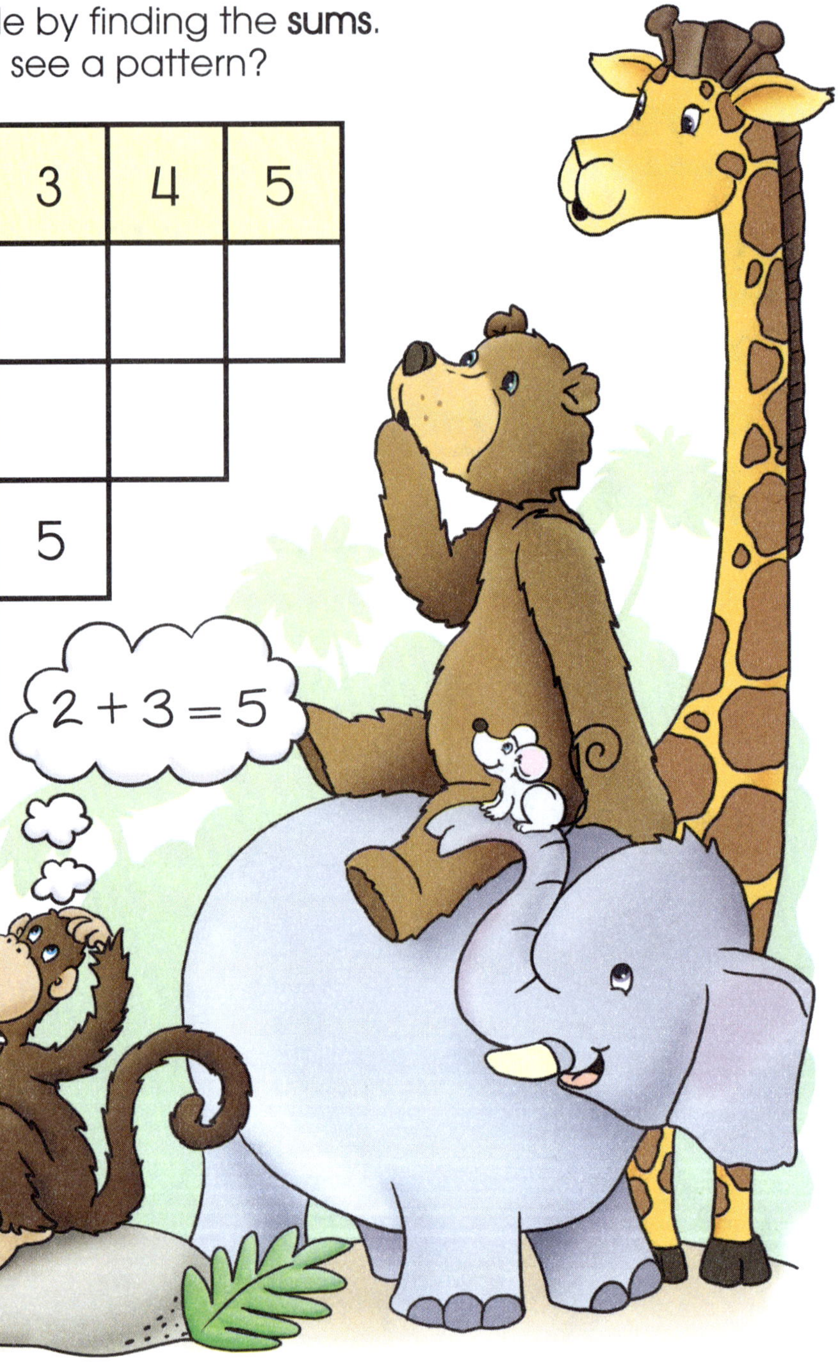

2 + 3 = 5

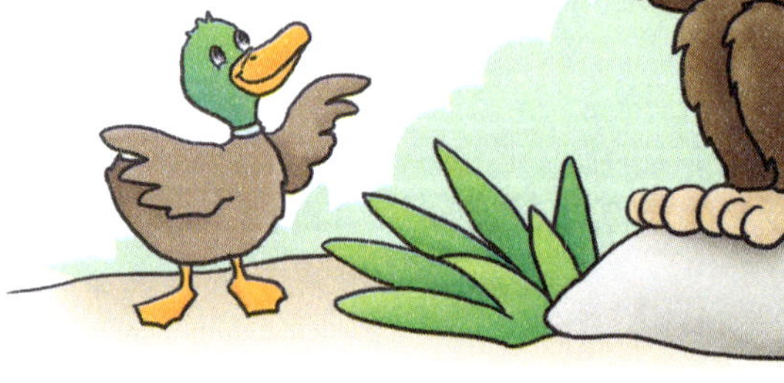

0 = 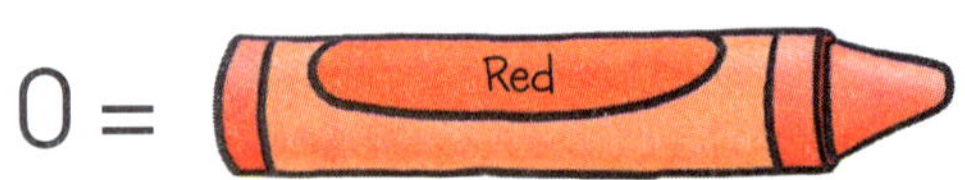

1 = 

2 = Blue

3 = Orange

4 = Yellow

5 = Green

Watch the signs!

Write the **sum** or **difference**. The addition facts table on page 14 may help you.

1. $3 + 1 =$ ______
2. $3 - 1 =$ ______
3. $2 + 0 =$ ______
4. $5 - 1 =$ ______
5. $2 + 3 =$ ______
6. $4 - 3 =$ ______
7. $2 - 0 =$ ______
8. $1 + 2 =$ ______
9. $4 + 1 =$ ______

10. $\begin{array}{r} 3 \\ + \ 1 \\ \hline \end{array}$

11. $\begin{array}{r} 2 \\ - \ 1 \\ \hline \end{array}$

12. $\begin{array}{r} 5 \\ + \ 0 \\ \hline \end{array}$

13. $\begin{array}{r} 4 \\ - \ 1 \\ \hline \end{array}$

14. $\begin{array}{r} 3 \\ - \ 2 \\ \hline \end{array}$

15. $\begin{array}{r} 0 \\ + \ 3 \\ \hline \end{array}$

16. $\begin{array}{r} 2 \\ + \ 2 \\ \hline \end{array}$

17. $\begin{array}{r} 3 \\ - \ 0 \\ \hline \end{array}$

6 + 3 = 9

Look at the picture. Read the number sentence. Write the **sum**.

1.

4 + 3 = ______

2.

2 + 6 = ______

3.

2 + 7 = ______

4.

4 + 2 = ______

5.

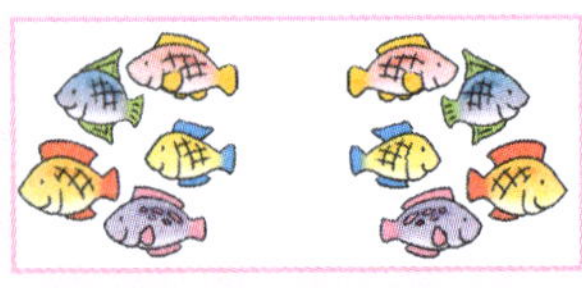

5 + 5 = ______

6.

1 + 6 = ______

7.

6 + 4 = ______

8.

4 + 5 = ______

Add 1 to the number.
Write the **sum**.

1. Add 1 to each number.
   Write the **sums**.

   6 ____

   8 ____

   7 ____

   9 ____

2. Add 2 to each number.
   Write the **sums**.

   5 ____

   7 ____

   8 ____

   6 ____

3. Add 3 to each number.
   Write the **sums**.

   5 ____

   6 ____

   4 ____

   7 ____

4. Add 4 to each number.
   Write the **sums**.

   5 ____

   3 ____

   4 ____

   6 ____

Fill in the addition facts table by finding the **sums**.

+	0	1	2	3	4	5	6	7	8	9
0	0						6			
1										
2						7				
3								10		
4										
5										
6										
7		8								
8										
9										

Write the **sums**.

9 + 1 = _____

8 + 2 = _____

7 + 3 = _____

6 + 4 = _____

5 + 5 = _____

Look at the addition facts table on page 18.
Find these facts in the table. What do you notice?

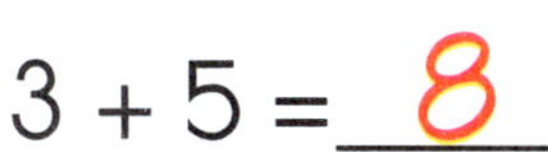

3 + 5 = 8 7 + 0 = 7

5 + 3 = 8 0 + 7 = 7

Write the **sums**. The addition facts table on page 18 may help you.

1. 6 + 3 = ____ 2. 5 + 2 = ____ 3. 7 + 3 = ____

 3 + 6 = ____ 2 + 5 = ____ 3 + 7 = ____

4. 9 + 1 = ____ 5. 6 + 2 = ____ 6. 8 + 0 = ____

 1 + 9 = ____ 2 + 6 = ____ 0 + 8 = ____

Write the **sum** and another fact that uses the same numbers.

7. 4 + 5 = ____ 8. 3 + 4 = ____ 9. 6 + 0 = ____

 ___ + ___ = ___ ___ + ___ = ___ ___ + ___ = ___

10. 8 + 2 = ____ 11. 0 + 9 = ____ 12. 1 + 7 = ____

 ___ + ___ = ___ ___ + ___ = ___ ___ + ___ = ___

Write addition facts for the numbers.

13. 2, 7, 9 14. 4, 6, 10 15. 0, 8, 8

 ___ + ___ = ___ ___ + ___ = ___ ___ + ___ = ___

 ___ + ___ = ___ ___ + ___ = ___ ___ + ___ = ___

A number line can help you find **differences**.

9 – 3 = 6

0 1 2 3 4 5 6 7 8 9 10

Count back from **9**.

$$\begin{array}{r} 9 \\ -\ 3 \\ \hline 6 \end{array}$$

Write the **difference**.

1. 8 – 3 = ____
2. 7 – 2 = ____
3. 10 – 4 = ____
4. 9 – 1 = ____
5. 6 – 0 = ____
6. 8 – 4 = ____

7. $\begin{array}{r} 6 \\ -\ 4 \\ \hline \end{array}$
8. $\begin{array}{r} 8 \\ -\ 2 \\ \hline \end{array}$
9. $\begin{array}{r} 5 \\ -\ 5 \\ \hline \end{array}$
10. $\begin{array}{r} 9 \\ -\ 4 \\ \hline \end{array}$
11. $\begin{array}{r} 10 \\ -\ 3 \\ \hline \end{array}$
12. $\begin{array}{r} 7 \\ -\ 4 \\ \hline \end{array}$
13. $\begin{array}{r} 9 \\ -\ 7 \\ \hline \end{array}$
14. $\begin{array}{r} 10 \\ -\ 8 \\ \hline \end{array}$

15. Write a subtraction equation for this number line.

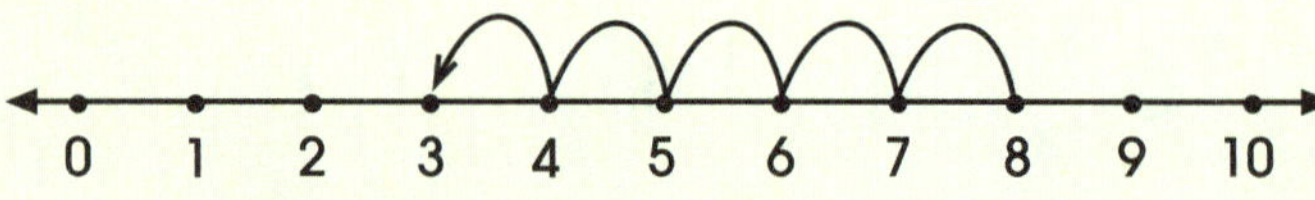

____ – ____ = ____

SUBTRACTION FACT PAIRS

Look at these subtraction facts:

8 − 3 = 5　　9 − 0 = 9

8 − 5 = 3　　9 − 9 = 0

Write the **differences**.

1. 7 − 3 = ____　　7 − 4 = ____
2. 9 − 5 = ____　　9 − 4 = ____
3. 7 − 0 = ____　　7 − 7 = ____
4. 9 − 1 = ____　　9 − 8 = ____
5. 10 − 2 = ____　　10 − 8 = ____
6. 8 − 6 = ____　　8 − 2 = ____

Write the **difference** and another fact that uses the same numbers.

7. 9 − 5 = ____　　___ − ___ = ___
8. 7 − 5 = ____　　___ − ___ = ___
9. 6 − 0 = ____　　___ − ___ = ___
10. 10 − 2 = ____　　___ − ___ = ___
11. 8 − 8 = ____　　___ − ___ = ___
12. 8 − 1 = ____　　___ − ___ = ___

Write subtraction facts for the numbers.

13. 3, 6, 9
___ − ___ = ___
___ − ___ = ___

14. 2, 8, 10
___ − ___ = ___
___ − ___ = ___

15. 0, 9, 9
___ − ___ = ___
___ − ___ = ___

Write the **differences**.
Color the picture.

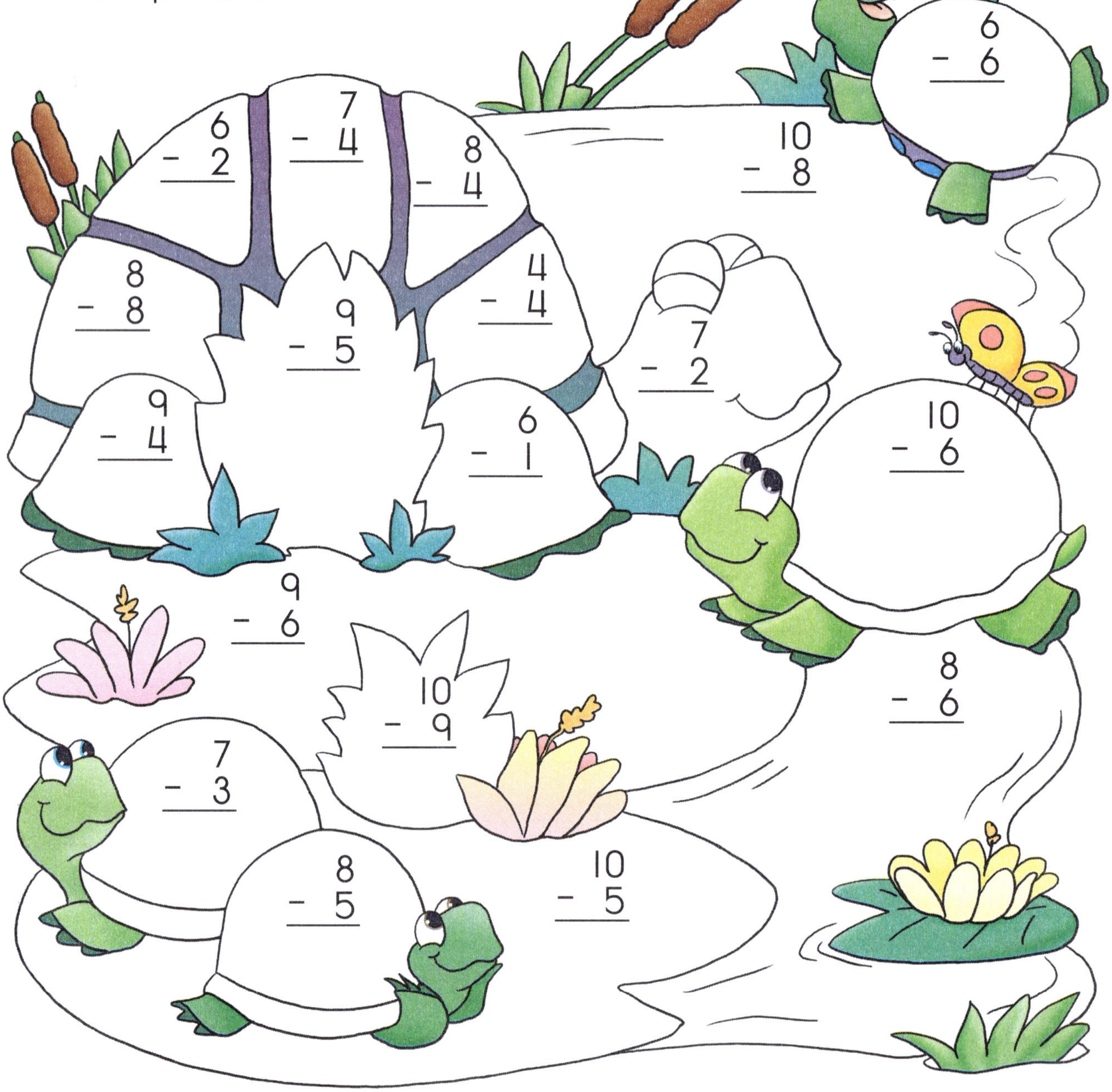

$6 - 2$

$7 - 4$

$8 - 4$

$6 - 6$

$10 - 8$

$8 - 8$

$9 - 5$

$4 - 4$

$7 - 2$

$9 - 4$

$6 - 1$

$10 - 6$

$9 - 6$

$10 - 9$

$8 - 6$

$7 - 3$

$8 - 5$

$10 - 5$

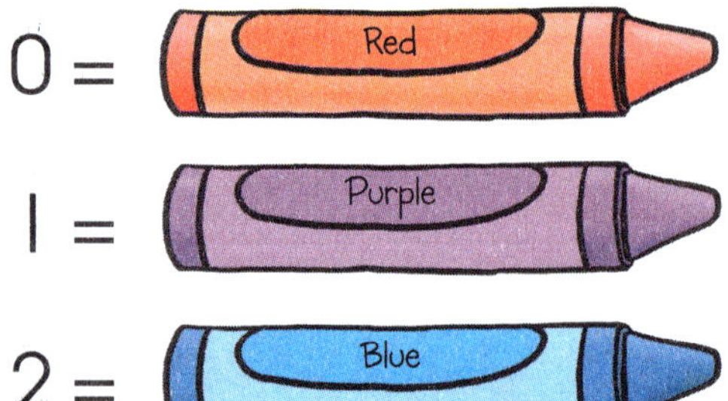

Write the **sum** or **difference**.

1. 8 + 1 = _____
2. 7 – 2 = _____
3. 9 + 0 = _____
4. 10 – 1 = _____
5. 6 + 3 = _____
6. 8 – 3 = _____
7. 8 – 0 = _____
8. 7 + 2 = _____
9. 4 + 6 = _____

Beeeee sure to watch those signs!

10. $\begin{array}{r} 1 \\ +\ 9 \\ \hline \end{array}$

11. $\begin{array}{r} 5 \\ -\ 1 \\ \hline \end{array}$

12. $\begin{array}{r} 7 \\ +\ 0 \\ \hline \end{array}$

13. $\begin{array}{r} 9 \\ -\ 2 \\ \hline \end{array}$

14. $\begin{array}{r} 3 \\ -\ 0 \\ \hline \end{array}$

15. $\begin{array}{r} 3 \\ +\ 7 \\ \hline \end{array}$

16. $\begin{array}{r} 5 \\ +\ 5 \\ \hline \end{array}$

17. $\begin{array}{r} 6 \\ -\ 0 \\ \hline \end{array}$

Match.

Circle groups of 10.	10 and More	Number
1.	10 and 3	11
		12
2.	10 and 5	13
		14
3.	10 and 1	15
		16
4.	10 and 7	17
		18
5.	10 and 10	19
		20
6.	10 and 6	

I through 10	1	2	3	4	5	6	7	8	9	10
11 and more	11	12	13	14	15	16	17	18	19	20

Write the missing numbers.

1. 11, 12, ____ , 14, ____ , 16, ____ , 18, ____ , 20

2. 11, ____ , ____ , ____ , 15, ____ , ____ , ____ , 19

3. 5, ____ , ____ , 8, ____ , ____ , 11, ____ , ____ , 14

4. ____ , ____ , 13, ____ , ____ , ____ , 17, ____ , ____ , 20

5. Connect the dots.

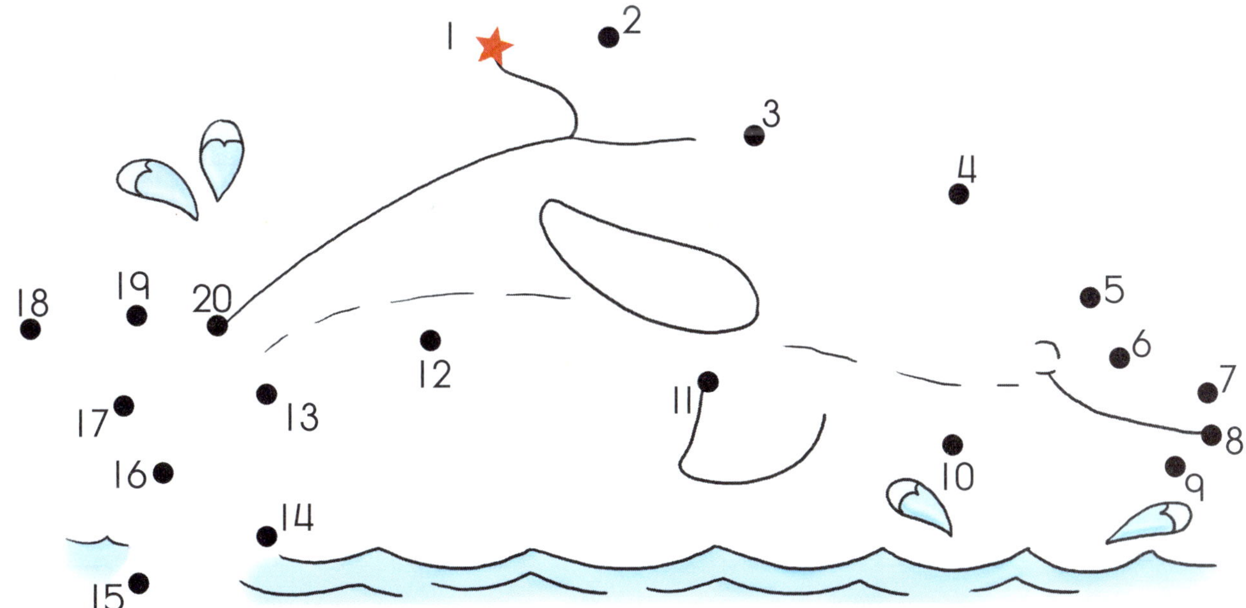

Write a number sentence about the domino.

1. 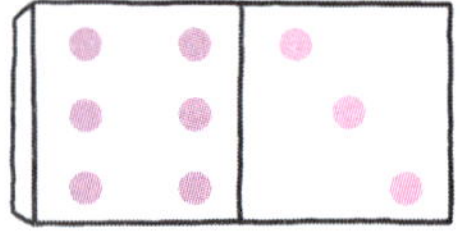

___ + ___ = ___

2. 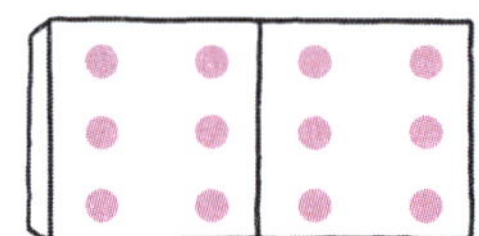

___ + ___ = ___

3. 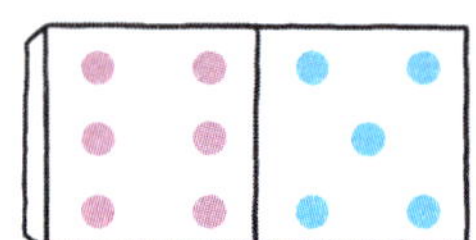

___ + ___ = ___

4. 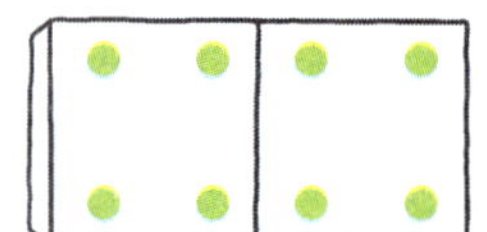

___ + ___ = ___

5. 

___ + ___ = ___

6. 

___ + ___ = ___

7. ___ + ___ = ___

8. ___ + ___ = ___

9. ___ + ___ = ___

Draw dots on the domino to find the **sum** for the problem. Write the **sum**.

10. 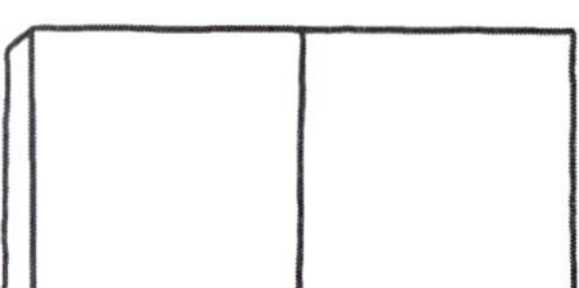

6 + 5 = ___

11. 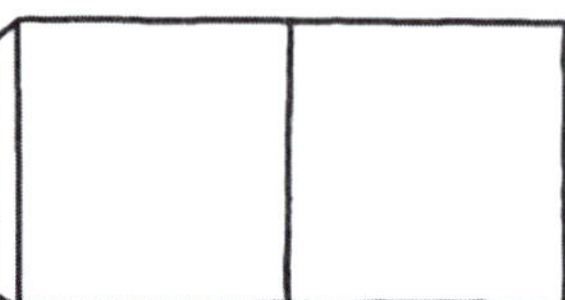

6 + 6 = ___

12. 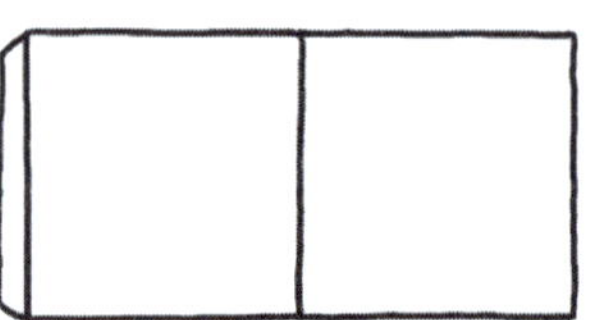

4 + 6 = ___

A number line can help you find the **sum**.

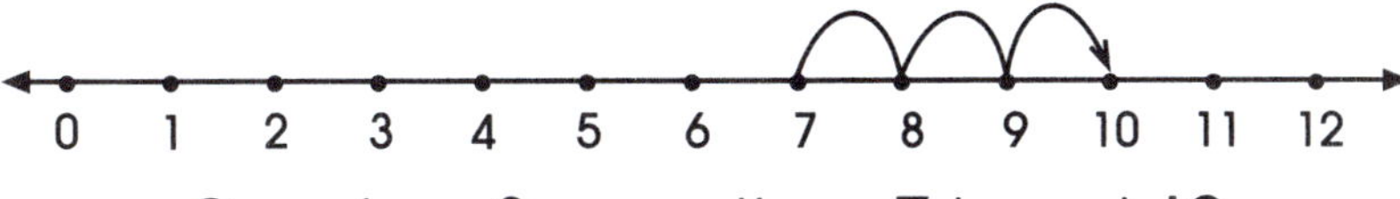

Count on **3** more than **7** to get **10**.

Write the **sum**.

1. $\begin{array}{r} 5 \\ +\ 6 \\ \hline \end{array}$
2. $\begin{array}{r} 8 \\ +\ 3 \\ \hline \end{array}$
3. $\begin{array}{r} 9 \\ +\ 1 \\ \hline \end{array}$
4. $\begin{array}{r} 4 \\ +\ 4 \\ \hline \end{array}$
5. $\begin{array}{r} 7 \\ +\ 5 \\ \hline \end{array}$
6. $\begin{array}{r} 3 \\ +\ 9 \\ \hline \end{array}$
7. $\begin{array}{r} 7 \\ +\ 2 \\ \hline \end{array}$
8. $\begin{array}{r} 9 \\ +\ 2 \\ \hline \end{array}$
9. $\begin{array}{r} 6 \\ +\ 6 \\ \hline \end{array}$
10. $\begin{array}{r} 7 \\ +\ 4 \\ \hline \end{array}$
11. $\begin{array}{r} 5 \\ +\ 5 \\ \hline \end{array}$
12. $\begin{array}{r} 8 \\ +\ 4 \\ \hline \end{array}$

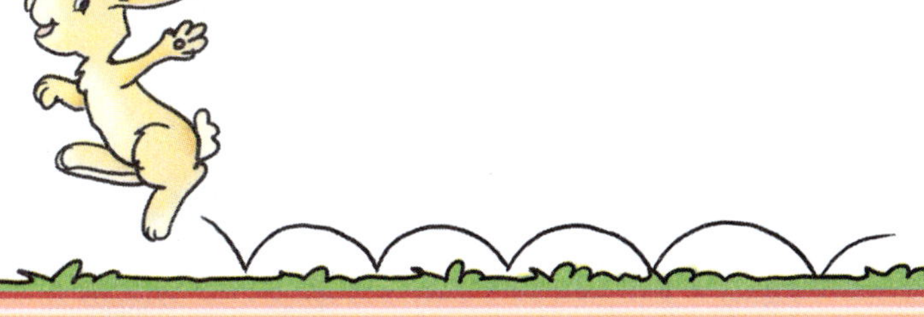

MORE SUBTRACTION FACTS

10 – 3 = 7

0 1 2 3 4 5 6 7 8 9 10 11 12

10 – 7 = 3

0 1 2 3 4 5 6 7 8 9 10 11 12

Write the **differences**.

1. 10 – 2 = ____

   10 – 8 = ____

2. 12 – 8 = ____

   12 – 4 = ____

3. 12 – 3 = ____

   12 – 9 = ____

4. 12 – 6 = ____

5. 12 – 5 = ____

   12 – 7 = ____

6. 11 – 3 = ____

   11 – 8 = ____

7. 11 – 4 = ____

   11 – 7 = ____

8. 11 – 5 = ____

   11 – 6 = ____

$$\begin{array}{r} 11 \\ -\ 7 \\ \hline 4 \end{array}$$

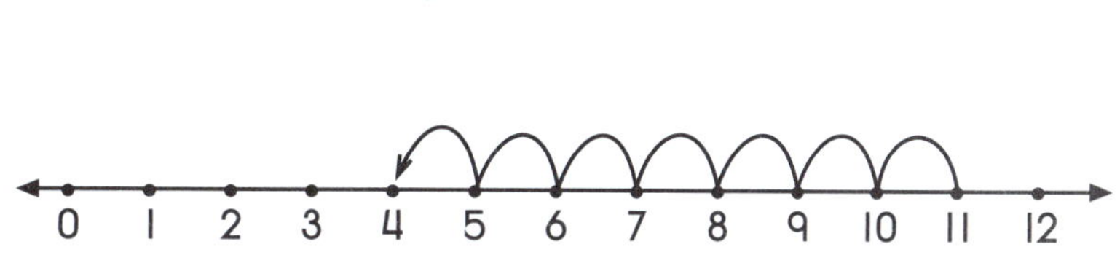

Write the **difference**.

1. $\begin{array}{r} 11 \\ -\ 5 \\ \hline \end{array}$

2. $\begin{array}{r} 10 \\ -\ 4 \\ \hline \end{array}$

3. $\begin{array}{r} 9 \\ -\ 5 \\ \hline \end{array}$

4. $\begin{array}{r} 12 \\ -\ 6 \\ \hline \end{array}$

5. $\begin{array}{r} 11 \\ -\ 3 \\ \hline \end{array}$

6. $\begin{array}{r} 10 \\ -\ 2 \\ \hline \end{array}$

7. $\begin{array}{r} 12 \\ -\ 4 \\ \hline \end{array}$

8. $\begin{array}{r} 11 \\ -\ 2 \\ \hline \end{array}$

9. $\begin{array}{r} 12 \\ -\ 7 \\ \hline \end{array}$

10. $\begin{array}{r} 12 \\ -\ 5 \\ \hline \end{array}$

11. $\begin{array}{r} 11 \\ -\ 4 \\ \hline \end{array}$

12. $\begin{array}{r} 12 \\ -\ 8 \\ \hline \end{array}$

Write the **sums** and **differences**.

Follow the path around the animals that like water.
Write the **sums** and **differences**.
Some examples are done for you.

WHICH PROBLEMS GIVE THE ANSWER?

Circle the problems that equal each number.
The first one is done for you.

1. Circle the problems that equal 9.

   10 – 1   2 + 7   8 + 1   3 + 5   11 – 3

2. Circle the problems that equal 5.

   3 + 3   6 – 1   5 + 1   5 + 0   9 – 4

3. Circle the problems that equal 8.

   10 – 2   4 + 4   6 + 3   2 + 6   12 – 6

4. Circle the problems that equal 10.

   12 – 3   6 + 4   7 + 3   4 + 5   11 – 1

5. Circle the problems that equal 12.

   4 + 7   12 – 0   8 + 4   7 + 5   6 + 5

6. Circle the problems that equal 6.

   3 + 3   12 – 6   5 + 1   9 + 3   11 – 4

7. Circle the problems that equal 11.

   6 + 4   9 + 2   5 + 6   7 + 5   8 + 3

8. Circle the problems that equal 7.

   7 + 0   11 – 4   4 + 3   2 + 6   12 – 1

Write the **differences**.
Color the picture.

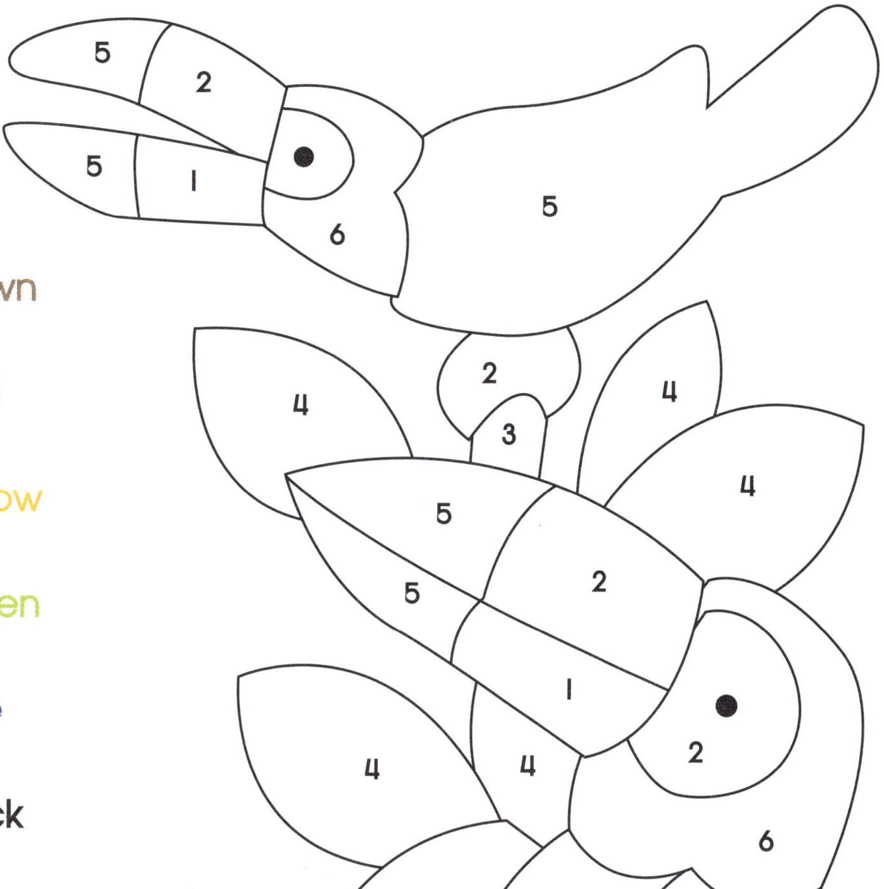

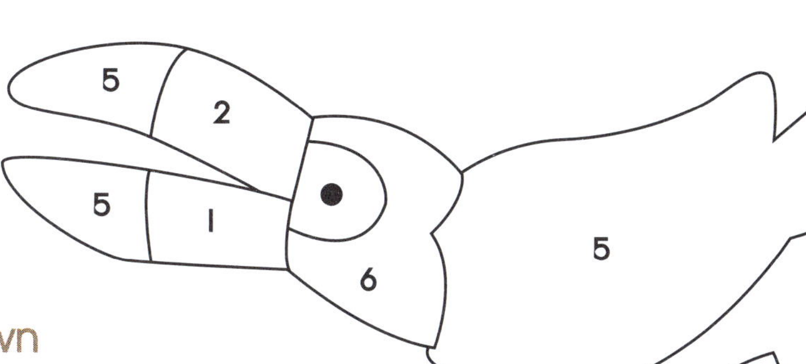

12 – 9 = ______ Brown

10 – 9 = ______ Red

11 – 9 = ______ Yellow

12 – 8 = ______ Green

12 – 6 = ______ Blue

11 – 6 = ______ Black

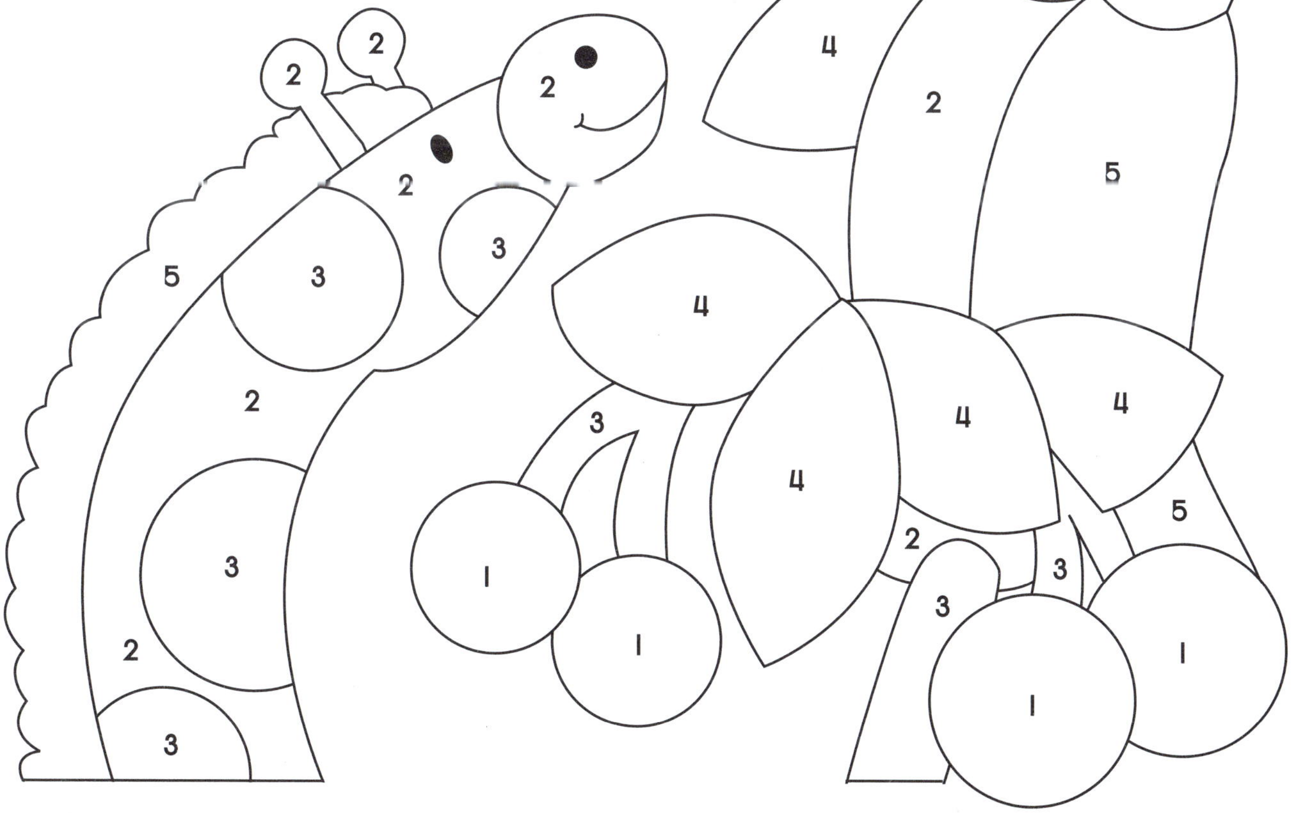

1 tens 1 ones

How many? 11

Count the objects. Circle the objects in groups of ten.
Write how many **tens** and **ones** there are. Then write the number.

1. ______ tens ______ ones

How many? ______

2. ______ tens ______ ones

How many? ______

3. ______ tens ______ ones

How many? ______

4. ______ tens ______ ones

How many? ______

5. ______ tens ______ ones

How many? ______

6. ______ tens ______ ones

How many? ______

2 tens 3 ones

tens ones
23

Count the **tens** and **ones**. Write how many **tens** and **ones** there are.

1. ______ tens ______ ones

tens ones
______

2. ______ tens ______ ones

tens ones
______

3. ______ tens ______ ones

tens ones
______

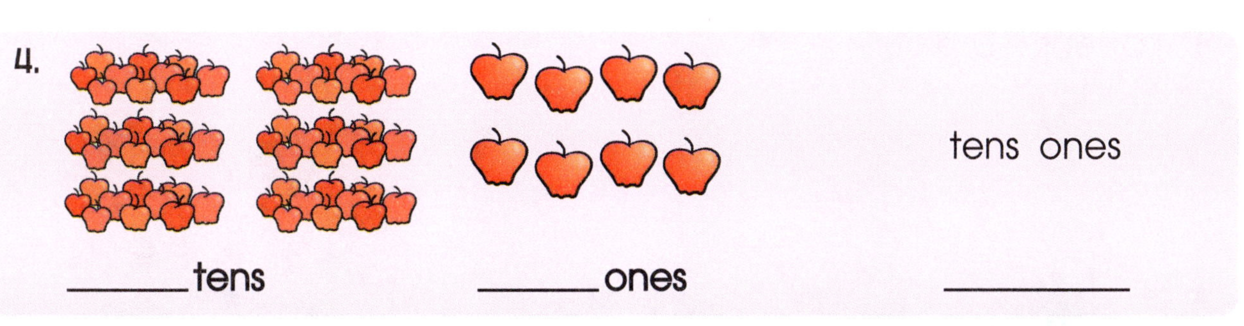

4. ______ tens ______ ones

tens ones
______

MATCHING NUMBERS WITH TENS & ONES

Write the number.
Match the number to the correct picture.

1. 2 tens 6 ones 26

2. 4 tens 1 one ______

3. 7 tens 0 ones ______

4. 5 tens 8 ones ______

5. 6 tens 2 ones ______

6. 8 tens 5 ones ______

7. 3 tens 7 ones ______

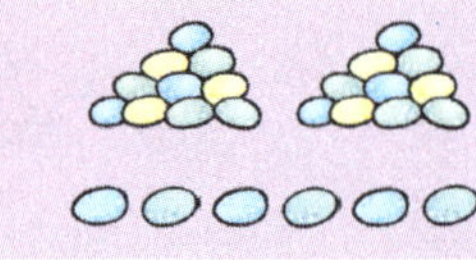

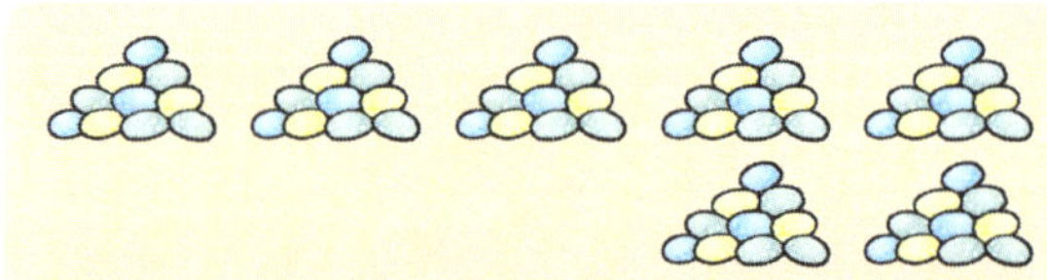

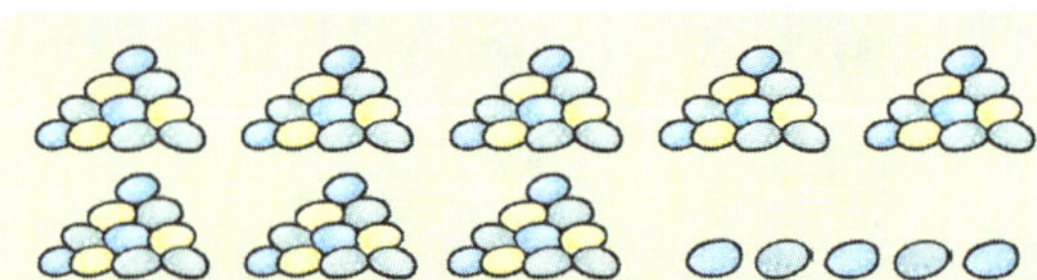

Read each number.
Write how many **tens** and **ones** there are.

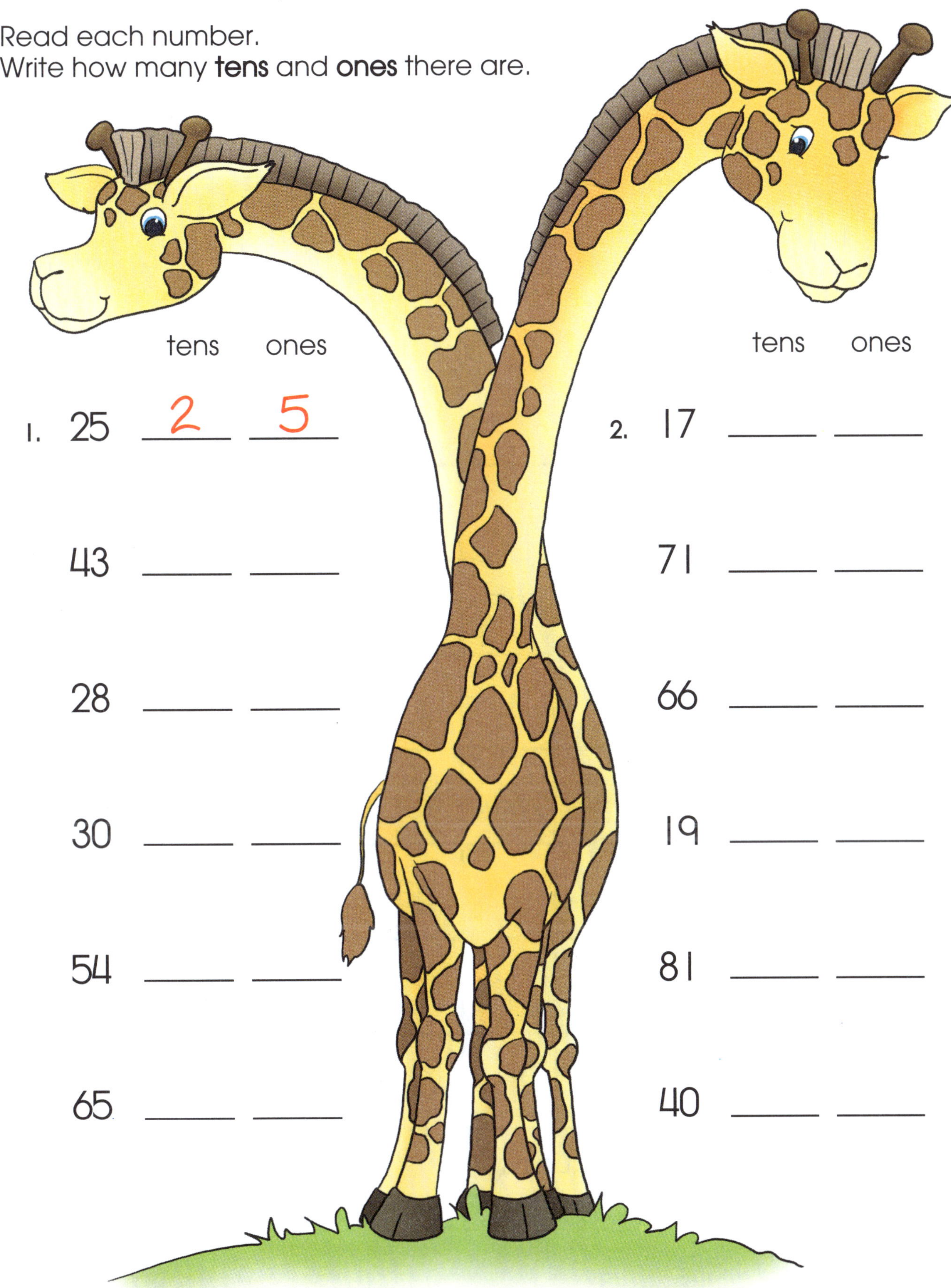

		tens	ones
1.	25	2	5
	43	____	____
	28	____	____
	30	____	____
	54	____	____
	65	____	____

		tens	ones
2.	17	____	____
	71	____	____
	66	____	____
	19	____	____
	81	____	____
	40	____	____

Count to **100**.
Write the missing numbers.

1									
2	12						72		
			33						
						64			
				45					
		26							
					58				
10					60				100

Count by **2**s. Circle those squares.

Write the missing numbers.

1. 1, 2, ____, 4, 5, ____, 7, ____, ____, 10

2. 41, ____, ____, ____, 45, 46, ____, 48, ____, 50

3. ____, 72, 73, ____, 75, ____, ____, 78, ____, ____

4. 31, ____, ____, ____, 35, ____, 37, ____, ____, ____

5. ____, ____, 83, ____, ____, ____, ____, 88, ____, 90

6. 61, ____, ____, ____, ____, ____, ____, ____, ____

7. 91, ____, 93, ____, ____, ____, ____, ____, 99, ____

Connect the dots.
Start at the ▲ and count by **ones** to **21**.
Start at the ■ and count by **tens** to **100**.

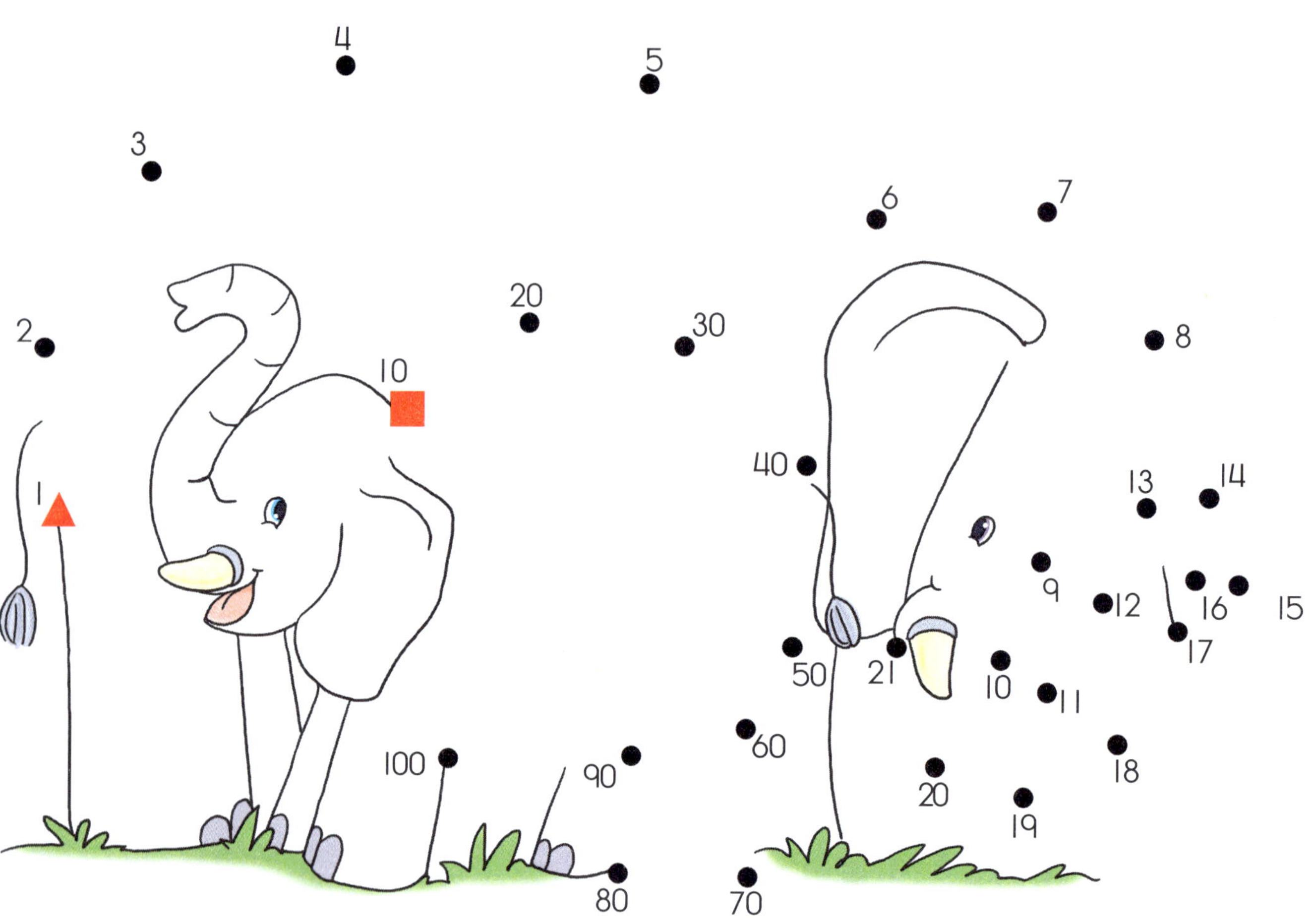

Count by **tens** to **100**. Write the missing numbers.

10	____	30	____	____
____	70	____	____	____

Write the number that comes **before**.

1. 17 18
2. ______ 33
3. ______ 24
4. ______ 67
5. ______ 81
6. ______ 30
7. ______ 45
8. ______ 27

Write the number that comes **after**.

9. 22 23
10. 11 ______
11. 18 ______
12. 37 ______
13. 27 ______
14. 6 ______
15. 38 ______
16. 69 ______

Write how many **tens** and **ones** there are in each group.
Then write the numbers. Circle the **greater** number.

1.

3 tens 2 ones — 2 tens 3 ones

32 — 23

2.

____ tens ____ ones — ____ tens ____ ones

______ — ______

3.

____ tens ____ ones — ____ tens ____ ones

______ — ______

4.

____ tens ____ ones — ____ tens ____ ones

______ — ______

5.

____ tens ____ ones — ____ tens ____ ones

______ — ______

6.

____ tens ____ ones — ____ tens ____ ones

______ — ______

Circle the number that is **greater**.

1.	23	14	2.	50	48	3.	25	31
4.	19	21	5.	35	27	6.	10	15
7.	18	10	8.	13	31	9.	43	34

Circle the number that is **less**.

10.	55	48	11.	25	31	12.	23	36
13.	62	59	14.	18	13	15.	25	31
16.	58	69	17.	44	54	18.	78	82

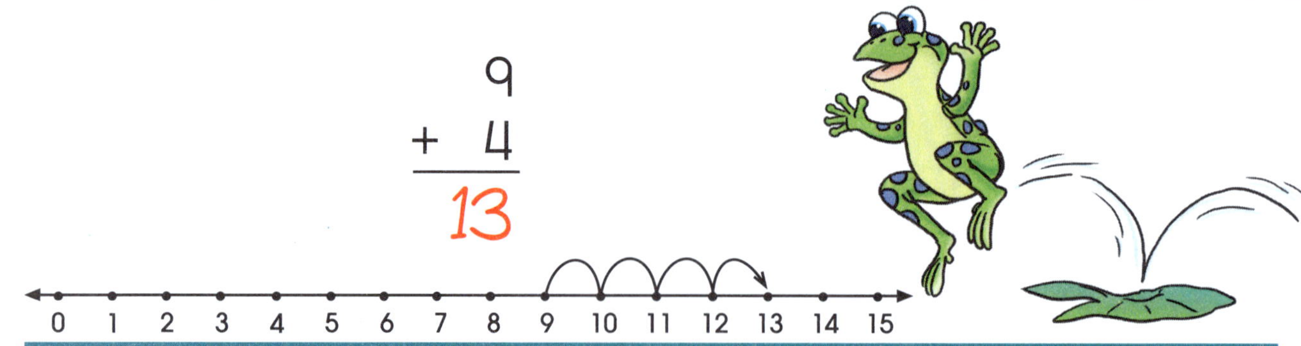

Write the **sum**.

1. $\begin{array}{r} 8 \\ +\ 5 \\ \hline \end{array}$
2. $\begin{array}{r} 7 \\ +\ 7 \\ \hline \end{array}$
3. $\begin{array}{r} 9 \\ +\ 6 \\ \hline \end{array}$
4. $\begin{array}{r} 8 \\ +\ 4 \\ \hline \end{array}$
5. $\begin{array}{r} 7 \\ +\ 6 \\ \hline \end{array}$
6. $\begin{array}{r} 5 \\ +\ 9 \\ \hline \end{array}$
7. $\begin{array}{r} 8 \\ +\ 7 \\ \hline \end{array}$
8. $\begin{array}{r} 6 \\ +\ 6 \\ \hline \end{array}$
9. $\begin{array}{r} 6 \\ +\ 8 \\ \hline \end{array}$
10. $\begin{array}{r} 7 \\ +\ 5 \\ \hline \end{array}$
11. $\begin{array}{r} 4 \\ +\ 9 \\ \hline \end{array}$
12. $\begin{array}{r} 8 \\ +\ 3 \\ \hline \end{array}$
13. $\begin{array}{r} 7 \\ +\ 4 \\ \hline \end{array}$
14. $\begin{array}{r} 9 \\ +\ 0 \\ \hline \end{array}$
15. $\begin{array}{r} 7 \\ +\ 8 \\ \hline \end{array}$
16. $\begin{array}{r} 5 \\ +\ 5 \\ \hline \end{array}$

Write the **sum**.

1. $6 + 7 =$ _____
2. $4 + 9 =$ _____
3. $6 + 6 =$ _____
4. $8 + 6 =$ _____
5. $7 + 5 =$ _____
6. $8 + 0 =$ _____
7. $7 + 8 =$ _____
8. $5 + 9 =$ _____
9. $7 + 7 =$ _____

Write the missing number.

10. $6 +$ ____ $= 14$
11. $9 +$ ____ $= 15$
12. $8 +$ ____ $= 12$
13. ____ $+ 7 = 13$
14. $8 +$ ____ $= 8$
15. ____ $+ 4 = 11$
16. $3 +$ ____ $= 10$
17. $7 +$ ____ $= 15$
18. ____ $+ 9 = 14$

Think of an addition fact to help you find the **difference**.

14 – 6 = 8

Write the **difference**.

1. 11 – 7 = ____ 2. 13 – 9 = ____ 3. 12 – 5 = ____

4. 15 – 9 = ____ 5. 10 – 9 = ____ 6. 14 – 7 = ____

7. 12 – 3 = ____ 8. 15 – 8 = ____ 9. 13 – 8 = ____

10. 14 – 5 = ____ 11. 13 – 6 = ____ 12. 7 – 0 = ____

13. 12 – 8 = ____ 14. 9 – 9 = ____ 15. 14 – 9 = ____

16. 15 – 7 = ____ 17. 13 – 5 = ____ 18. 11 – 2 = ____

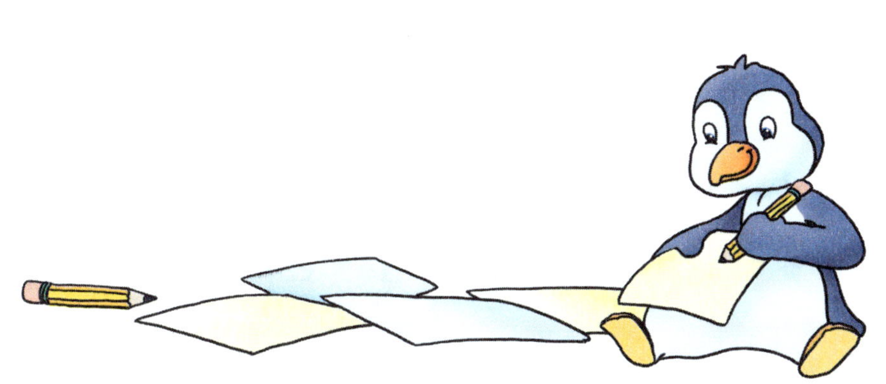

Write the **sum** or **difference**.

1. $\begin{array}{r} 9 \\ +\ 3 \\ \hline \end{array}$

2. $\begin{array}{r} 11 \\ -\ 6 \\ \hline \end{array}$

3. $\begin{array}{r} 8 \\ +\ 7 \\ \hline \end{array}$

4. $\begin{array}{r} 11 \\ -\ 5 \\ \hline \end{array}$

5. $\begin{array}{r} 12 \\ -\ 9 \\ \hline \end{array}$

6. $\begin{array}{r} 14 \\ -\ 6 \\ \hline \end{array}$

7. $\begin{array}{r} 8 \\ +\ 5 \\ \hline \end{array}$

8. $\begin{array}{r} 0 \\ +\ 9 \\ \hline \end{array}$

9. $\begin{array}{r} 9 \\ +\ 6 \\ \hline \end{array}$

10. $\begin{array}{r} 12 \\ -\ 5 \\ \hline \end{array}$

11. $\begin{array}{r} 13 \\ -\ 7 \\ \hline \end{array}$

12. $\begin{array}{r} 12 \\ -\ 3 \\ \hline \end{array}$

13. $\begin{array}{r} 14 \\ -\ 5 \\ \hline \end{array}$

14. $\begin{array}{r} 9 \\ +\ 4 \\ \hline \end{array}$

15. $\begin{array}{r} 8 \\ -\ 8 \\ \hline \end{array}$

16. $\begin{array}{r} 7 \\ +\ 7 \\ \hline \end{array}$

Here are four more new addition facts to remember:

8 + 8 = 16 8 + 9 = 17

9 + 7 = 16 9 + 9 = 18

Write the **sum**.

1. 8 + 6 = ____
2. 8 + 7 = ____
3. 8 + 8 = ____
4. 7 + 7 = ____
5. 7 + 8 = ____
6. 7 + 9 = ____
7. 9 + 7 = ____
8. 9 + 8 = ____
9. 9 + 9 = ____

10. $\begin{array}{r} 8 \\ +\ 5 \\ \hline \end{array}$

11. $\begin{array}{r} 6 \\ +\ 7 \\ \hline \end{array}$

12. $\begin{array}{r} 9 \\ +\ 6 \\ \hline \end{array}$

13. $\begin{array}{r} 7 \\ +\ 4 \\ \hline \end{array}$

14. $\begin{array}{r} 9 \\ +\ 8 \\ \hline \end{array}$

15. $\begin{array}{r} 9 \\ +\ 7 \\ \hline \end{array}$

16. $\begin{array}{r} 6 \\ +\ 8 \\ \hline \end{array}$

17. $\begin{array}{r} 9 \\ +\ 9 \\ \hline \end{array}$

Fill in each addition number wheel.
Add the outer number to the middle number.

1. +6: 6, 8, 0, 5, 2, 4, 7, 9 — 14

2. +7: 8, 5, 1, 9, 2, 3, 7, 6

3. +8: 4, 6, 1, 3, 0, 2, 5, 7

4. +9: 3, 5, 0, 9, 8, 1, 4, 6

Color the picture.

Even numbers =

Odd numbers =

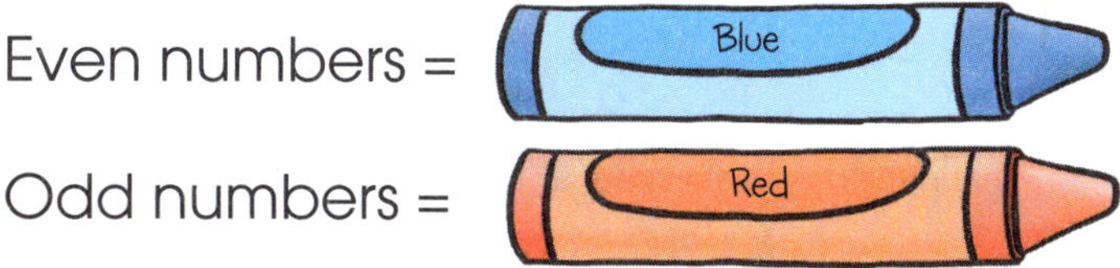

Fill in the addition facts table by finding the **sums**.

+	0	1	2	3	4	5	6	7	8	9
0	0			3						
1								8		
2			4							
3										
4						9				
5									13	
6	6									
7					11					
8										
9			11			14				

Write the **sum**.

1. 1 + 1 = ______
2. 2 + 2 = ______
3. 3 + 3 = ______
4. 4 + 4 = ______
5. 5 + 5 = ______
6. 6 + 6 = ______
7. 7 + 7 = ______
8. 8 + 8 = ______
9. 9 + 9 = ______

Circle all of the **doubles** in the addition facts table.

If you know a **double**, it's easy to remember a **double plus 1** fact.

7 + 7 = 14

7 + 8 = 15

Write the **sums**.
Use the addition facts table on page 50 if you need help.

1. 4 + 4 = ____
   4 + 5 = ____
2. 6 + 6 = ____
   6 + 7 = ____
3. 8 + 8 = ____
   8 + 9 = ____
4. 5 + 5 = ____
   5 + 6 = ____
5. 3 + 3 = ____
   3 + 4 = ____
6. 7 + 7 = ____
   7 + 8 = ____

7. $\begin{array}{r} 6 \\ +\ 6 \\ \hline \end{array}$ $\begin{array}{r} 6 \\ +\ 7 \\ \hline \end{array}$

8. $\begin{array}{r} 7 \\ +\ 7 \\ \hline \end{array}$ $\begin{array}{r} 7 \\ +\ 8 \\ \hline \end{array}$

9. $\begin{array}{r} 5 \\ +\ 5 \\ \hline \end{array}$ $\begin{array}{r} 5 \\ +\ 6 \\ \hline \end{array}$

10. $\begin{array}{r} 8 \\ +\ 8 \\ \hline \end{array}$ $\begin{array}{r} 8 \\ +\ 9 \\ \hline \end{array}$

When you know one fact, you can think of another fact.

Look at these subtraction facts:

16 – 9 = 7

16 – 7 = 9

Write the **differences**.

1. 12 – 3 = ____   12 – 9 = ____
2. 14 – 5 = ____   14 – 9 = ____
3. 15 – 7 = ____   15 – 8 = ____
4. 17 – 9 = ____   17 – 8 = ____
5. 13 – 5 = ____   13 – 8 = ____
6. 11 – 6 = ____   11 – 5 = ____

Write the **difference** and another fact that uses the same numbers.

7. 14 – 6 = ____   ____ – ____ = ____
8. 17 – 8 = ____   ____ – ____ = ____
9. 12 – 9 = ____   ____ – ____ = ____
10. 15 – 7 = ____   ____ – ____ = ____
11. 13 – 4 = ____   ____ – ____ = ____
12. 15 – 9 = ____   ____ – ____ = ____

Fill in the squares in the diamond puzzles.

8 + 7 = 15 15 – 7 = 8

7 + 8 = 15 15 – 8 = 7

The addition and subtraction facts are related in a **fact family**. All of the facts use the same numbers.

Write the missing numbers.

1. 4 + 7 = ____
   7 + 4 = ____
   11 – 4 = ____
   11 – 7 = ____

2. 9 + 7 = ____
   7 + 9 = ____
   16 – 7 = ____
   16 – 9 = ____

3. 7 + 0 = ____
   0 + 7 = ____
   7 – 0 = ____
   7 – 7 = ____

4. 8 + 5 = ____
   5 + ____ = 13
   13 – 5 = ____
   13 – 8 = ____

5. 8 + 9 = ____
   9 + 8 = ____
   ____ – 9 = 8
   ____ – 8 = 9

6. 9 + 9 = ____
   18 – 9 = ____

Write addition and subtraction facts for the numbers.

7. 6, 9, 15
   ____ + ____ = ____
   ____ + ____ = ____
   ____ – ____ = ____
   ____ – ____ = ____

8. 9, 9, 0
   ____ + ____ = ____
   ____ + ____ = ____
   ____ – ____ = ____
   ____ – ____ = ____

9. 5, 7, 12
   ____ + ____ = ____
   ____ + ____ = ____
   ____ – ____ = ____
   ____ – ____ = ____

Add any two numbers first. Then add the third number to find the **sum**.

Look for a **ten**. Adding **10** to a number is easy to do!

$$\begin{array}{r} 4 \\ 6 \\ +\ 4 \\ \hline 14 \end{array} \quad (4 + 6 = 10)$$

$$\begin{array}{r} 4 \\ 6 \\ +\ 4 \\ \hline 14 \end{array} \quad (4 + 4 = 8)$$

Look for a **double**. Add the third number to it.

Write the **sum**.

1. $\begin{array}{r} 3 \\ 4 \\ +\ 4 \\ \hline \end{array}$

2. $\begin{array}{r} 5 \\ 3 \\ +\ 5 \\ \hline \end{array}$

3. $\begin{array}{r} 3 \\ 7 \\ +\ 7 \\ \hline \end{array}$

4. $\begin{array}{r} 2 \\ 9 \\ +\ 2 \\ \hline \end{array}$

5. $\begin{array}{r} 4 \\ 4 \\ +\ 2 \\ \hline \end{array}$

6. $\begin{array}{r} 3 \\ 9 \\ +\ 3 \\ \hline \end{array}$

7. $\begin{array}{r} 4 \\ 4 \\ +\ 4 \\ \hline \end{array}$

8. $\begin{array}{r} 3 \\ 4 \\ +\ 7 \\ \hline \end{array}$

9. $\begin{array}{r} 5 \\ 7 \\ +\ 5 \\ \hline \end{array}$

10. $\begin{array}{r} 8 \\ 0 \\ +\ 8 \\ \hline \end{array}$

Read the problem. Find and write the number.
Use the space to figure out the problem.

1. Start with 3.
   Double it.
   Add 8.
   What is the number? ______

2. Start with 5.
   Add 3.
   Add 9.
   What is the number? ______

3. Start with 8.
   Subtract 7.
   Add 3.
   Double it.
   What is the number? ______

4. Start with 8.
   Subtract 5.
   Add 1.
   Subtract 4.
   What is the number? ______

5. Start with 4.
   Double it.
   Double it.
   What is the number? ______

This race is for 2 players.
Take turns giving the answer to every other problem.
The player who has more correct answers is the winner.

Write **how many** there are.

1. 

______

2.

______

Circle groups of ten. Count the ones. Write **how many** there are.

3.

______ tens ______ ones = ______

4. 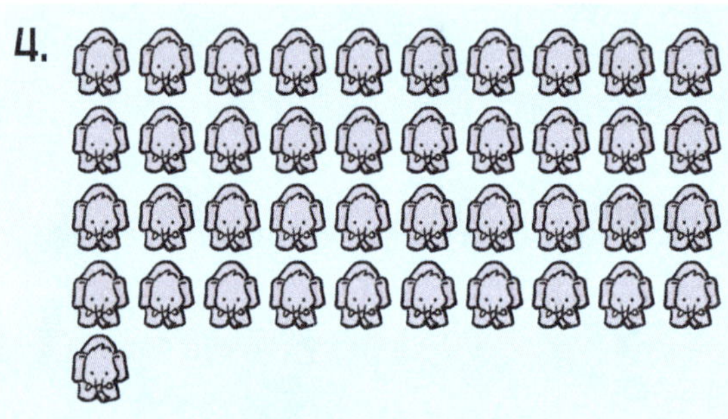

______ tens ______ ones = ______

5. Count the objects in each group. Write the numbers.
Circle the number that is **less**.

______

______

Circle the number that is **greater**.

6. 29 37

7. 43 34

8. 69 70

Write the missing numbers.

9. 31, ______, 33, ______, ______, ______, 37, ______, 39, ______

10. 75, ______, ______, 78, ______, ______, 81, ______, ______, 84

Write the **sum**.

1. 5 + 6 = ______ 2. 4 + 8 = ______ 3. 9 + 9 = ______

4. 7 + 0 = ______ 5. 8 + 9 = ______ 6. 8 + 6 = ______

Write the **difference**.

7. 13 − 8 = ______ 8. 5 − 5 = ______ 9. 14 − 7 = ______

10. 16 − 9 = ______ 11. 14 − 5 = ______ 12. 15 − 8 = ______

Add or **subtract**.

13. $\begin{array}{r} 12 \\ -\ \ 5 \\ \hline \end{array}$ 14. $\begin{array}{r} 4 \\ +\ \ 9 \\ \hline \end{array}$ 15. $\begin{array}{r} 8 \\ -\ \ 0 \\ \hline \end{array}$ 16. $\begin{array}{r} 15 \\ -\ \ 6 \\ \hline \end{array}$

17. $\begin{array}{r} 6 \\ +\ \ 6 \\ \hline \end{array}$ 18. $\begin{array}{r} 16 \\ -\ \ 8 \\ \hline \end{array}$ 19. $\begin{array}{r} 3 \\ 6 \\ +\ \ 7 \\ \hline \end{array}$ 20. $\begin{array}{r} 6 \\ 8 \\ +\ \ 4 \\ \hline \end{array}$

21. Write a fact family for these numbers: 7, 9, and 16.

___ + ___ = ___   ___ − ___ = ___

___ + ___ = ___   ___ − ___ = ___

Use the picture stories to answer the questions.

1. How many **in all**?

6 giraffes

2. How many **altogether**?

_______ parrots

3. What is the **total**?

_______ elephants

4. How many **in all**?

_______ lions

5. How many **altogether**?

_______ monkeys

6. What is the **total**?

_______ zebras

FEATHERED FRIENDS

The answer to an addition problem is called the **sum**.
You can write an **addition number sentence** like this: **2** + **1** = **3**.

2 + 1 = 3

How many in all? 3

Write an addition number sentence for each picture story.

1.

+

_____ + _____ = _____

How many in all? _____

2.

+

_____ + _____ = _____

What is the **total** number of ? _____

3.

+

_____ + _____ = _____

How many **altogether**? _____

Write an addition number sentence for each picture story.

1.

_____ + _____ = _____ fish

What is the **total** number of ? _____

2.

_____ + _____ = _____ sea horses

How many **altogether**? _____

3.

+

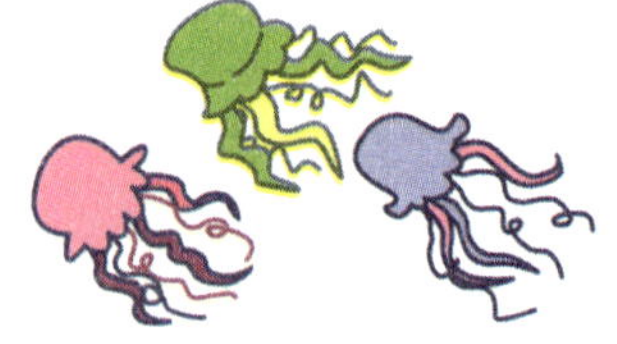

_____ + _____ = _____ jellyfish

How many **in all**? _____

4.

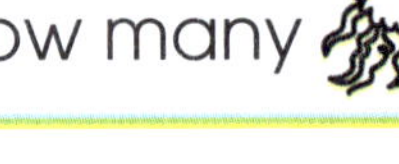

_____ + _____ = _____ fish

How many **altogether**? _____

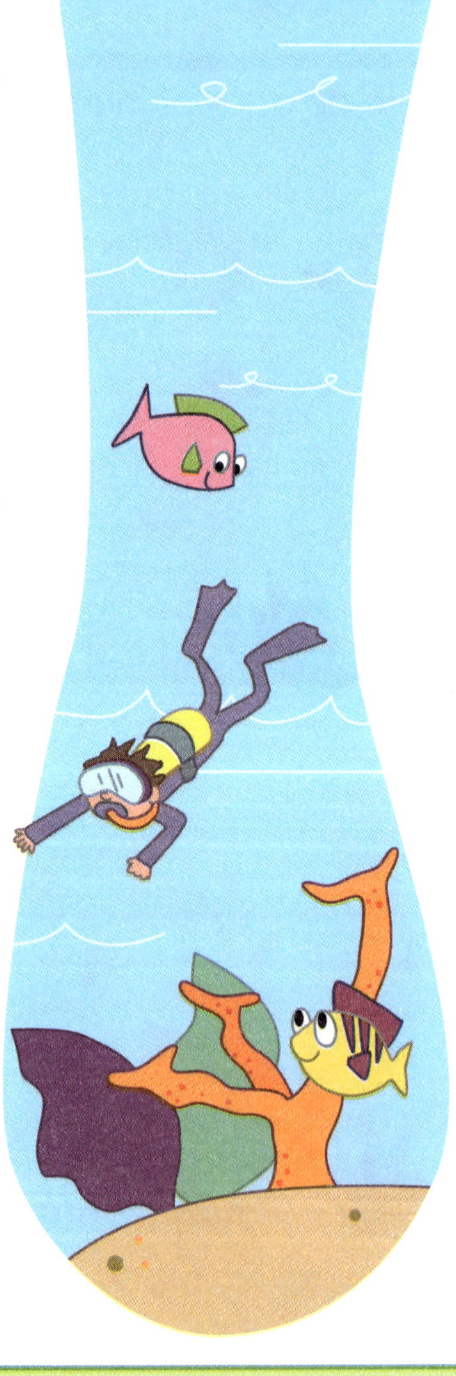

Remember, when you see these words, you should add: **in all**, **altogether**, **total**, and **sum**.

Amy has **3** cats.
Dan has **2** cats.
What is the **total** number of cats?

Solve

  3
+ 2
  5 cats

Read and solve each word problem.

1. Jason saw **2** birds.
   Then he saw **6** more birds.
   How many birds did he see **in all**?

Solve

______
______
______ birds

2. Katy has **1** turtle.
   Marco has **5** turtles.
   How many turtles do they have **altogether**?

Solve

______
______
______ turtles

3. Pedro has **4** dogs.
   Gary has **3** dogs.
   What is the **total** number of dogs?

Solve

______
______
______ dogs

Lauren saw **3** fish.
Evan saw **4** fish.
How many fish are there **in all**?

Solve

  3
+ 4
―――
  7 fish

Read and solve each word problem.

1. Nate saw **3** puppies.
   Then he saw **5** more puppies.
   What is the **total** number of puppies?

Solve

______

______

______ puppies

2. Julia saw **2** birds.
   Rob saw **3** birds.
   How many birds are there **altogether**?

Solve

______

______

______ birds

3. Abby saw **2** kittens.
   Logan saw **6** kittens.
   How many kittens are there **in all**?

Solve

______

______

______ kittens

Dylan saw **4** baseballs.
Kirk saw **2** baseballs.
How many baseballs did they see **in all**?

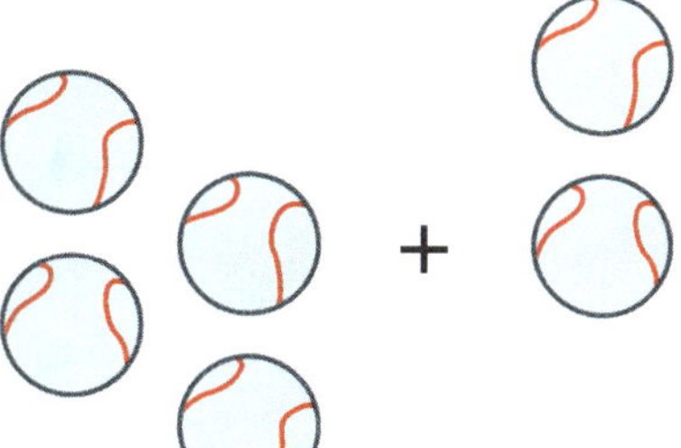

Solve

 4
+2
 6 baseballs

Read and solve each word problem.

1. Noah saw **3** hats.
Paul saw **5** hats.
How many hats did they see **altogether**?

Solve

_____
_____
_____ hats

2. Mindy saw **2** bats.
Then she saw **3** more bats.
What was the **total** number of bats she saw?

+

Solve

_____
_____
_____ bats

3. Carol saw **2** pennants.
Alexis saw **4** pennants.
How many pennants did they see **in all**?

+

Solve

_____
_____
_____ pennants

Use the picture stories to answer the questions.

1. How many are **left**?

3 frogs

2. How many are **left**?

_____ cats

3. How many are **left**?

_____ rabbits

4. How many are **left**?

_____ dogs

5. How many are **left**?

_____ mice

6. How many are **left**?

_____ birds

The answer to a subtraction problem is called the **difference**.
You can write a **subtraction number sentence** like this: **7** – **3** = **4**.

7 – 3 = 4
in all – going away = are left

Write a subtraction number sentence for each picture story.

1.

_____ – _____ = _____
in all – going away = are left

2.

_____ – _____ = _____
in all – going away = are left

3.

_____ – _____ = _____
in all – going away = are left

Write a subtraction number sentence for each picture story.

1.

7 - 2 = 5

How many are **left**? ______

2.

______ - ______ = ______

How many are **left**? ______

3.

______ - ______ = ______

How many are **left**? ______

4.

______ - ______ = ______

How many are **left**? ______

Remember, when you see these words, you should subtract: **going away, left, more/less,** and **difference**.

There are **6** frogs.
There are **4** lily pads.
How many **more** frogs are there?

Solve

6
−4
2 frogs

Read and solve each word problem.

1. There are **5** fish.
   There are **4** cattails.
   How many **more** fish are there?

Solve

______

______

______ fish

2. There are **8** flowers.
   There are **4** butterflies.
   How many **more** flowers are there?

Solve

______

______

______ flowers

3. There are **7** turtles.
   There are **5** logs.
   How many **more** turtles are there?

Solve

______

______

______ turtles

6 bees were on a flower.
3 bees flew away.
How many bees were **left**?

Solve

6
-3
3 bees

Read and solve each word problem.

1. **5** bees were at the hive.
   3 bees flew away.
   How many bees were **left**?

Solve

______
______
______ bees

2. **6** bears were in the woods.
   4 bears went away.
   How many bears were **left**?

Solve

______
______
______ bears

3. Bear had **6** jars of honey.
   He gave away **2** jars.
   How many jars of honey did he have **left**?

Solve

______
______
______ jars

There are **8** green frogs.
There are **4** yellow frogs.
How many **more** green frogs are there?

Solve

$$\begin{array}{r} 8 \\ -\ 4 \\ \hline 4 \end{array}$$

4 frogs

Read and solve each word problem.

1. There were **8** grasshoppers. **4** jumped away. How many grasshoppers were **left**?

Solve

______

______

______ grasshoppers

2. There are **6** brown rabbits. There are **4** yellow rabbits. How many **more** brown rabbits are there?

Solve

______

______

______ brown rabbits

3. **9** frogs were sitting on a lily pad. **4** frogs jumped off. How many frogs were **left**?

Solve

______

______

______ frogs

4. There are **7** purple spiders. There are **3** blue spiders. How many **more** purple spiders are there?

Solve

______

______

______ purple spiders

Match each picture word problem to the correct number sentence.

1. How many bees are **left**?

$4 + 3 = 7$

2. How many birds are **left**?

$7 - 4 = 3$

3. How many butterflies are there **in all**?

$2 + 5 = 7$

4. How many ducks are **left**?

$6 - 2 = 4$

5. What is the **total** number of owls?

$5 - 3 = 2$

Match each picture word problem to the correct number sentence.

1. How many toucans are there **altogether**?

$$\begin{array}{r} 5 \\ +\ 4 \\ \hline 9 \end{array}$$

2. How many monkeys are **left**?

$$\begin{array}{r} 3 \\ +\ 6 \\ \hline 9 \end{array}$$

3. How many iguanas are there **in all**?

$$\begin{array}{r} 6 \\ -\ 2 \\ \hline 4 \end{array}$$

4. How many jaguars are **left**?

$$\begin{array}{r} 4 \\ -\ 1 \\ \hline 3 \end{array}$$

Circle the correct question and number sentence for each word problem.

1. **10** ladybugs were in the garden.
   5 ladybugs left.

How many ladybugs were there in all? 5 + 5 = 10

How many ladybugs were left? 10 – 5 = 5

2. **11** beetles were on a log.
   3 more beetles came along.

How many beetles were there in all? 11 + 3 = 14

How many beetles were left? 11 – 3 = 8

3. **8** ants were on a watermelon.
   7 more ants were on the ground.

How many ants were there in all? 8 + 7 = 15

How many ants were left? 8 – 7 = 1

4. **12** bees were at a hive.
   3 bees flew away.

How many bees were there in all? 12 + 3 = 15

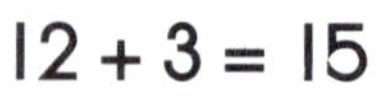

How many bees were left? 12 – 3 = 9

Christy had **7** oranges.
She bought **3** more.
How many does she have **altogether**?

Solve

7
+ 3
10 oranges

Read and solve each word problem.

1. Ethan picked **8** apples.
He ate **2** of them.
How many does he have **left**?

Solve

______
______
______ apples

2. Nick has **5** pears.
Jill has **4** pears.
How many do they have **in all**?

Solve

______
______
______ pears

3. Pat had **7** bananas.
He ate **4** bananas.
How many does he have **left**?

Solve

______
______
______ bananas

8 birds were in the tree.
3 birds flew away.
How many birds were **left**?

Solve

  8
- 3
---
  5 birds

Read and solve each word problem.

1. There are 7 green kites.
   There are 4 orange kites.
   What is the **total** number of kites?

Solve

______

______

______ kites

2. 6 squirrels are brown.
   6 squirrels are gray.
   How many squirrels are there **in all**?

Solve

______

______

______ squirrels

3. There are 8 swings.
   2 swings are taken.
   How many swings are **left**?

Solve

______

______

______ swings

11 pigs are in the pen.
5 pigs are in the mud outside the pen.
How many pigs are there **altogether**?

Solve

11
+ 5
16 pigs

Read and solve each word problem.

1. 7 sheep are in the pen.
   5 sheep are in the yard.
   How many **more** sheep are in the pen?

Solve

______

______

______ sheep

2. 8 cows are white.
   5 cows are brown.
   How many cows are there **in all**?

Solve

______

______

______ cows

3. There were 12 eggs in the nest.
   4 eggs hatched.
   How many eggs were **left**?

Solve

______

______

______ eggs

Look at the pictures above to find out how much each toy costs. Then solve the problems.

1. Lisa bought  4¢

and a  + 5¢

How much did she spend? 9¢

2. Jerry bought a  ____¢

and a ◯ ____¢

How much did he spend? ____¢

3. Tyler had  ____¢

He bought a  ◯ ____¢

How much did he have left? ____¢

4. Jenny had  ____¢

She bought a ◯ ____¢

How much did she have left? ____¢

Look at the pictures above to find out how much each snack costs. Then solve the problems.

1. Jackie had 10¢. She bought a How much did she have left?

2. Josh bought a and an How much did he spend?

3. Hanna bought and a How much did she spend?

4. Marcie had 15¢. She bought an How much did she have left?

5. Ted bought a and a How much did he spend?

6. Will had 12¢. He bought How much did he have left?

Use the picture graph to answer the questions.

Name	Number of Baseballs
Sam	⚾ ⚾ ⚾ ⚾
Dana	⚾ ⚾ ⚾ ⚾ ⚾
Beth	⚾ ⚾ ⚾
Tom	⚾ ⚾
Jim	⚾ ⚾ ⚾ ⚾ ⚾ ⚾
Heidi	⚾ ⚾ ⚾ ⚾ ⚾

1. How many baseballs does Sam have? ______
2. How many baseballs does Dana have? ______
3. How many baseballs does Beth have? ______
4. How many baseballs does Tom have? ______
5. How many baseballs does Jim have? ______
6. How many baseballs does Heidi have? ______
7. How many baseballs do Beth and Dana have **altogether**?

8. Jim has **more** baseballs than Sam.
   How many **more** baseballs does Jim have?

READING FUN

Use the picture graph to answer the questions.

Name	Number of Books Read
Ann	
Bret	
Chan	
Zach	
Emma	

1. How many books did Ann read? ______

2. How many books did Chan read? ______

3. How many books did Emma read? ______

4. Who read the most books? ________________

5. Who read the fewest books? ________________

6. How many books did Bret and Zach read **altogether**?

   _____ ◯ _____ = _____

7. How many books did Ann and Chan read **in all**?

   _____ ◯ _____ = _____

8. Emma read **more** books than Ann. How many **more** books did Emma read?

   _____ ◯ _____ = _____

Use the bar graph to answer the questions.

1. How many boxes of cookies did Kay sell? ______

2. How many boxes of cookies did Tim sell? ______

3. How many boxes of cookies did Tim and Jeff sell **in all**?

______ ◯ ______ = ______

4. How many boxes of cookies did Chris and Jeff sell **altogether**?

______ ◯ ______ = ______

5. Chris sold **more** boxes of cookies than Tim. How many **more** boxes of cookies did Chris sell?

______ ◯ ______ = ______

6. How many boxes of cookies did Tim and Kay sell **in all**?

______ ◯ ______ = ______

MAGIC MARBLES

Use the bar graph to answer the questions.

1. How many marbles does Joe have? ______

2. How many marbles does Mike have? ______

3. How many marbles does Cindy have? ______

4. Cindy has **more** marbles than Joe.
   How many **more** marbles does Cindy have?

5. Mike has **more** marbles than Joe.
   How many **more** marbles does Mike have?

6. How many marbles do Joe and Cindy have **altogether**?

Use the tally table to answer the questions.

Pet	Number of Votes
Bird	𝍸
Cat	𝍸 𝍸
Dog	𝍸 𝍸 //
Fish	𝍸 /
Pony	///

1. How many votes did the pony get? ______
2. How many votes did the bird get? ______
3. How many votes did the fish get? ______
4. Which animal got the most votes? ______________
5. Which animal got the fewest votes? ______________
6. The cat got **more** votes than the fish.
   How many **more** votes did the cat get?

   _____ ◯ _____ = _____

7. How many votes did the bird and the fish get **in all**?

   _____ ◯ _____ = _____

Use the table to answer the questions.

Favorite Fruit			
Fruit	First Grade	Second Grade	Third Grade
Apple	9	8	6
Banana	10	9	6
Orange	6	5	9

1. How many children in second grade like apples best? ______
2. How many children in first grade like bananas best? ______
3. Which fruit do children in third grade like best? __________
4. Which fruit do children in second grade like best? __________
5. How many children in second and third grade like apples best?

   ______ ◯ ______ = ______

6. How many children in second grade like bananas more than they like oranges?

   ______ ◯ ______ = ______

7. How many children are in third grade?

1. Write the missing numbers in the calendar.

June						
Sunday	Monday	Tuesday	Wednesday	Thursday	Friday	Saturday
		1	2		4	5
6		8		10		12
13	14		16		18	
20		22		24		26
	28		30			

2. What day comes after Tuesday? ____________

3. What day comes before Friday? ____________

4. What day of the week is June 15? ____________

5. What is the date of the first Monday? ____________

6. What is the date of the second Friday? ____________

7. How many days are in one week? ____________

8. How many days are in two weeks? _____ ◯ _____ = _____

9. How many days are in June? ____________

The movie starts at **5:00**.
It is **2** hours long. At what time does the movie end?

7:00

Start

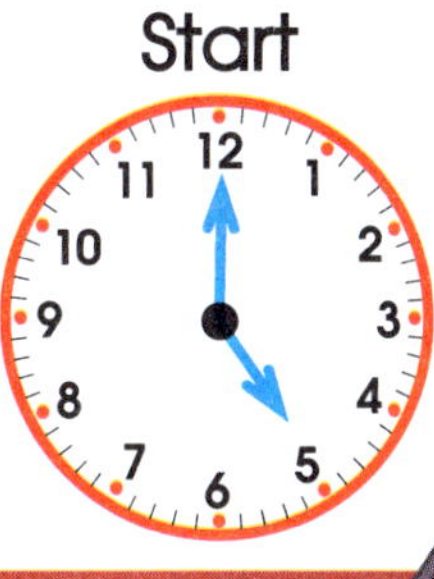

End

Read and solve each story problem.
Draw hands on the clocks to show the starting time and ending time of each activity.

1. The game starts at **1:30**.
It is **3** hours long. At what time does the game end?

____ : ____

Start

End

2. The concert ended at **4:00**.
It was **2** hours long. At what time did the concert start?

____ : ____

Start

End

3. School starts at **8:30**.
It ends **7** hours later.
At what time does the school day end?

____ : ____

Start

End

4. Rachel woke up at **7:00**.
She slept for **10** hours.
At what time did she go to bed?

____ : ____

Start

End

Jane has **8** balloons.
~~Jake has **4** balloons.~~
Brandon has **9** balloons.
How many balloons do Jane and Brandon have?

Solve

8
+9
17 balloons

Read each word problem. Cross out the information you do not need. Then solve each word problem.

1. Emily is **12** years old.
   Her brother is **5** years old.
   Her sister is **8** years old.
   How much older than her brother is Emily?

Solve

_____
_____
_____ years

2. Alex bought **7** gifts.
   Randy bought **8** gifts.
   Ashley bought **5** gifts.
   How many gifts did Randy and Ashley buy?

Solve

_____
_____
_____ gifts

3. Mark has **10** pizza slices.
   Jada has **7** pizza slices.
   Jose has **9** pizza slices.
   Brittany has **5** pizza slices.
   How many more pizza slices than Brittany does Jada have?

Solve

_____
_____
_____ pizza slices

Finish each story by filling in the blanks with the numbers that make sense.

1. There are more girls than boys in the band.

There are __9__ girls in the band.

There are ______ boys in the band.

There is a **total** of ______ children in the band.

8

9 17

2. Brad bought **2** more apples than oranges.

He bought __8__ apples.

He bought ______ oranges.

He bought ______ plums.

He bought ______ pieces of fruit **in all**.

5 6

8 19

3. Tony has **2** more dogs than Tina.

Tony has __5__ dogs.

Tina has ______ dogs.

Tina and Tony have ______ dogs **altogether**.

Tammy has one more dog than Tony.

Tammy and Tony have a **total** of ______ dogs.

3 5

8 11

PENNIES, NICKELS & DIMES

Penny 1¢ 1 cent

When we count **pennies**, we count by **ones**.

Nickel 5¢ 5 cents

When we count **nickels**, we count by **fives**.

Dime 10¢ 10 cents

When we count **dimes**, we count by **tens**.

Count the coins. Write the amount on the line.

1.

_____¢ _____¢ _____¢ _____¢ _____¢ _____¢ _____¢

2.

_____¢ _____¢ _____¢ _____¢ _____¢ _____¢ _____¢

3.

_____¢ _____¢ _____¢ _____¢ _____¢ _____¢

COUNTING COINS

Count on to find the total amount.
Write the amount on the line.

10¢ 20¢ 25¢ 30¢ 35¢ 35¢

1.

___¢ ___¢ ___¢ ___¢ ___¢ ___¢ ___¢

2.

___¢ ___¢ ___¢ ___¢ ___¢ ___¢ ___¢

3.

___¢ ___¢ ___¢ ___¢ ___¢ ___¢ ___¢

4.

___¢ ___¢ ___¢ ___¢ ___¢ ___¢ ___¢

What is the price of each toy?
Count the coins, and write the total amount on each price tag.

1.

10¢ 20¢ 25¢ 26¢ 27¢ 28¢

2.

___¢ ___¢ ___¢ ___¢ ___¢ ___¢ ___¢

3.

___¢ ___¢ ___¢ ___¢ ___¢ ___¢

4.

___¢ ___¢ ___¢ ___¢ ___¢ ___¢

5.

___¢ ___¢ ___¢ ___¢ ___¢

Count the money in each purse.
Write the amount on the line.

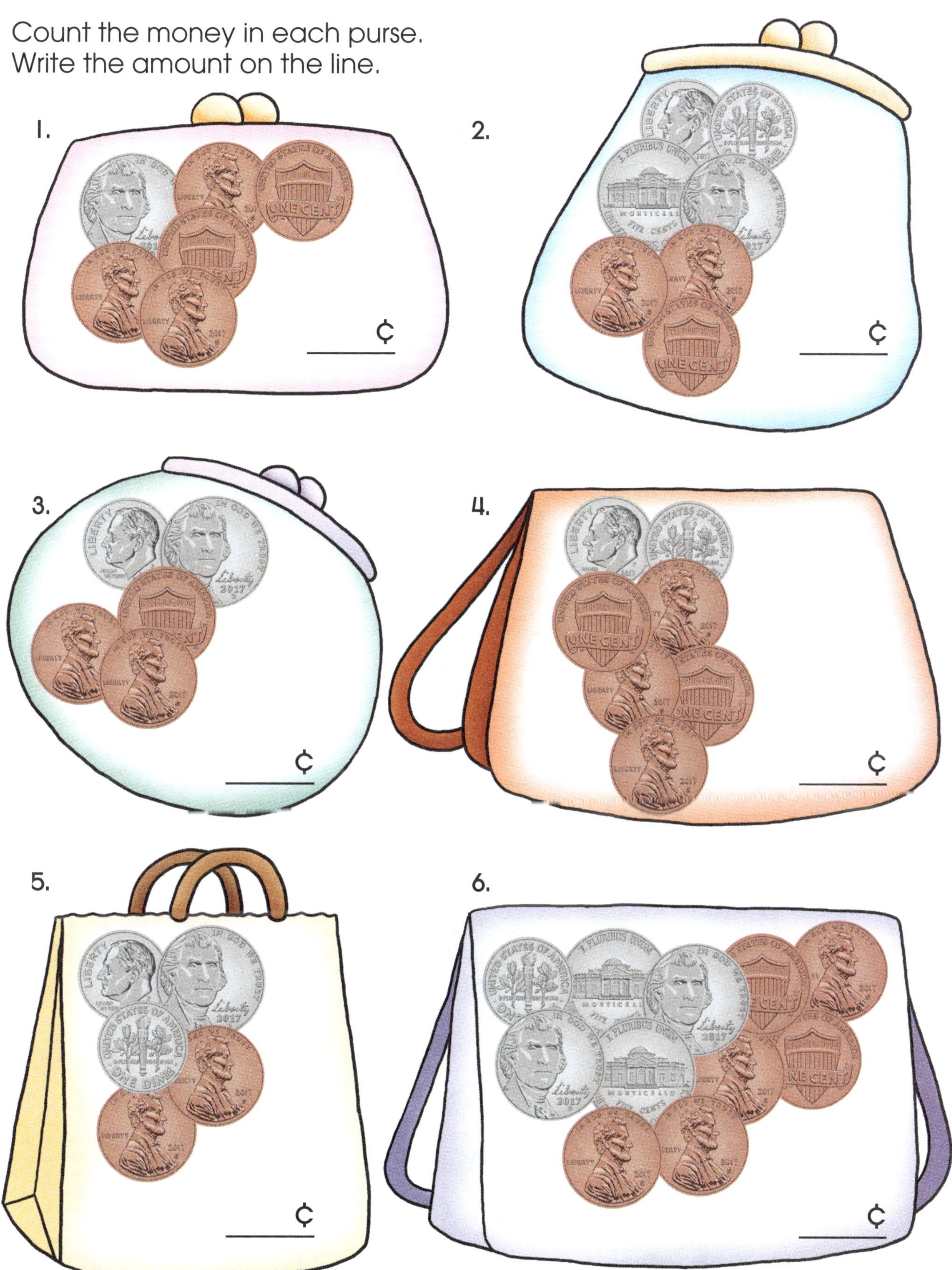

MATCHING AMOUNTS

Count the money in each purse.
Write the amount on the line.
Match the amount with the item.

1.

2.

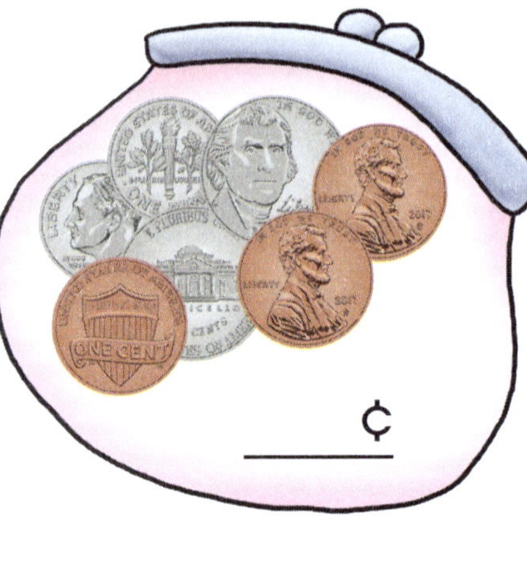

3.

4.

61¢

5.

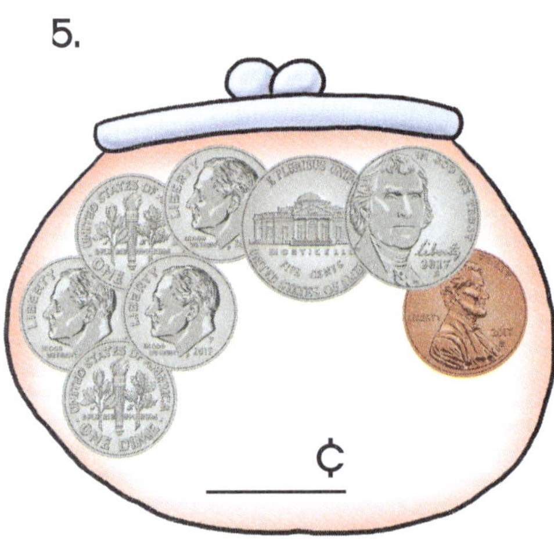

6.

1 quarter = 25¢ **2** dimes and 1 nickel = 25¢ **5** nickels = 25¢

Count each group of coins. Write the amounts.
Cross out the groups that are not equal to a quarter.

1. ____¢

2. ____¢

3. ____¢

4. ____¢

25¢
50¢
75¢
How much does each item cost?
Write the amount on the price tag.
1.
36¢
2.
¢
3.
¢
4.
¢
5.
¢

PAYING WITH COINS

Is there enough money to pay for each item? Count the coins. Then circle **yes** or **no**.

1.

25¢ 35¢ 45¢ 50¢ 51¢

yes no

2.

___¢ ___¢ ___¢ ___¢

yes no

3.

___¢ ___¢ ___¢ ___¢

yes no

4.

___¢ ___¢ ___¢ ___¢ ___¢

yes no

5.

___¢ ___¢ ___¢ ___¢

yes no

Circle the coins you will need to buy the flowers.

SHOWING THE VALUE OF A HALF DOLLAR

1 half dollar = 50¢ 2 quarters = 50¢ 5 dimes = 50¢ 10 nickels = 50¢

Circle the coins in each group to show 50¢.

1. 

2. 

3. 

4. 

Count the money in each bank. Write the amount on the line.
Circle each amount that is equal to 50¢.

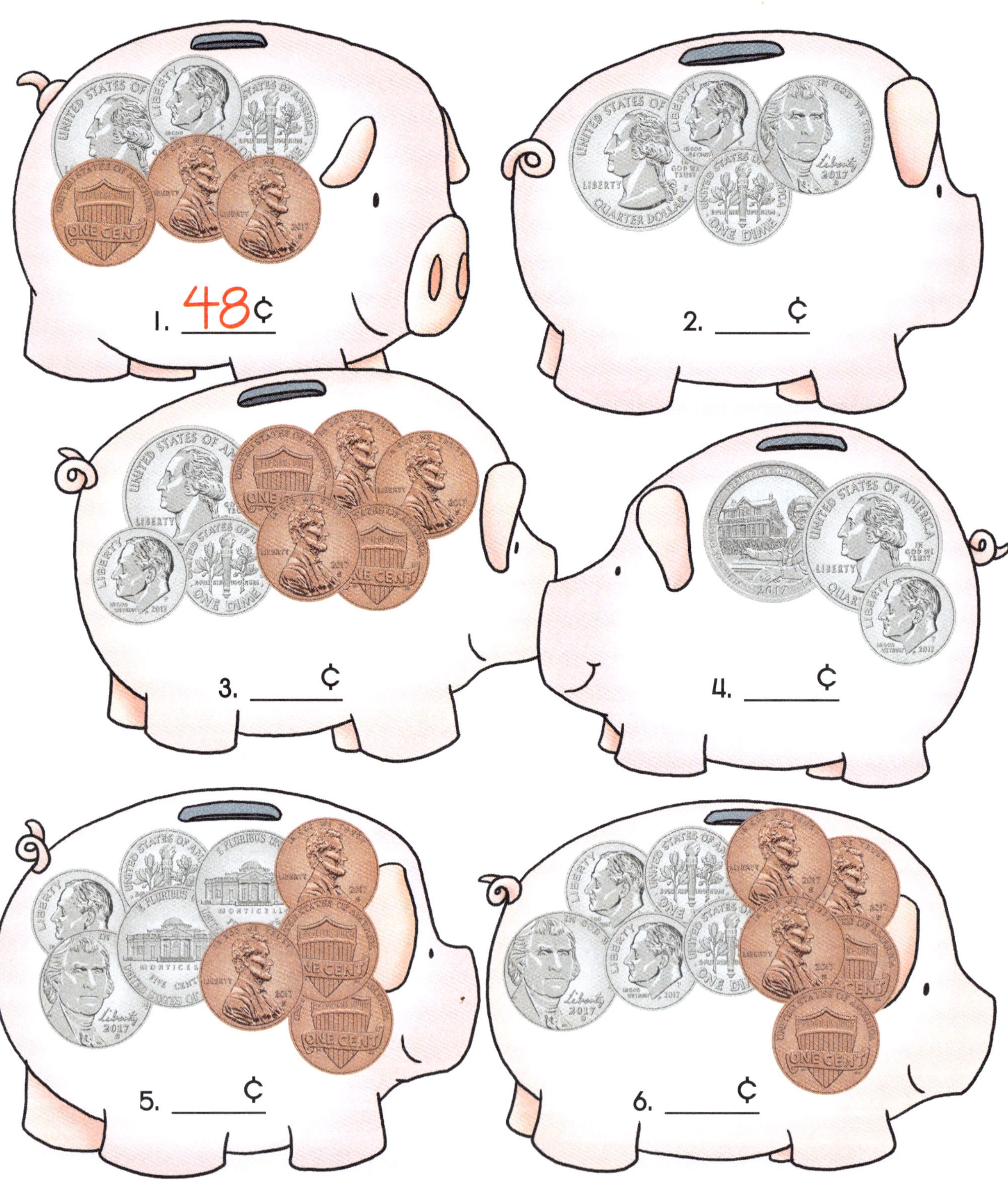

COMPARING AMOUNTS—WHICH IS MORE?

Count each group of coins. Write the amounts.
Circle the item that costs **more**.

1.

22¢

31¢

2.

____¢

____¢

3.

____¢

____¢

4.

____¢

____¢

COMPARING AMOUNTS—WHICH IS LESS?

Count each group of coins. Write the amounts.
Circle the amount that is **less**.

1.

25¢ 20¢

2.

____¢ ____¢

3.

____¢ ____¢

4.

____¢ ____¢

5.

____¢ ____¢

6.

____¢ ____¢

7.

____¢ ____¢

8.

____¢ ____¢

MAKING AMOUNTS

Draw the number of coins needed to make the amount.
Watch out!
There may be more circles than coins needed.

MAKING AMOUNTS

Draw Ⓗ for half-dollar.
Draw Ⓠ for quarter.
Draw Ⓓ for dime.
Draw Ⓝ for nickel.
Draw Ⓟ for penny.

Look at the price of each item.
Draw the fewest coins needed to pay for it.

1.

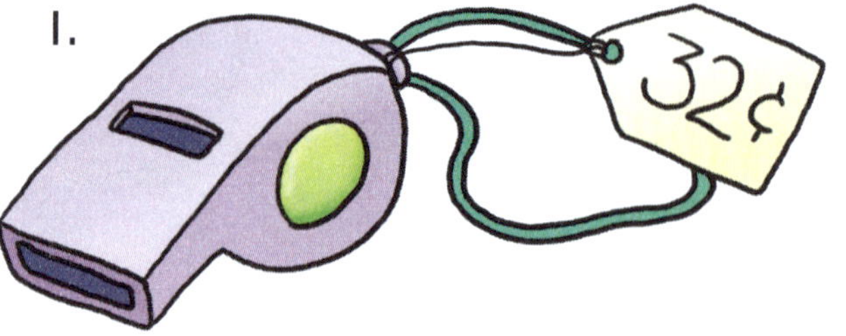

2.

3.

4.

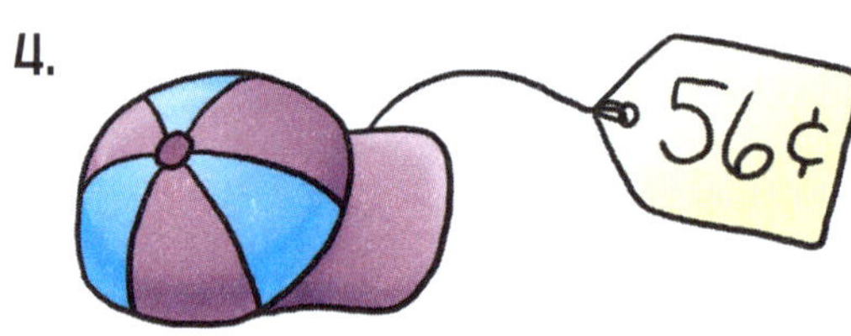

5.

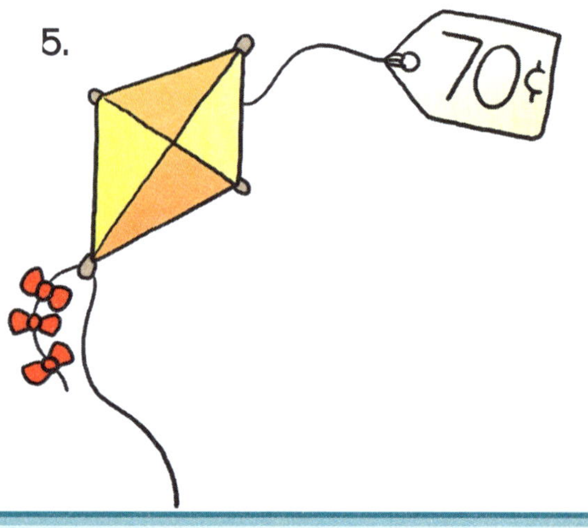

6.

Look at the pictures above to find out how much each toy costs. Add the amounts.

1.

32¢

+50¢

What is the total? 82¢

2.

___¢

+ ___¢

What is the total? ___¢

3.

___¢

+ ___¢

What is the total? ___¢

4.

___¢

+ ___¢

What is the total? ___¢

5.

___¢

+ ___¢

What is the total? ___¢

6.

___¢

+ ___¢

What is the total? ___¢

Find and write each amount of change.
Draw the coin or coins to show each amount.

Have	Buy	Change
1.	33¢	P P 35¢ − 33¢ = 2¢
2.	44¢	____¢ − ____¢ = ____¢
3.	65¢	____¢ − ____¢ = ____¢
4.	72¢	____¢ − ____¢ = ____¢
5.	90¢	____¢ − ____¢ = ____¢

Write how many coins are needed to make each amount using the fewest number of coins.

53¢	1				3
27¢					
18¢					
69¢					
76¢					
37¢					
92¢					

Make each amount using more coins.

53¢			5		3
27¢					
18¢					
69¢					
76¢					
37¢					
92¢					

Write the amounts in the puzzle.

Across

a. 6 dimes
b. 4 dimes and 2 pennies
c. 1 half dollar and 9 nickels
d. 6 nickels
e. 1 quarter
f. 1 dime and 5 pennies
g. 1 nickel and 5 pennies
h. 2 quarters
i. 3 quarters
j. 3 quarters, 1 nickel, and 4 pennies

a.
b.
c.
d.
e.
f.
g.
h.
i.
j.

Down

a. 6 dimes and 2 pennies
b. 9 nickels
c. 1 half dollar and 4 dimes
d. 3 dimes and 5 pennies
e. 5 nickels
f. 10 pennies
g. 2 nickels
h. 5 dimes and 5 pennies
i. 7 dimes and 4 pennies
j. 1 half dollar, 1 quarter, 1 dime, and 4 pennies

A clock has two hands. The hour hand shows the hour.
When the minute hand points to the 12, we say **o'clock**.

Read the hour hand first. Then read the minute hand.
Write the time in two ways.

1. 

3 o'clock

3:00

2.

_____ o'clock

_____ : _____

3. 

_____ o'clock

_____ : _____

4. 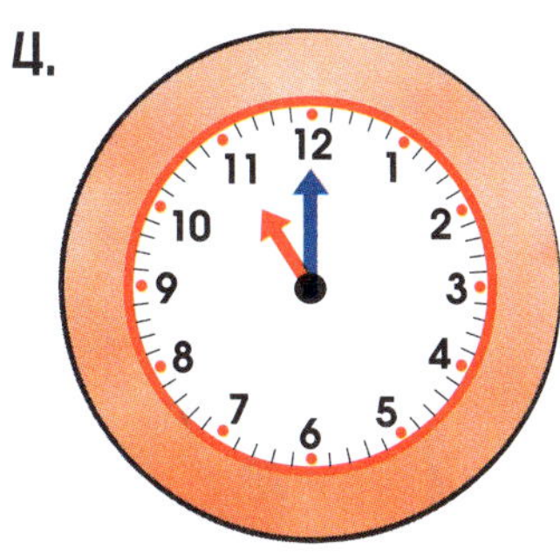

_____ o'clock

_____ : _____

5.

_____ o'clock

_____ : _____

6.

_____ o'clock

_____ : _____

SHOWING HOUR TIME

Write the time on the digital clock.
Draw hands on the clock face to show the time.

1. 5 o'clock

2. 10 o'clock

3. 6 o'clock

4. 12 o'clock

5. 3 o'clock

6. 8 o'clock

It takes the minute hand **5** minutes to move from one number to the next.

Count the minutes by **5**s.
Write the minutes on each line.

How many minutes are in an hour? ______

1. Look at the clock. Find the numbers 1 to 60 around the clock face. Circle these numbers: 15, 30, 45, 60.

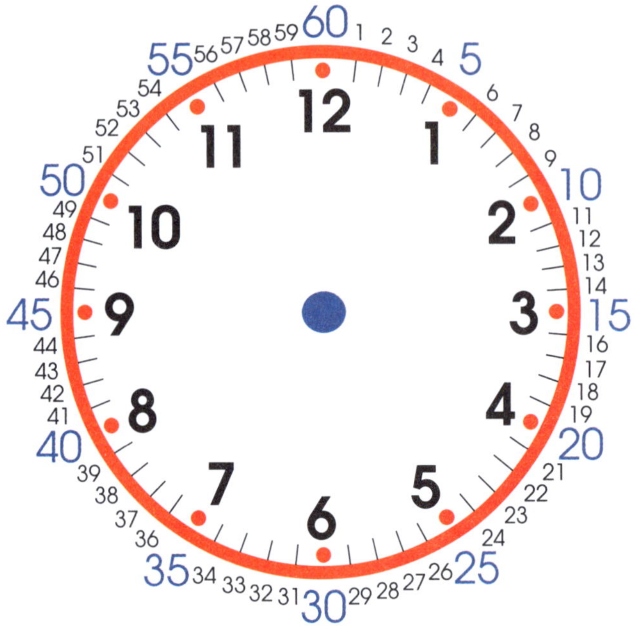

2. Start at the 12. Count around the clock face by 5s for the yellow part.

5, 10, ____

How many minutes are in this part of the clock?

____ minutes

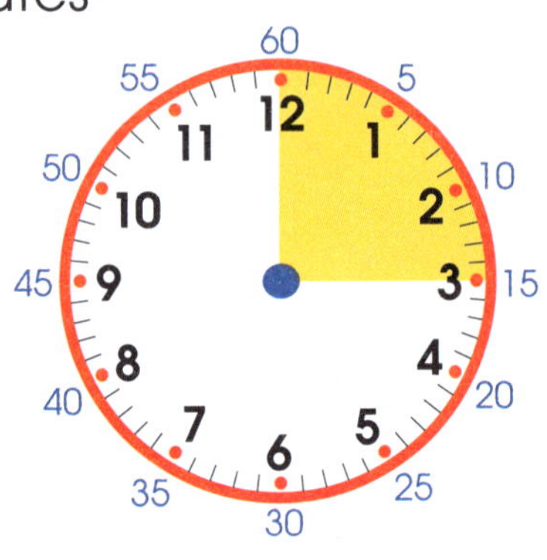

3. Start at the 12. Count around the clock face by 5s for the yellow part.

5, 10, ____,

____, ____, ____

How many minutes are in this part of the clock?

____ minutes

4. Start at the 12. Count around the clock face by 5s for the yellow part.

5, 10, ____, ____, ____,

____, ____, ____, ____

How many minutes are in this part of the clock?

____ minutes

The minute hand tells the minutes. When the minute hand points to the **6**, we say that it is **half past** the hour. The minute hand is *halfway* around the clock. The hour hand is ***halfway*** between the hour numbers.

The hour hand is halfway between the **2** and the **3**.
The minute hand points to the **6**.

The time is **half past 2** or **2:30**.

It is 30 minutes after 2.
It is **2:30**.

We can say: **"two thirty."**

Read the hour hand first. Then read the minute hand.
Write the time in two ways.

1.

Half past 4

4:30

2.

Half past ______

_____ : _____

3.

Half past ______

_____ : _____

4.

Half past ______

_____ : _____

5.

Half past ______

_____ : _____

6.

Half past ______

_____ : _____

Draw hands on the clock and fill in the blanks to show the time.

1. 

Half past 8

"eight thirty"

8:30

2. 

Half past ________

"________ thirty"

3. 

Half past ________

"twelve ________"

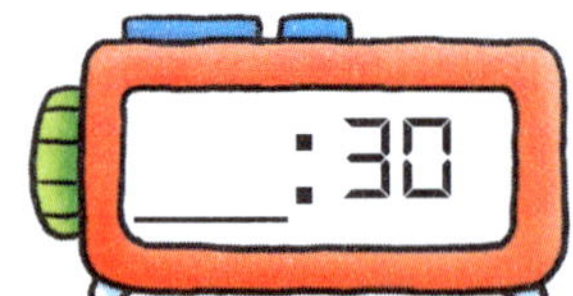

4. 

Half past 5

""

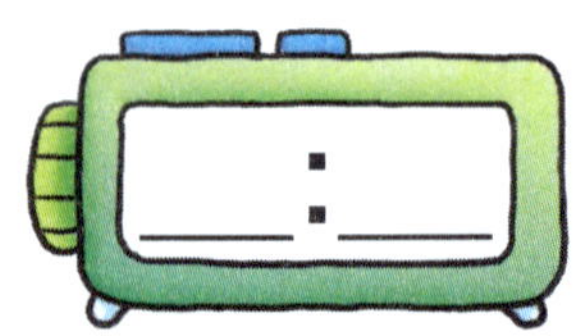

Write the time.

1. 1:30

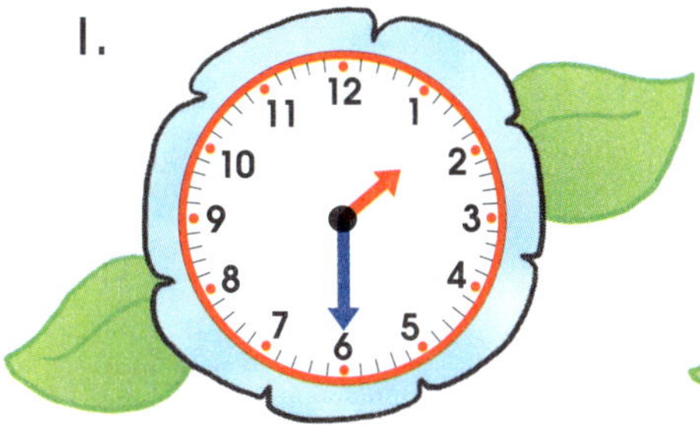

2. ___:___

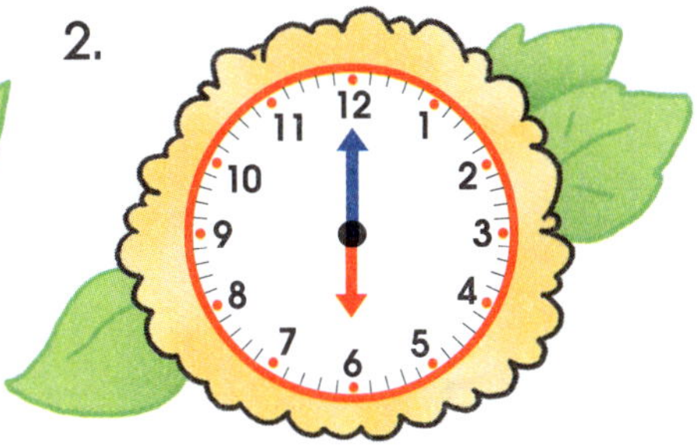

3. ___:___

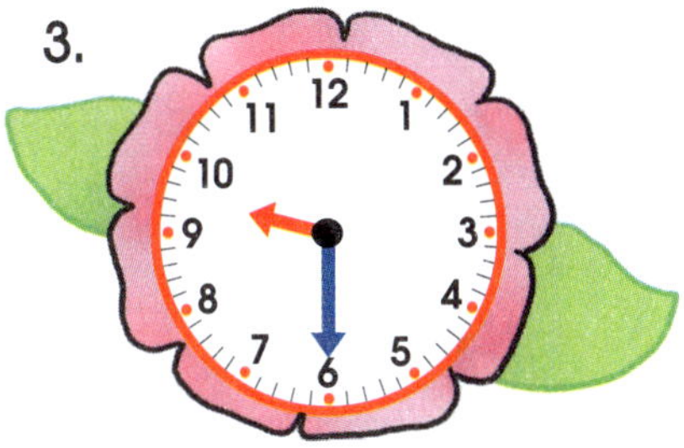

4. ___:___

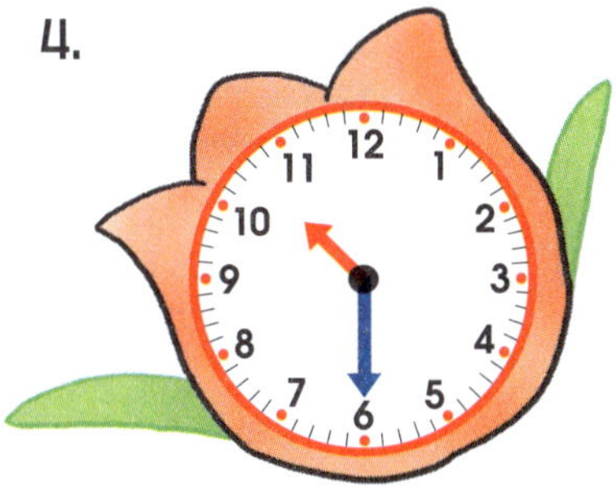

5. ___:___

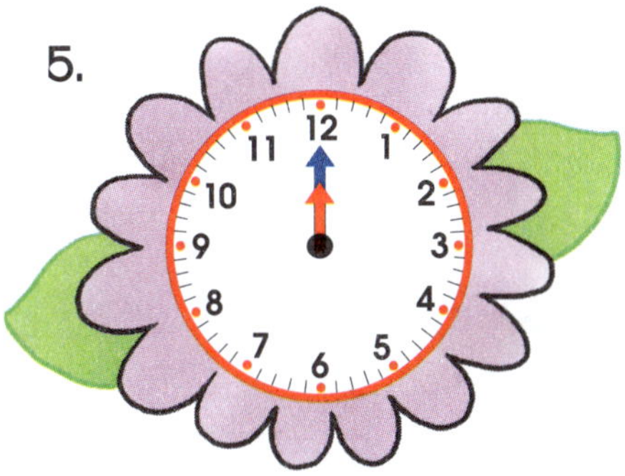

6. ___:___

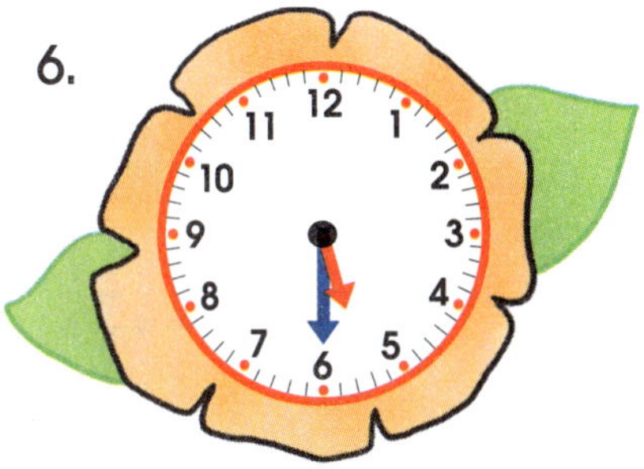

Draw hands on the clock face to show the time.

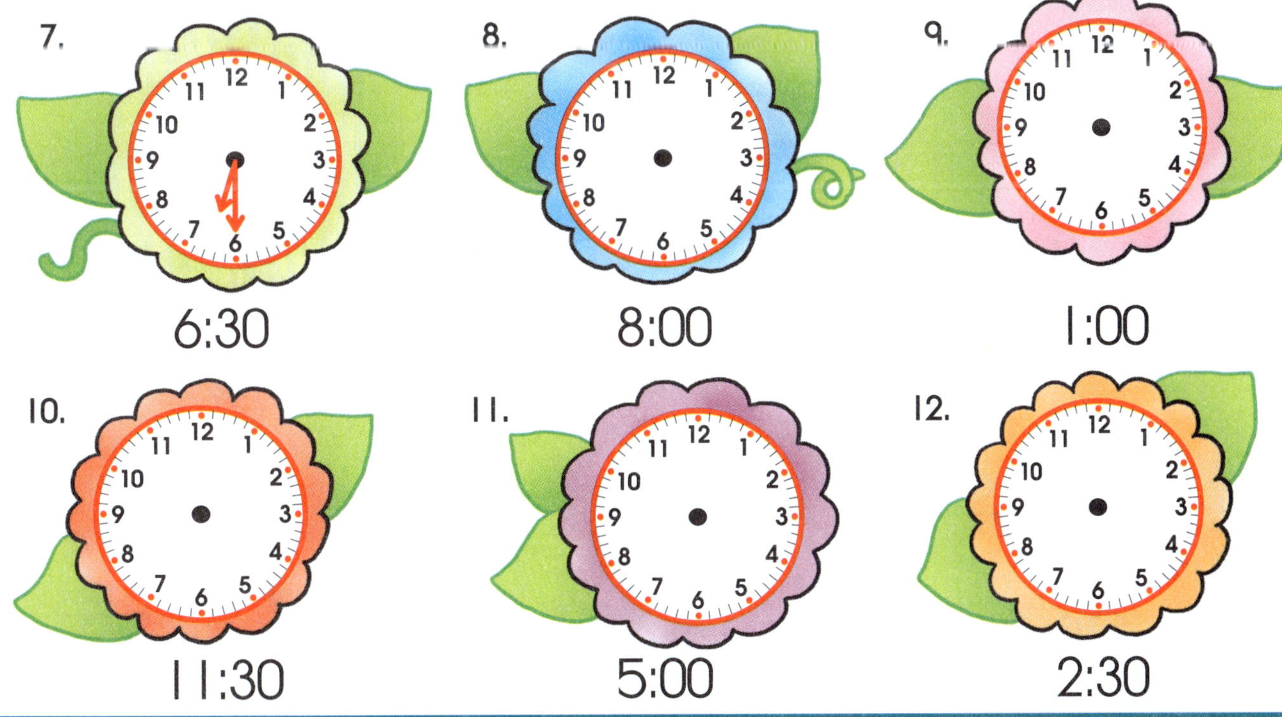

First, write the time or draw the hands in the **NOW** column.
Then, write the time for one hour earlier and one hour later.

One Hour Earlier | NOW | One Hour Later

1. 8:30

9:30

2. 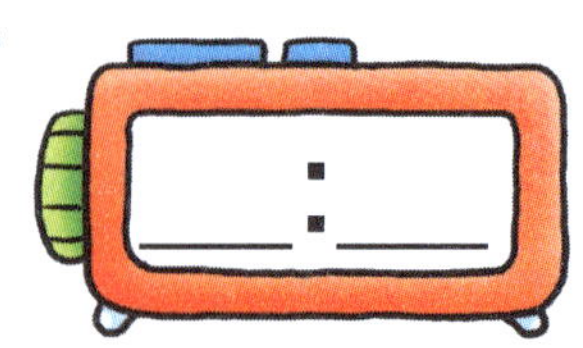

3:00

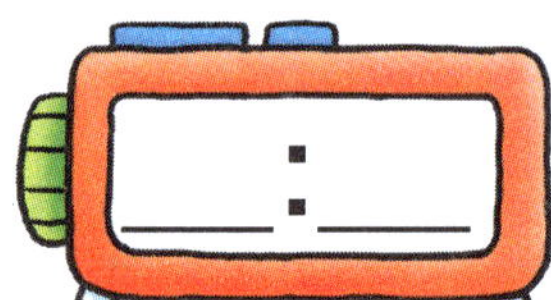

3. 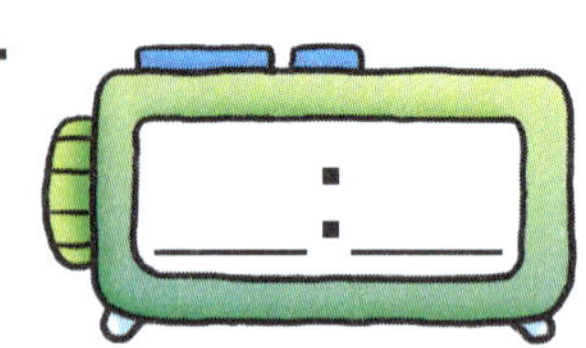

______

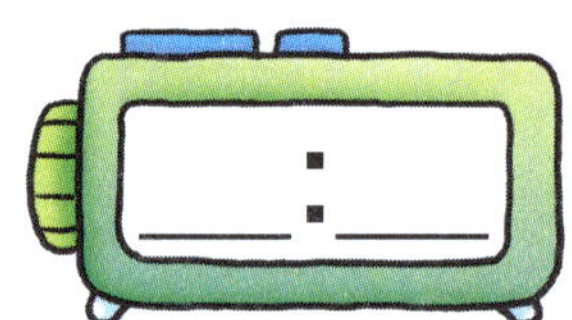

4. 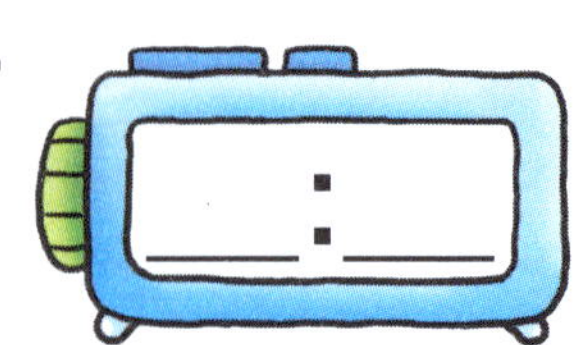

2:30

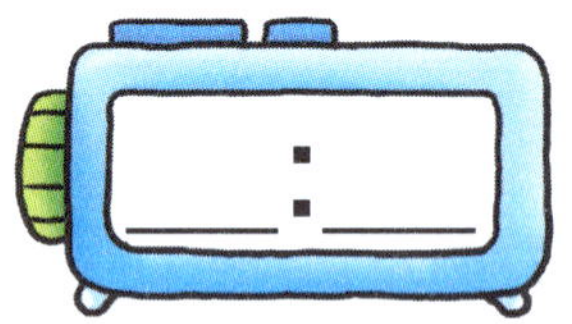

5. 

______

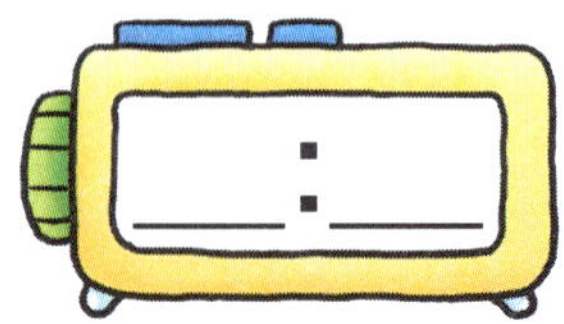

When the minute hand points to **3**, it is a quarter of the way around the clock. It is a **quarter past** the hour. The hour hand is a little past the hour number.

The time is quarter past **2**.

It is 15 minutes after **2**.
It is **2:15**.

We can say: "**quarter after 2**."

Read the hour hand first. Then read the minute hand.
Write the time in two ways.

1.

Quarter past 

______ : ______

2.

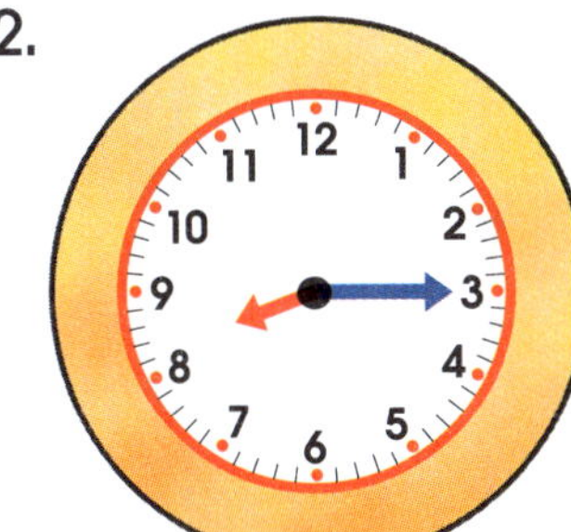

Quarter past ______

______ : ______

3.

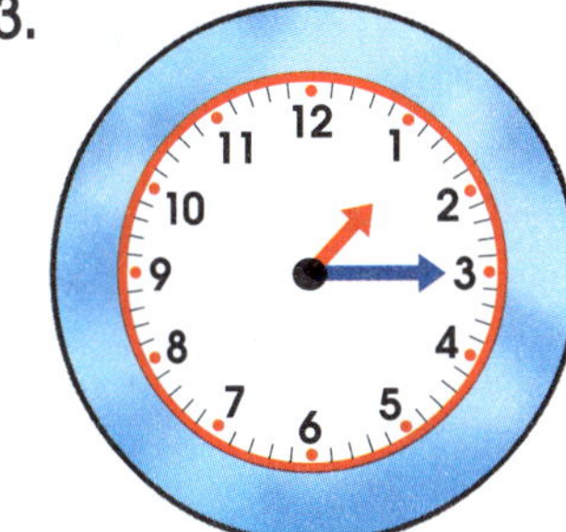

Quarter past ______

______ : ______

4.

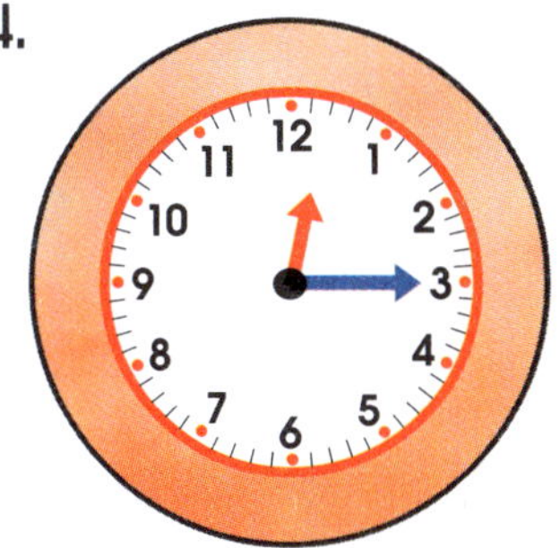

Quarter past ______

______ : ______

5.

Quarter past ______

______ : ______

6.

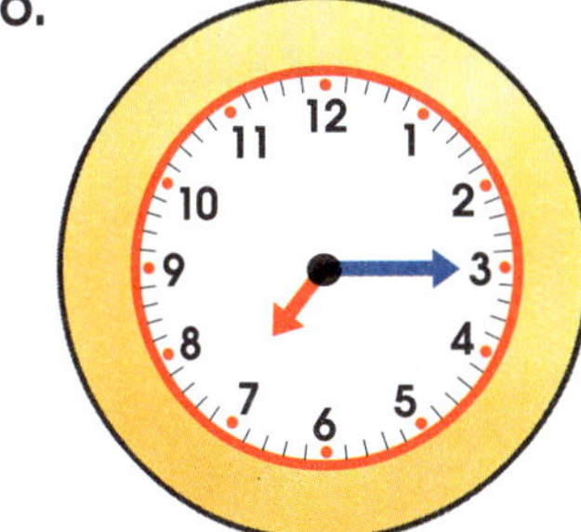

Quarter past ______

______ : ______

Draw hands on the clock and fill in the blanks to show the time.

1. 

Quarter past 7

"seven fifteen"

7:15

2. 

Quarter past 10

"__________ fifteen"

3. 

Quarter past ________

"__________ fifteen"

4. 

Quarter past 3

"________________"

When the minute hand points to the **9**, it is a **quarter to** the next hour. The hour hand is closer to the next hour.

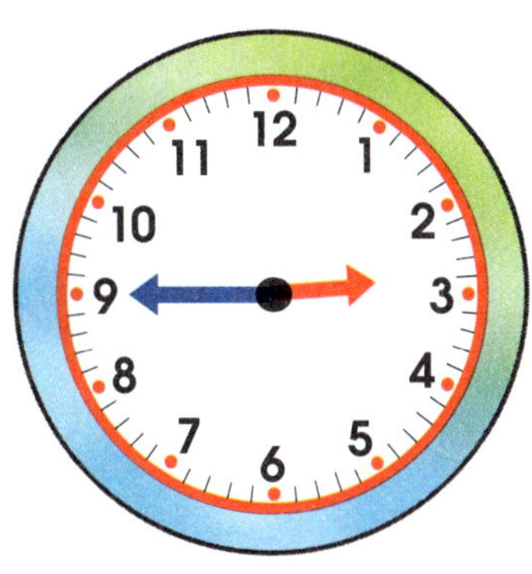

The time is **quarter to 3**.
It is 15 minutes to 3.
We can say: "**quarter to 3**."

OR

It is 45 minutes after 2.
It is **2:45**.
We can say: "**two forty-five**."

Read the hour hand first. Then read the minute hand.
Write the time in two ways.

1.

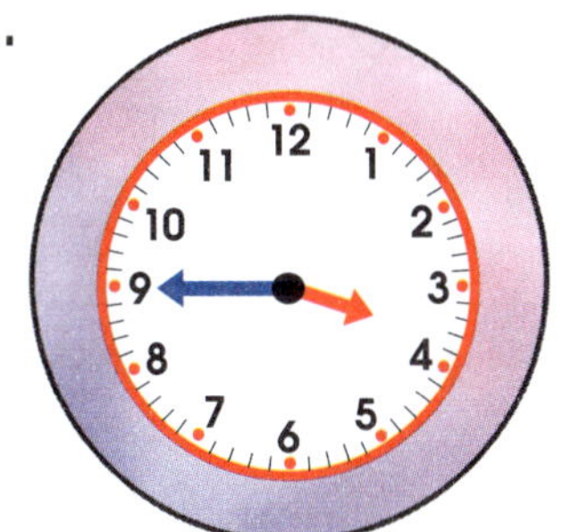

Quarter to 4

3:45

2.

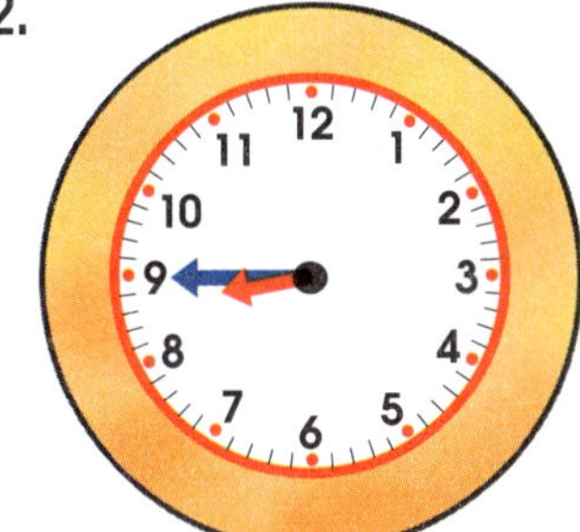

Quarter to ______

______ : ______

3.

Quarter to ______

______ : ______

4.

Quarter to ______

______ : ______

5.

Quarter to ______

______ : ______

6.

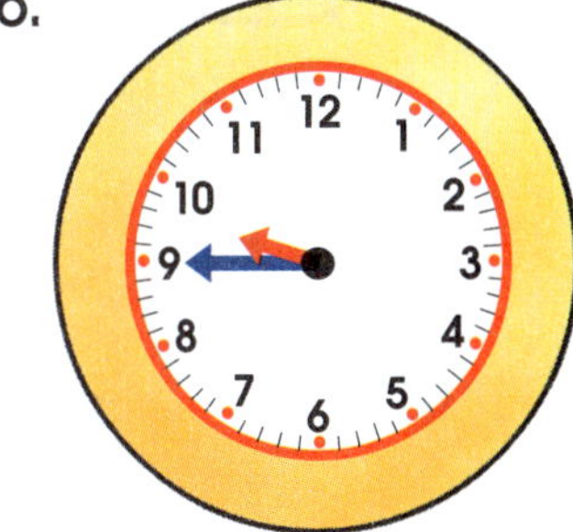

Quarter to ______

______ : ______

Write the time.

1. 

1:45

2. 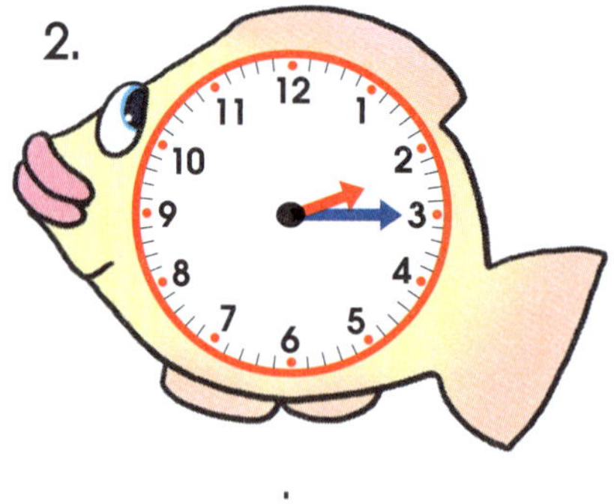

___:___

3. 

___:___

4. 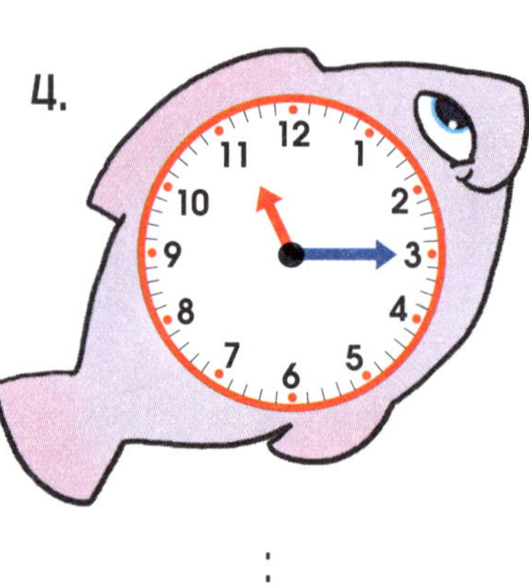

___:___

5. 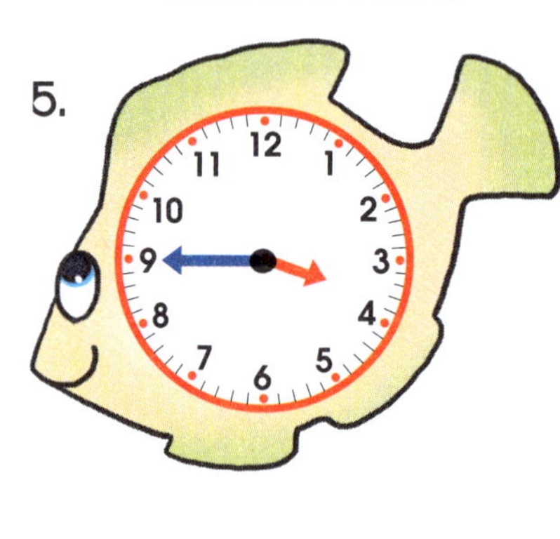

___:___

6. 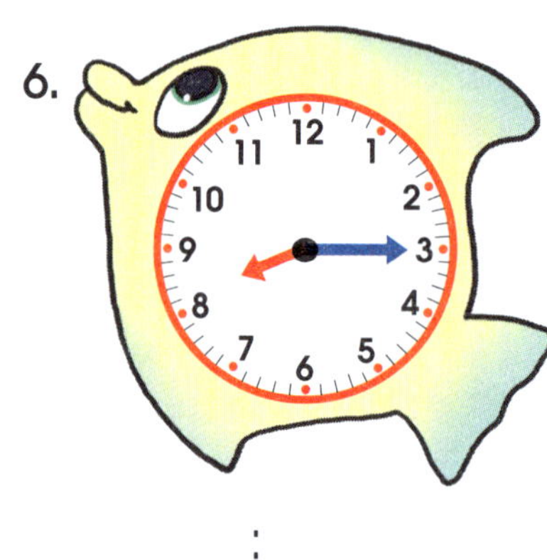

___:___

Draw hands on the clock face to show the time.

7. 2:45

8. 6:15

9. 

9:45

10. 10:45

11. 3:15

12. 12:15

Match the time on the card to the clock. There is more than one card that matches each clock.

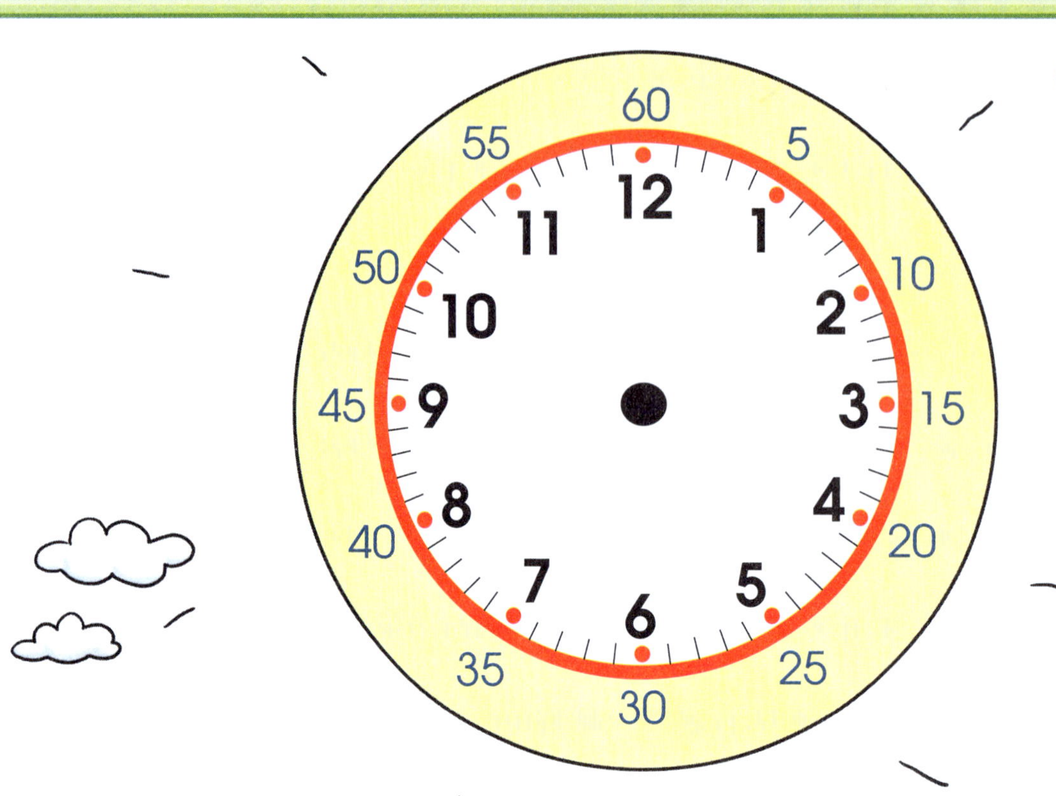

Write the time.

1. 4:05

2. ____ : ____

3. ____ : ____

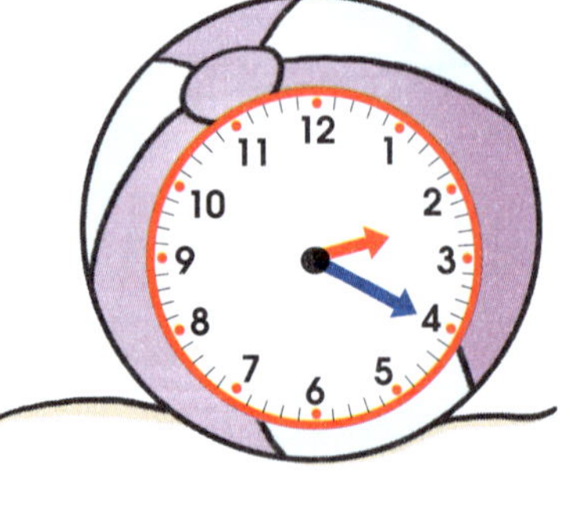

4. ____ : ____

5. ____ : ____

6. ____ : ____

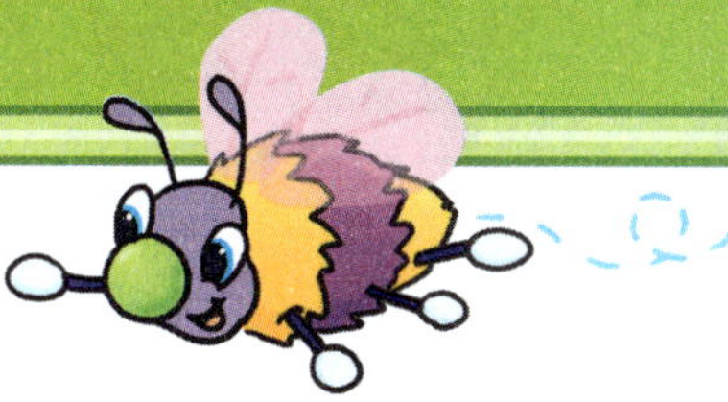

Write the time.

1. ____:____

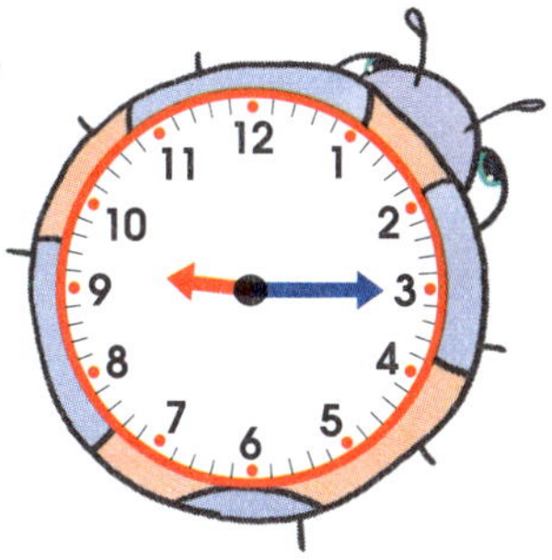

2. ____:____

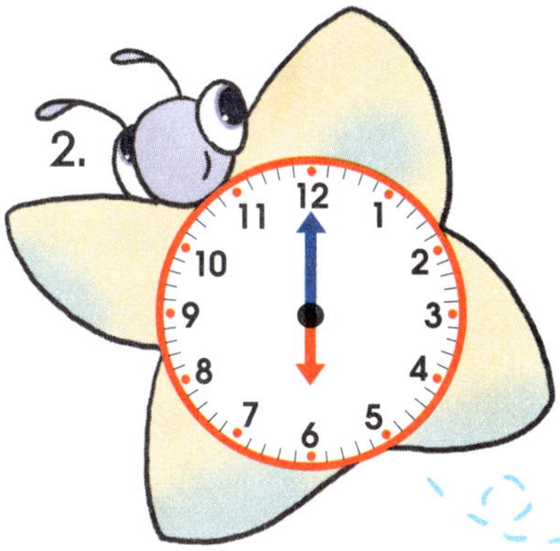

3. ____:____

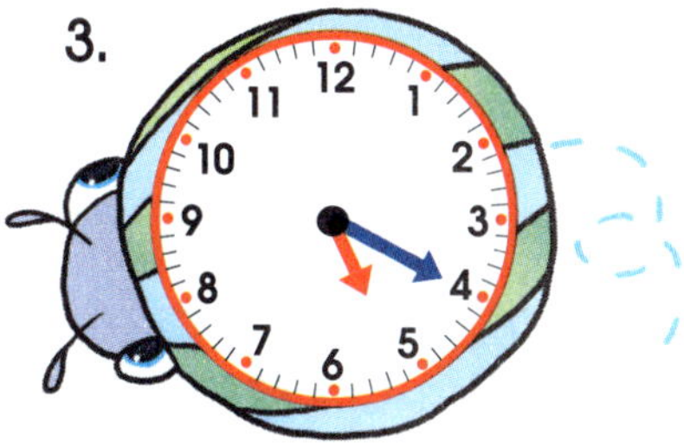

4. ____:____

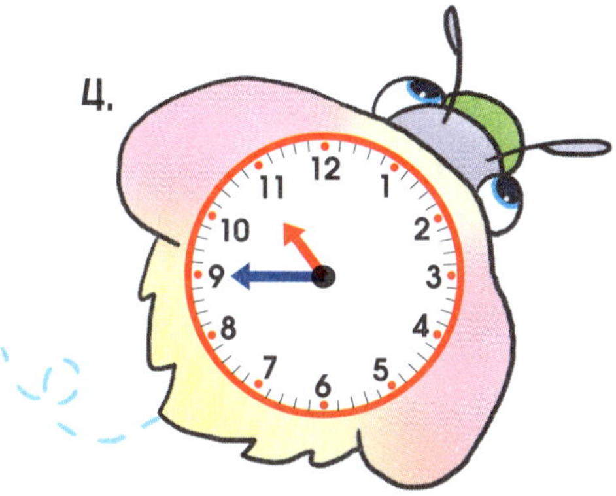

5. ____:____

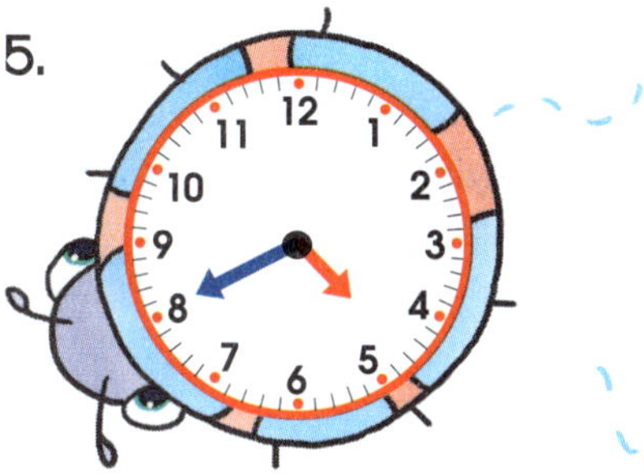

6. ____:____

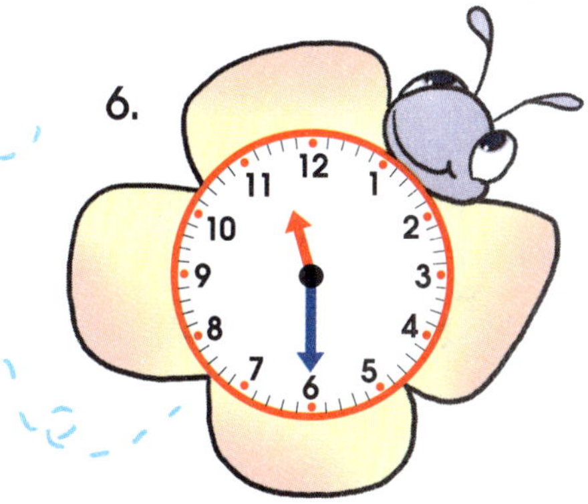

Draw hands on the clock face to show the time.

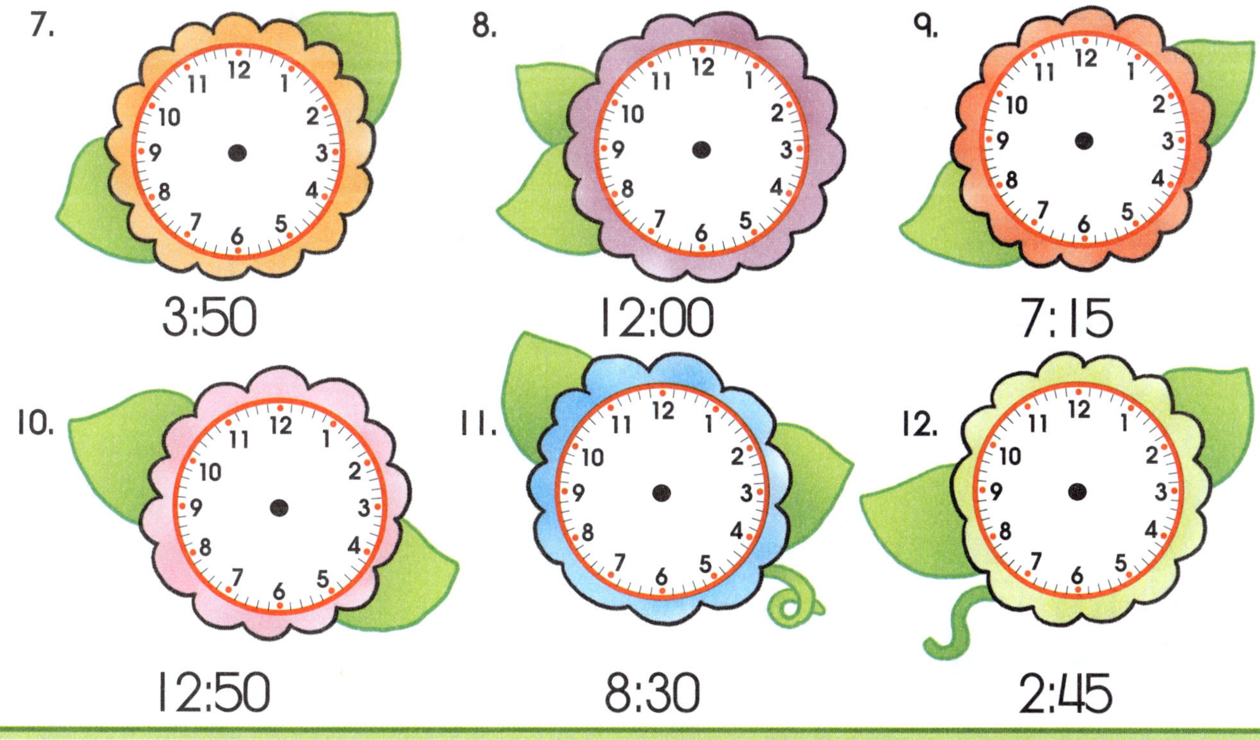

Draw hands to show the end time and write the end time.

Start | Amount of Time | End Time

1.

The game is 3 hours long.

7:00

2.

The movie is 2 hours long.

____ : ____

3.

Lunch time is 30 minutes long.

____ : ____

4.

The school day is 6 hours long.

____ : ____

5.

The trip to the zoo is 4 hours long.

____ : ____

Equal parts are the same size and shape.
Look at the shapes. One shape has 2 equal parts.

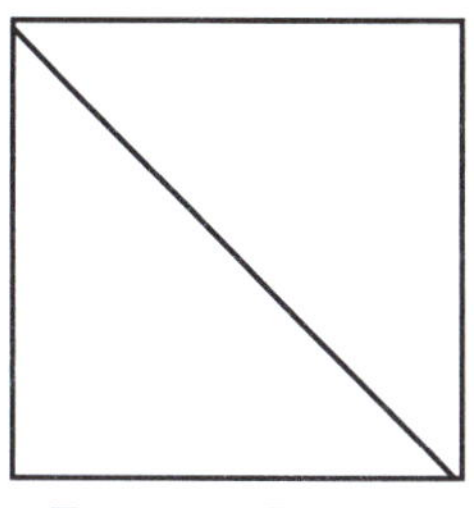

Equal Parts

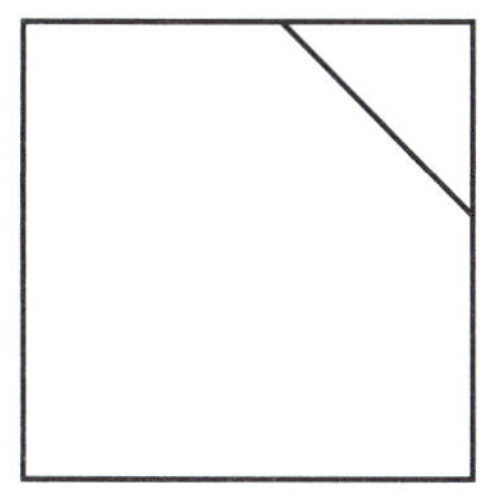

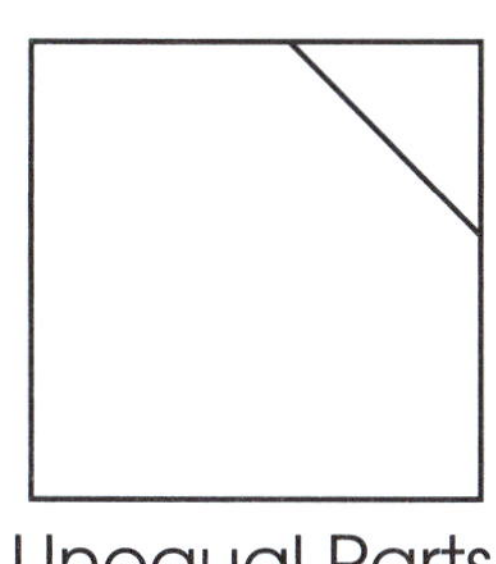

Unequal Parts

Circle the shapes that have equal parts.

1.

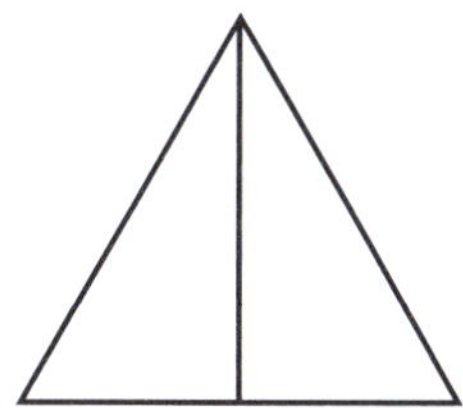

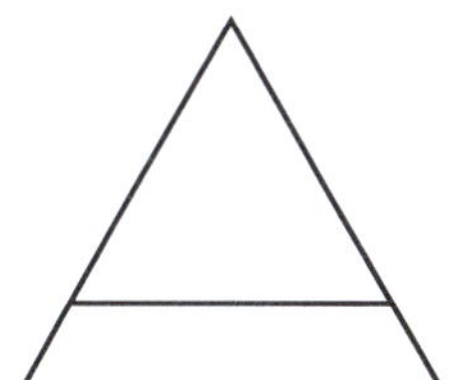

2.

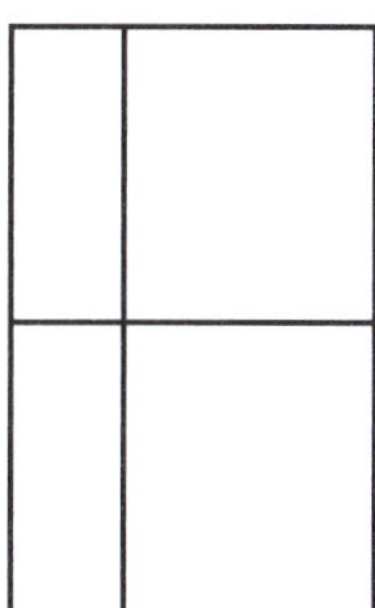

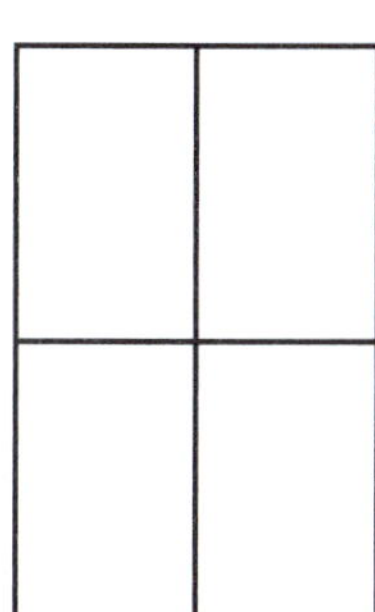

3.

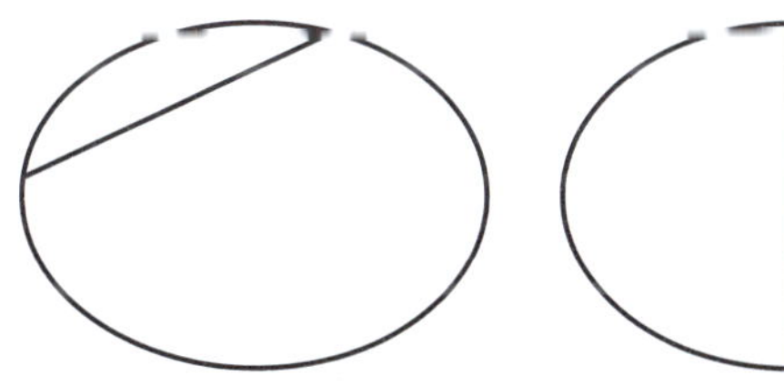

4.

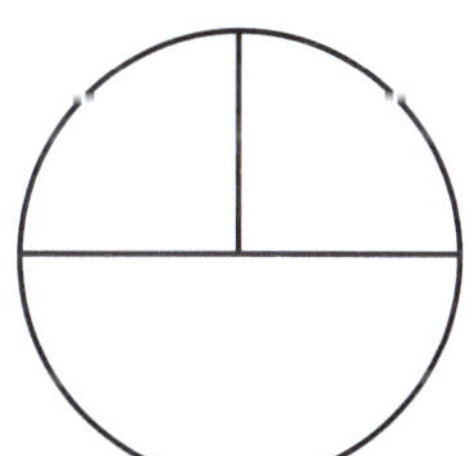

5.

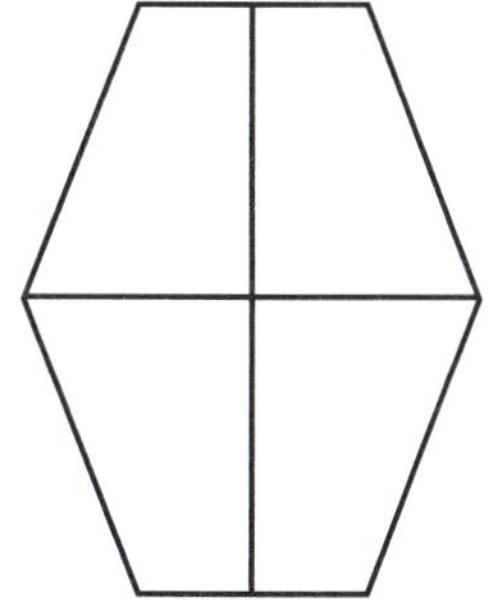

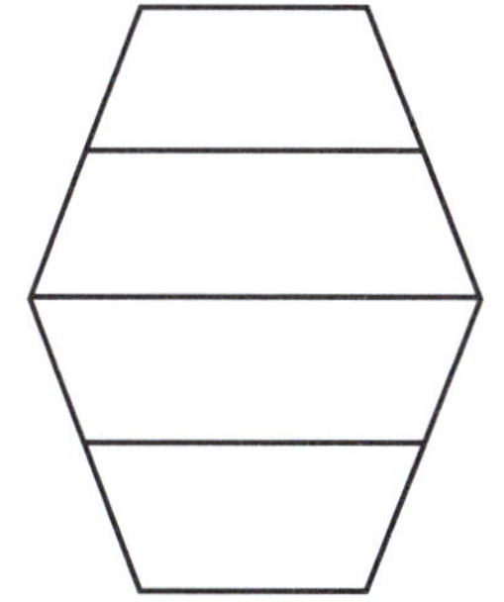

6.

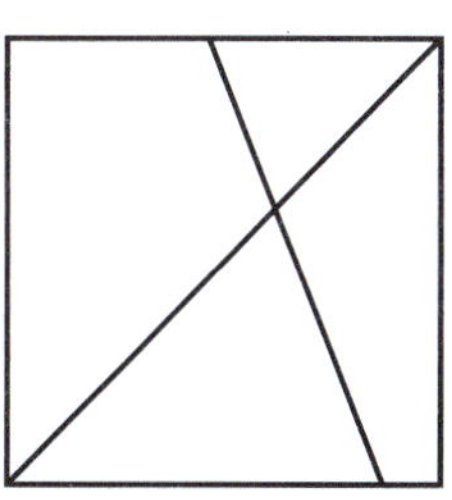

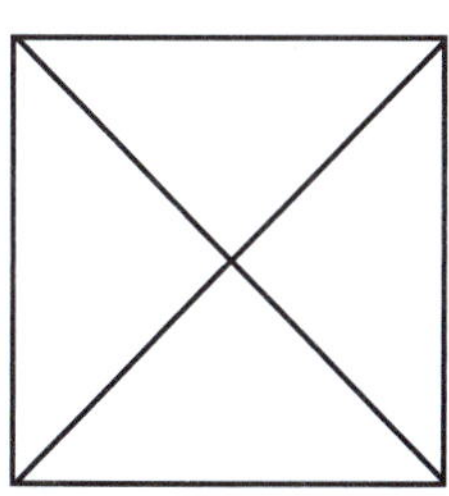

Look at the shapes. One shape has 4 equal parts.

4 Equal Parts 4 Not Equal Parts

Circle the shapes that have equal parts.

1.

2.

3.

4.

5.

6.

7.

8.

9.

Look at the shape. It has 2 equal parts. Each part is $\frac{1}{2}$ or **one-half**.

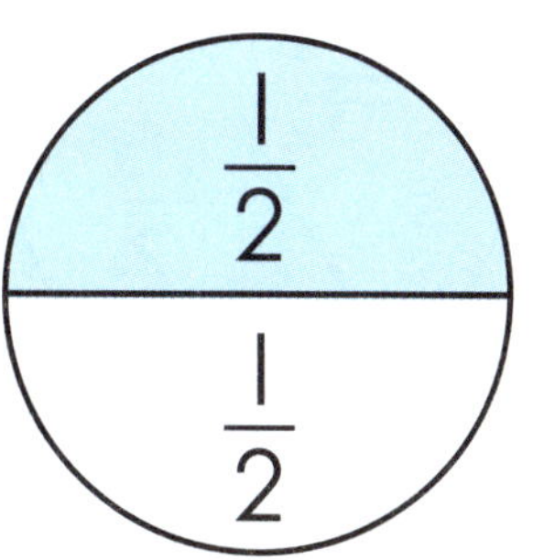

$\frac{1}{2}$ ←parts colored / ←equal parts

$\frac{1}{2}$ is a **fraction**.

A **fraction** is a number that tells about part of a shape or group.

Write the **fraction** $\frac{1}{2}$ on each part.

1\.

2\. 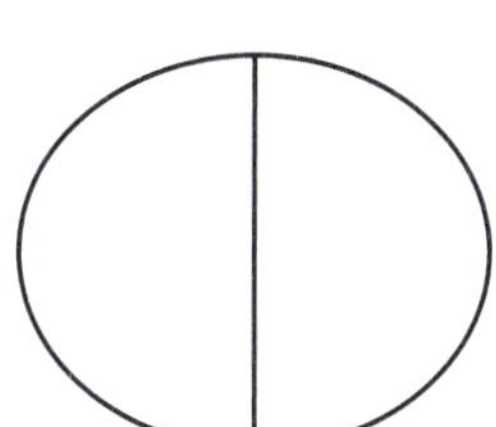

3\. 

4\. 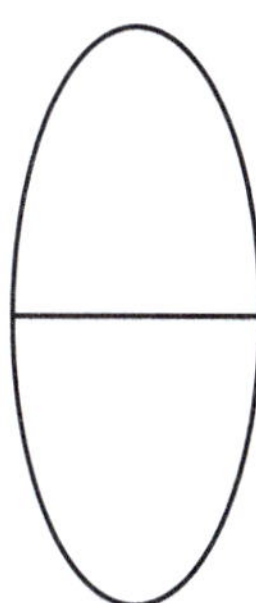

Color $\frac{1}{2}$ of each shape.

5\. 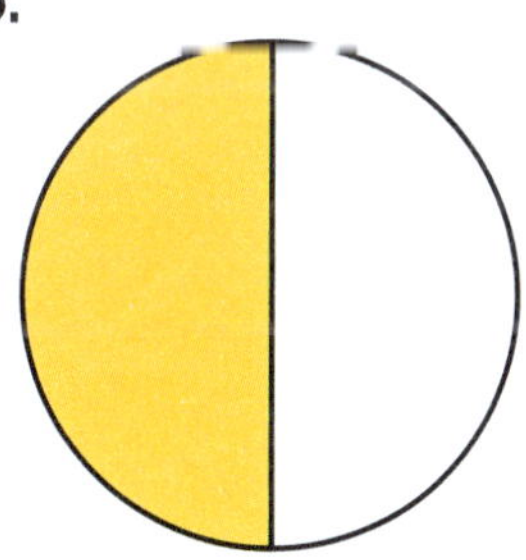

6\. 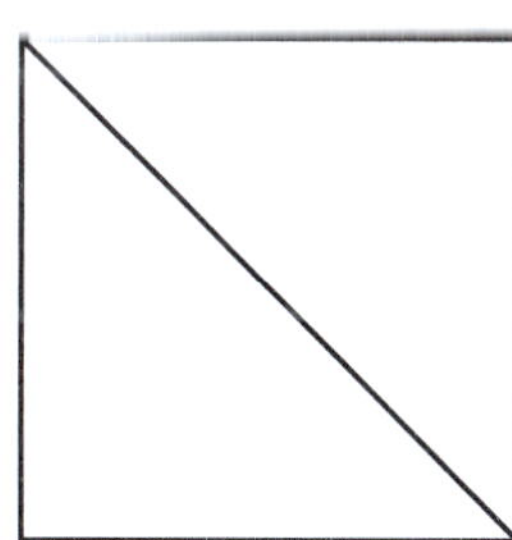

7\. 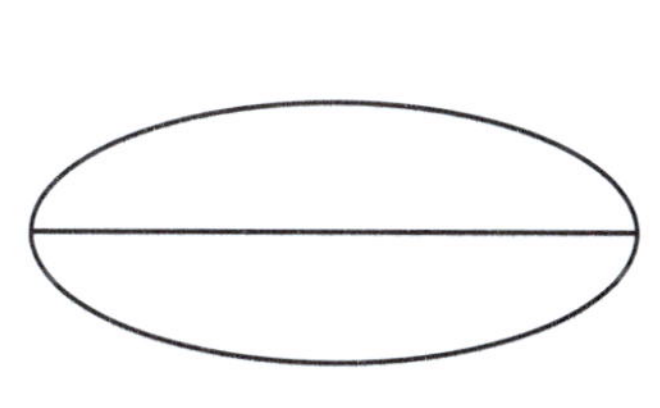

8\. 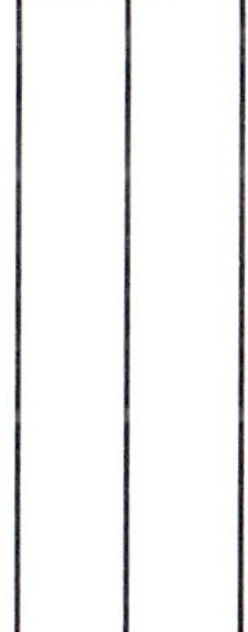

9\. 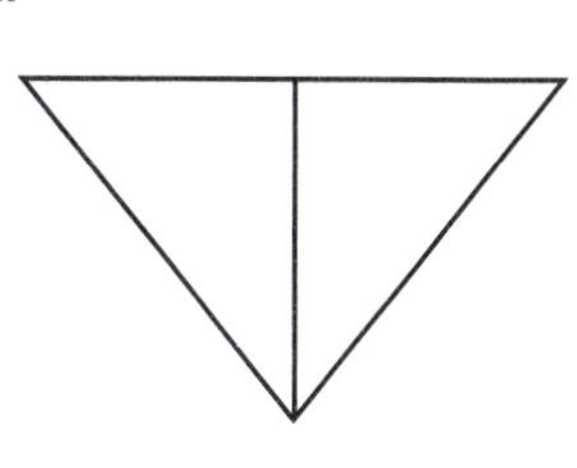

10\. 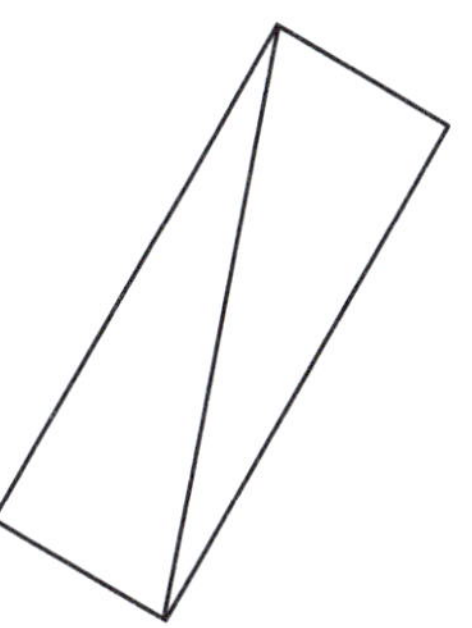

11\. 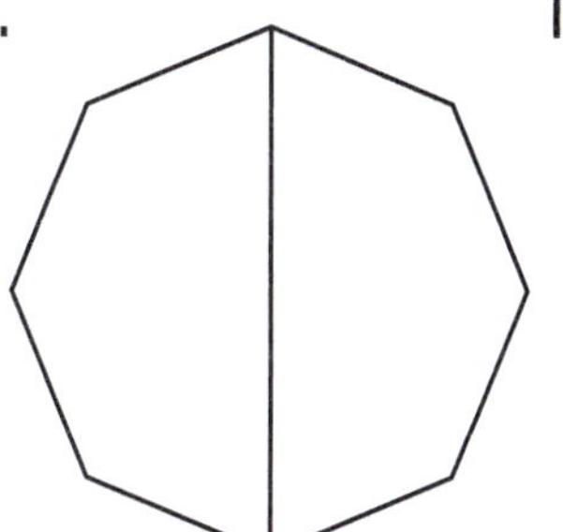

12\. 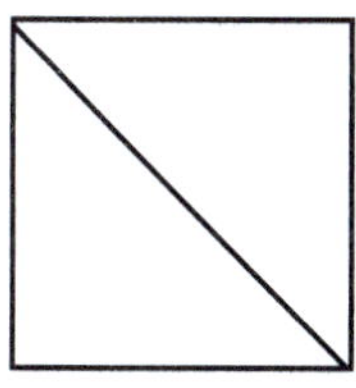

Cross out the shapes that do not have 2 equal parts.
On the shapes with 2 equal parts, write $\frac{1}{2}$ on each part and color $\frac{1}{2}$.

1.

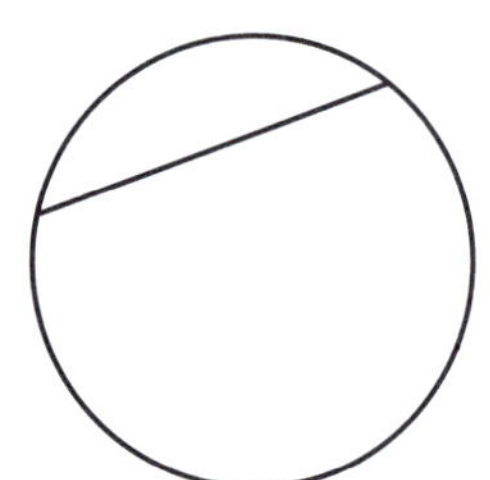

2.

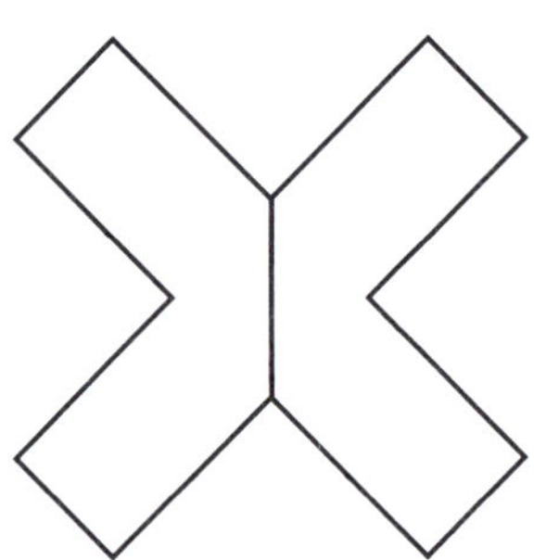

3.

4.

5.

6.

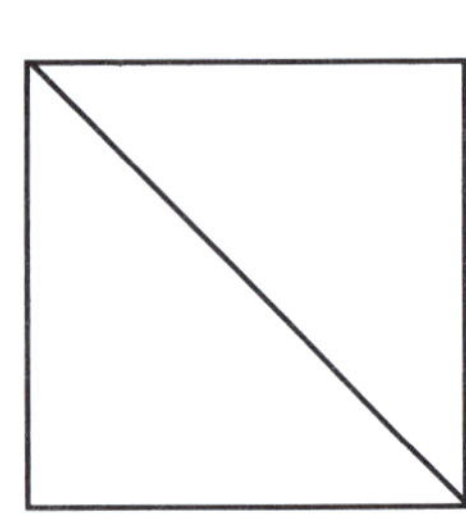

7.

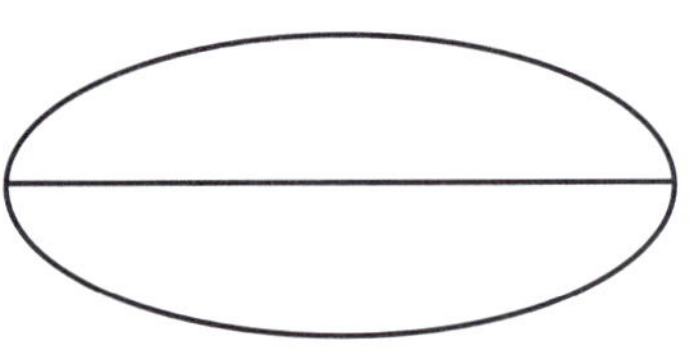

8.

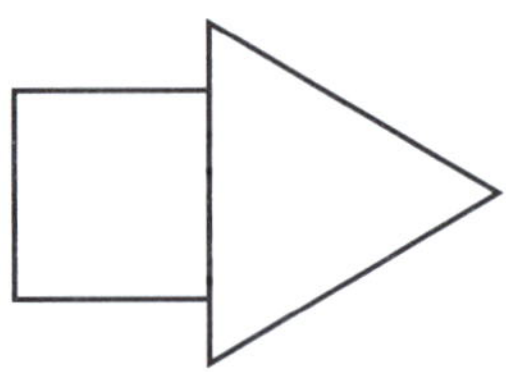

9.

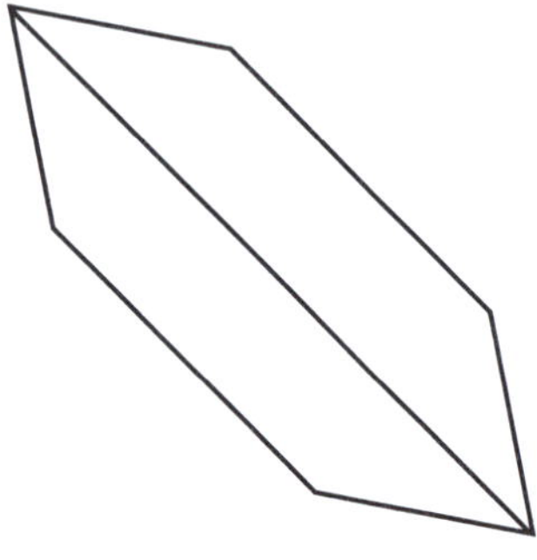

Look at the shape. It has 3 equal parts. Each part is $\frac{1}{3}$ or **one-third**.

$\frac{1}{3}$	$\frac{1}{3}$	$\frac{1}{3}$

$\frac{1}{3}$ ← parts colored / ← equal parts

Write the fraction $\frac{1}{3}$ on each part.

1. 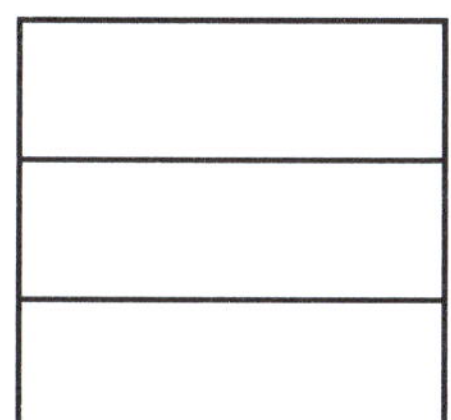
2. 
3. 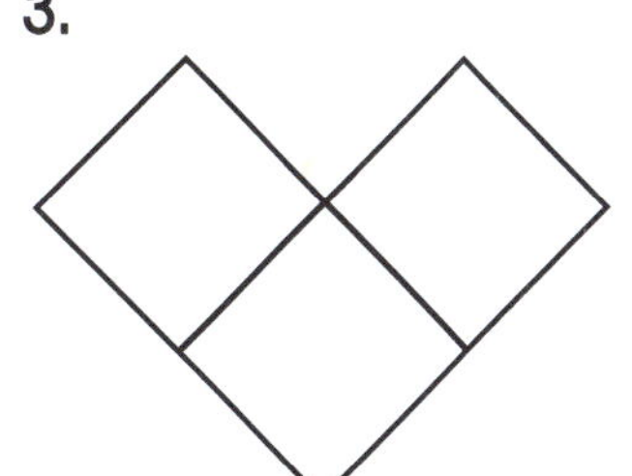
4. 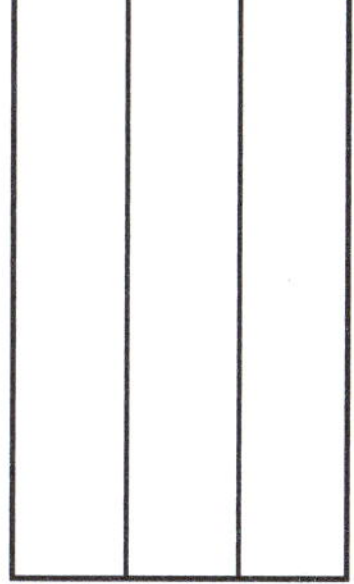

Color $\frac{1}{3}$ of each shape.

5. 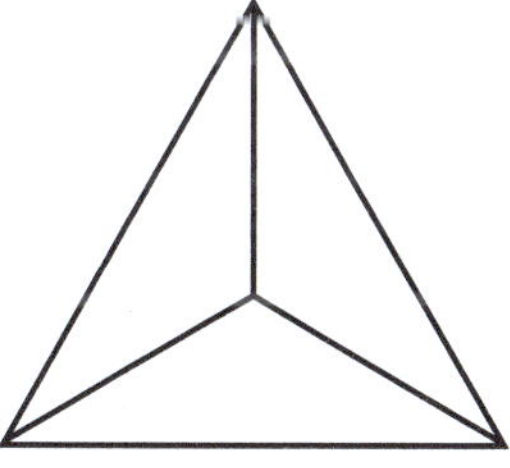
6. 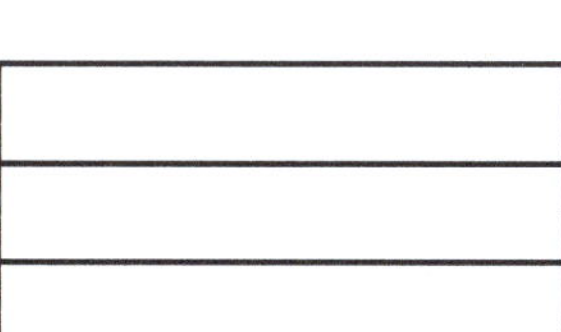
7. 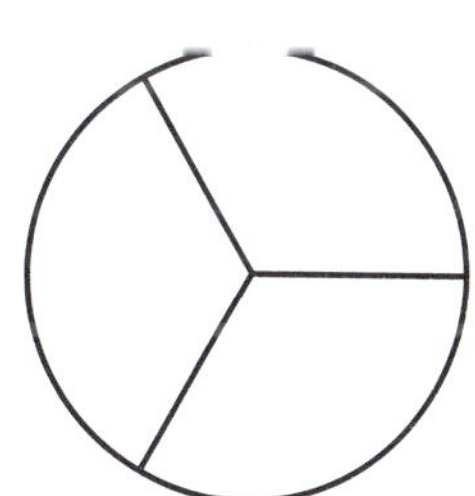
8. 
9. 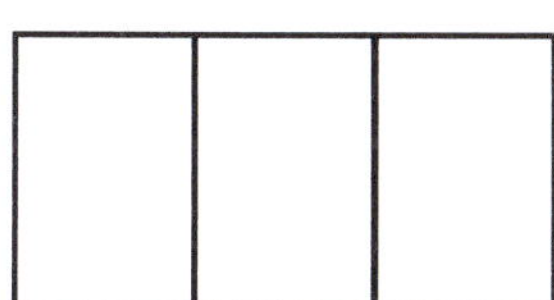
10. 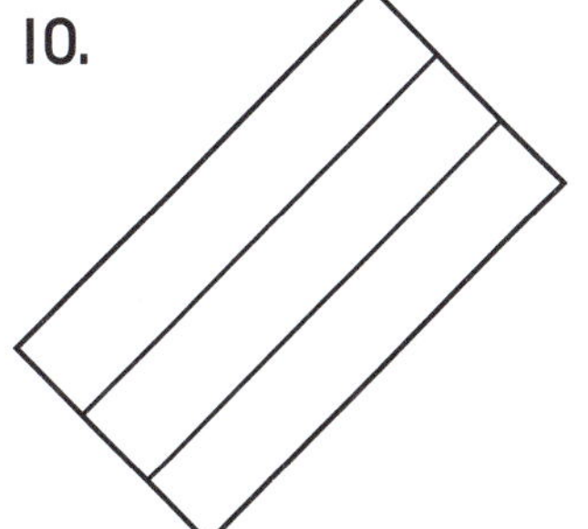
11. 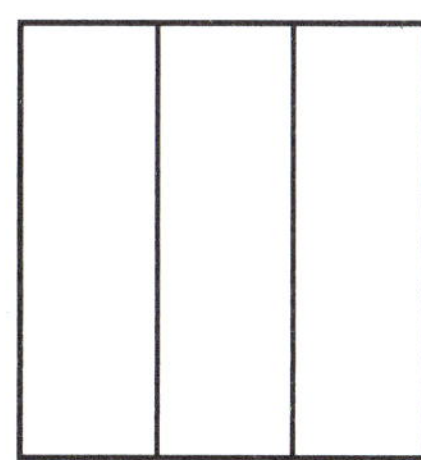
12. 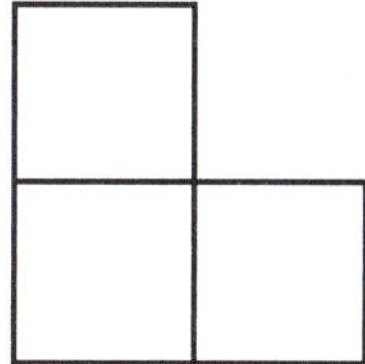

Look at the shape. It has 4 equal parts. Each part is $\frac{1}{4}$ or **one-fourth**.

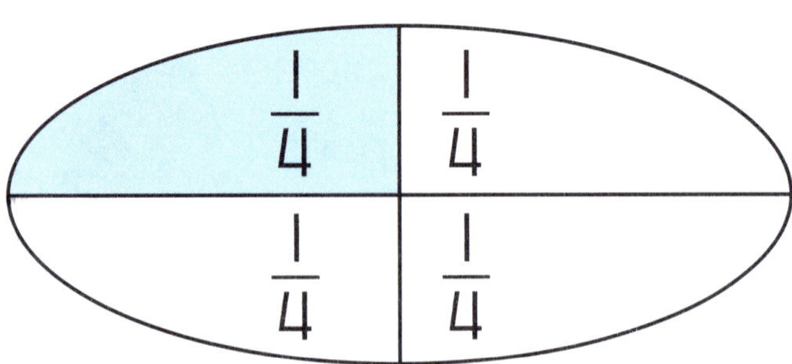

$\frac{1}{4}$ ←parts colored / ←equal parts

Write the fraction $\frac{1}{4}$ on each part.

1. 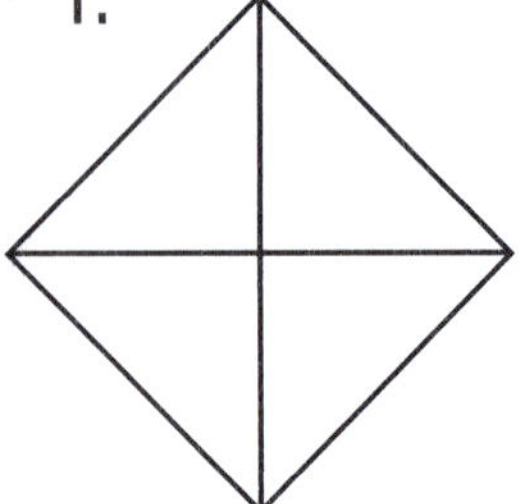
2. 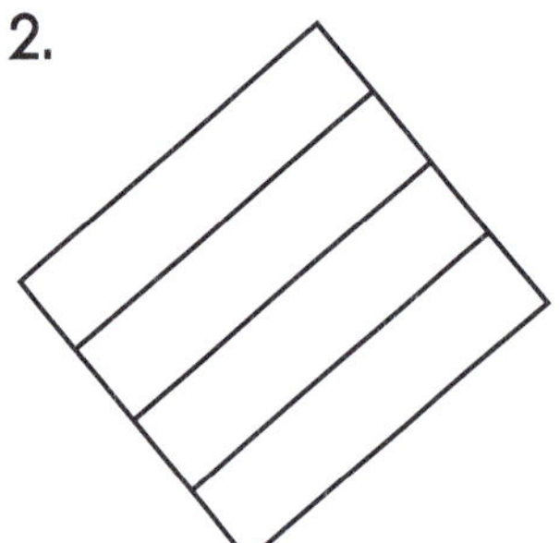
3. 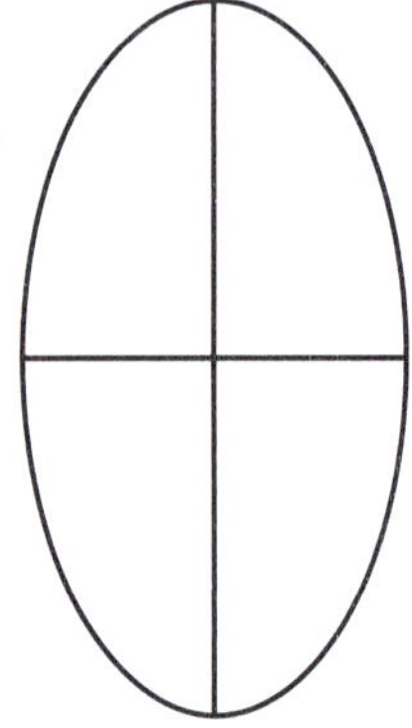
4. 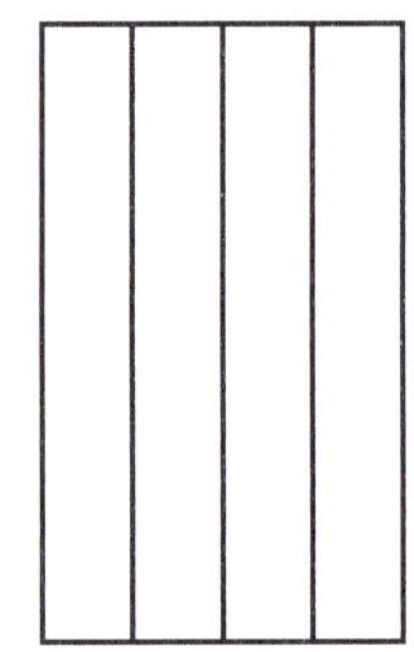

Color $\frac{1}{4}$ of each shape.

5. 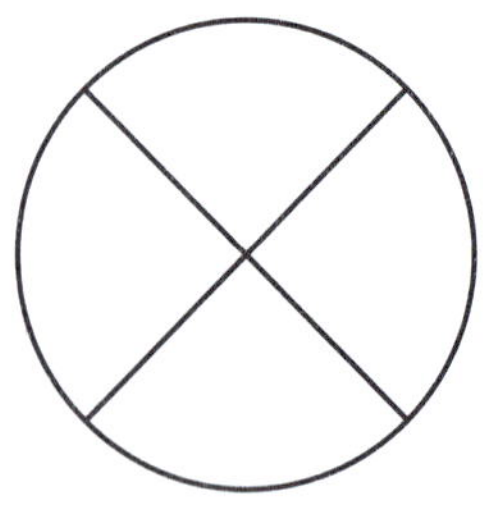
6. 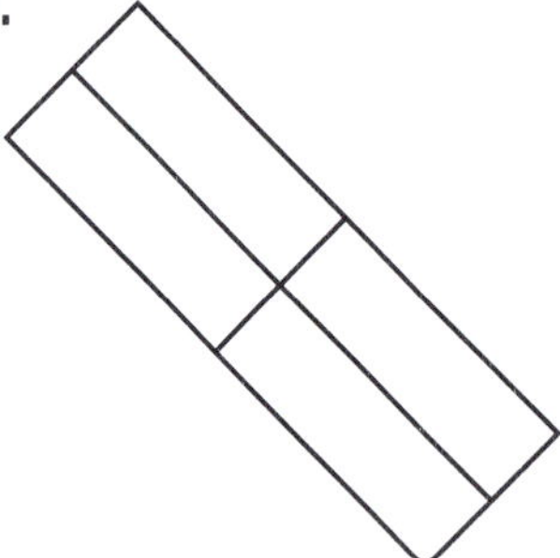
7. 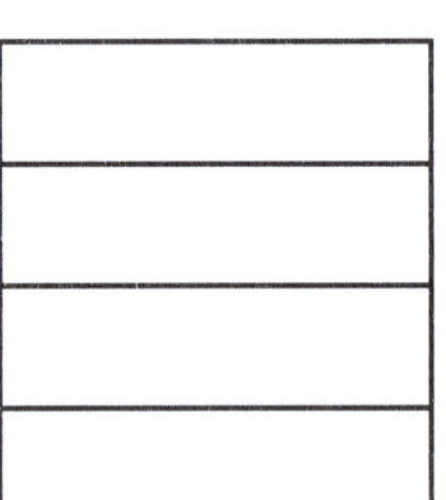
8. 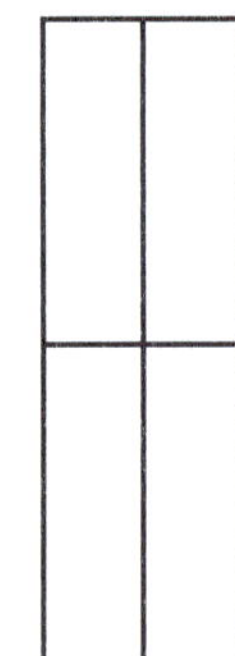
9. 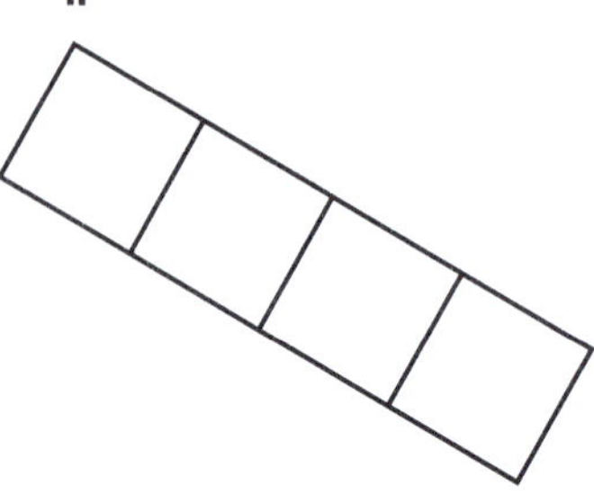
10. 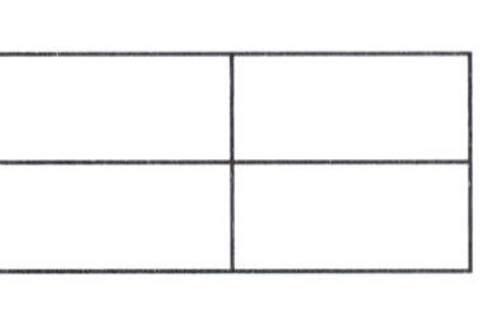
11. 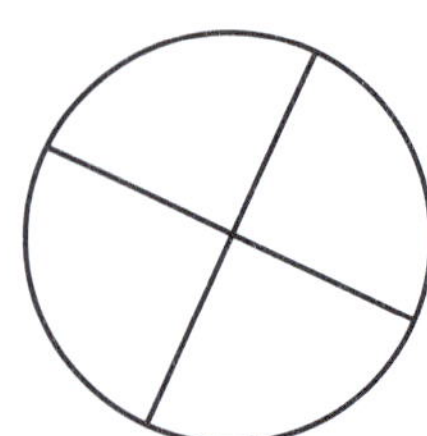
12. 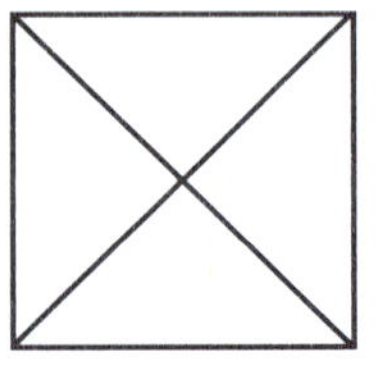

In a fraction, the top number tells how many parts are colored. The bottom number of a fraction tells how many equal parts there are in all.

$\frac{1}{2}$ $\frac{1}{3}$ $\frac{1}{4}$

Write the fraction to tell about the colored part of each shape.

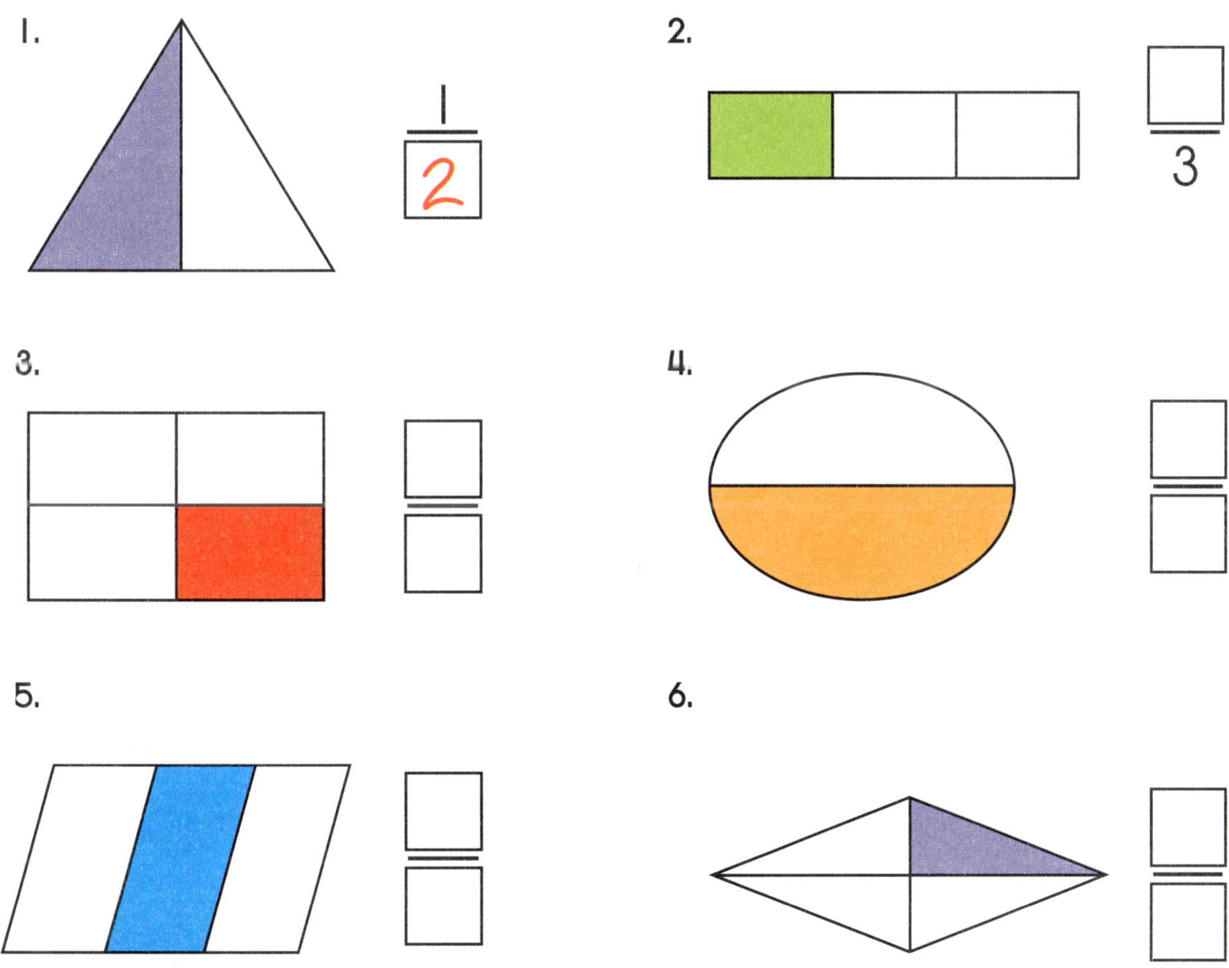

Circle the correct fraction.

1.
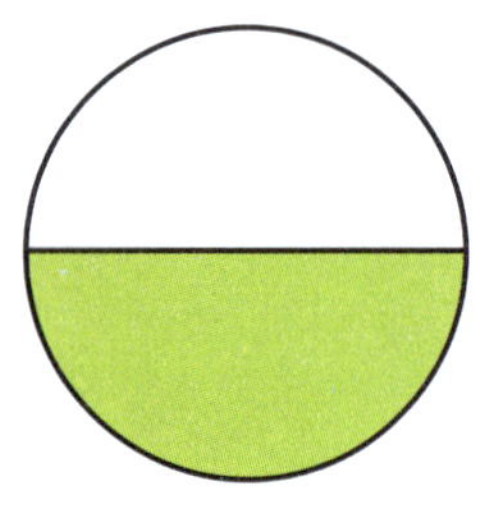

$\frac{1}{2}$ $\frac{1}{3}$ $\frac{1}{4}$

2.
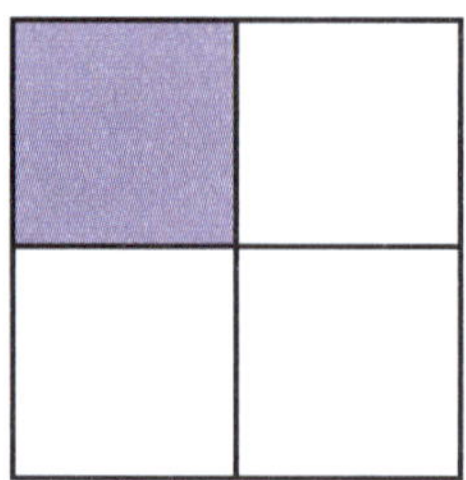

$\frac{1}{2}$ $\frac{1}{3}$ $\frac{1}{4}$

3.

$\frac{1}{2}$ $\frac{1}{3}$ $\frac{1}{4}$

4.
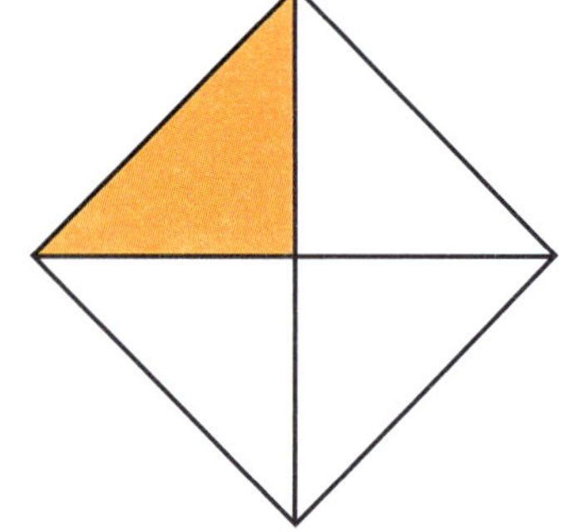

$\frac{1}{2}$ $\frac{1}{3}$ $\frac{1}{4}$

5.
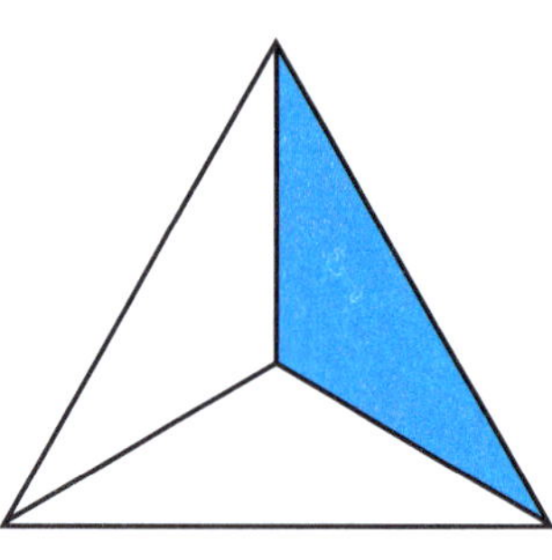

$\frac{1}{2}$ $\frac{1}{3}$ $\frac{1}{4}$

6.
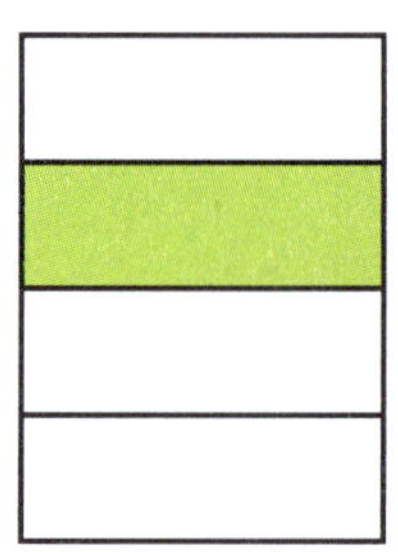

$\frac{1}{2}$ $\frac{1}{3}$ $\frac{1}{4}$

7.
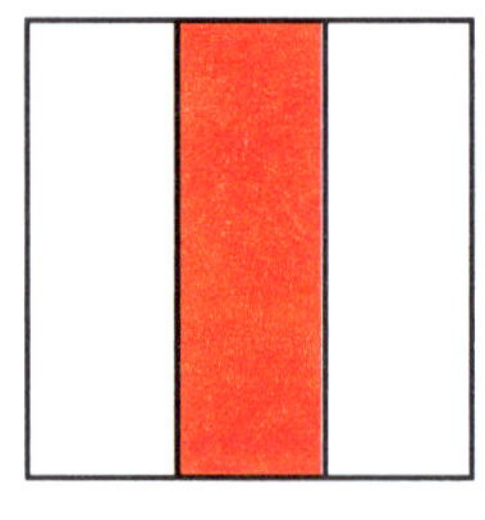

$\frac{1}{2}$ $\frac{1}{3}$ $\frac{1}{4}$

8.
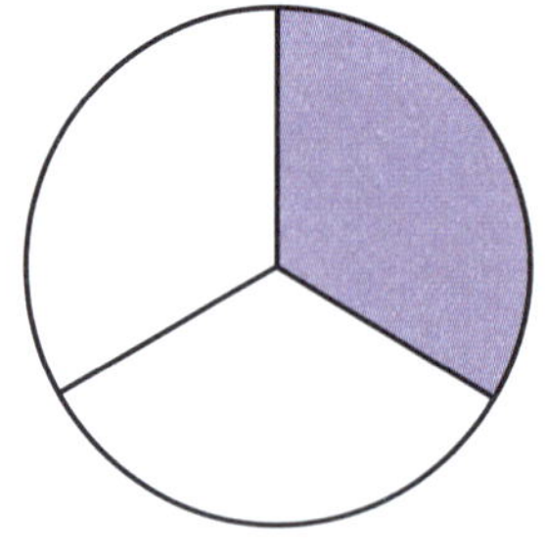

$\frac{1}{2}$ $\frac{1}{3}$ $\frac{1}{4}$

9.
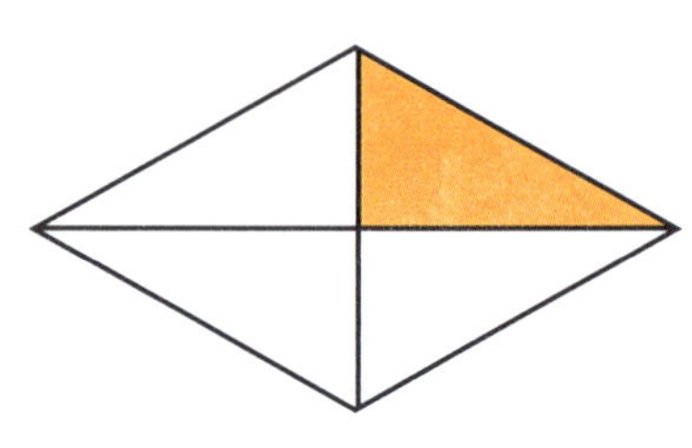

$\frac{1}{2}$ $\frac{1}{3}$ $\frac{1}{4}$

A fraction tells how many parts of a whole are being used.
These fractions tell about the colored part of each shape.

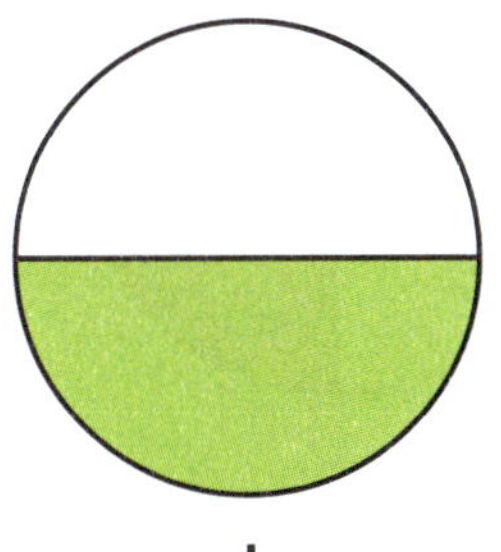

$\frac{1}{2}$

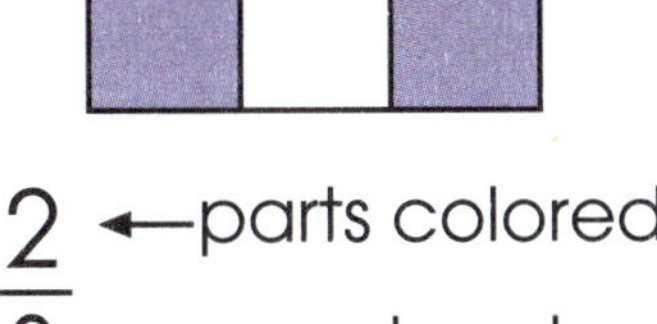

$\frac{2}{3}$ ←parts colored
←equal parts

$\frac{3}{4}$

Write the fraction to tell about the colored part of each shape.

1. 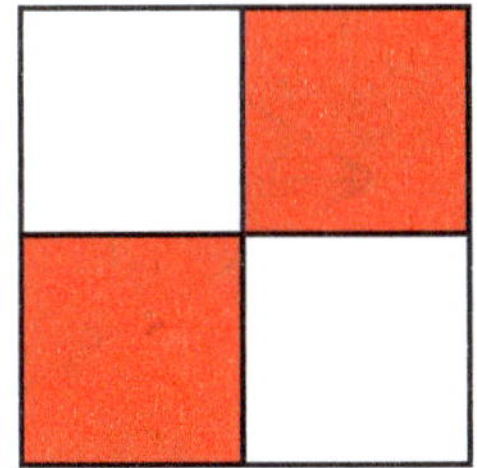 $\frac{2}{4}$

2. 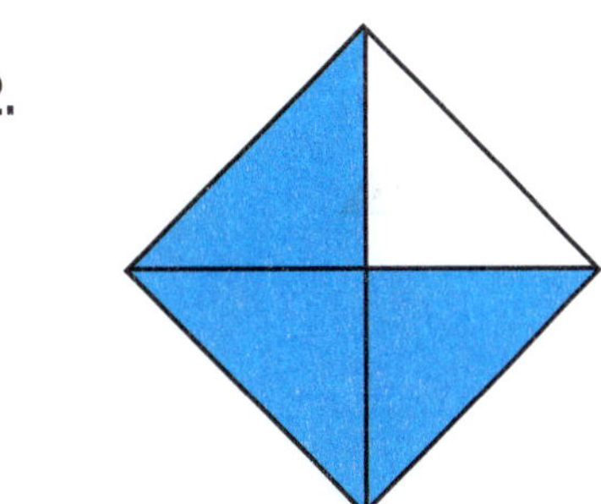 $\frac{3}{\square}$

3. 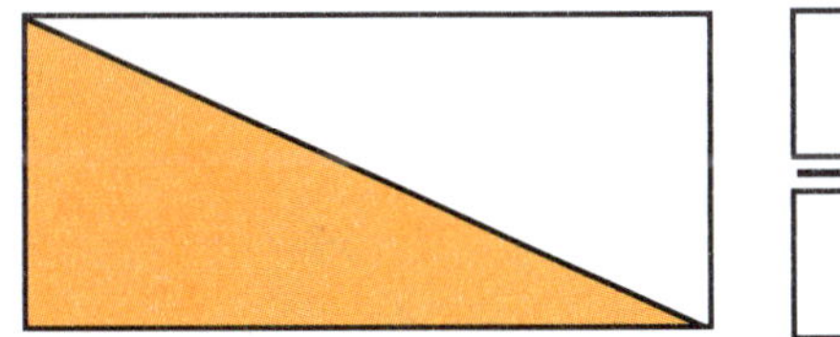

4.  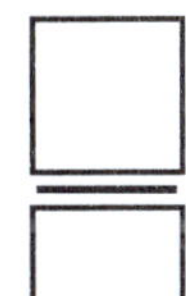

5. 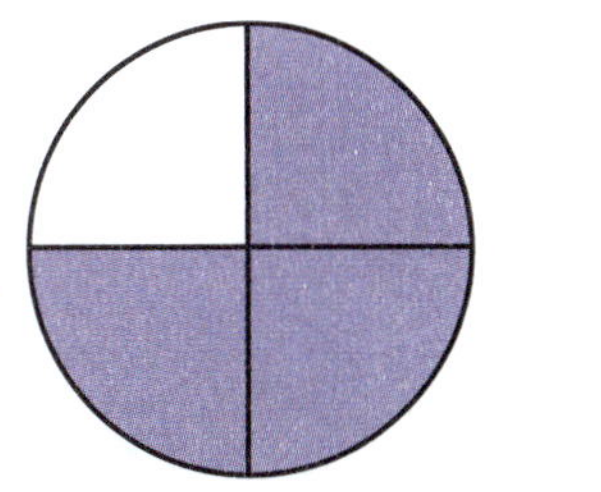

6. 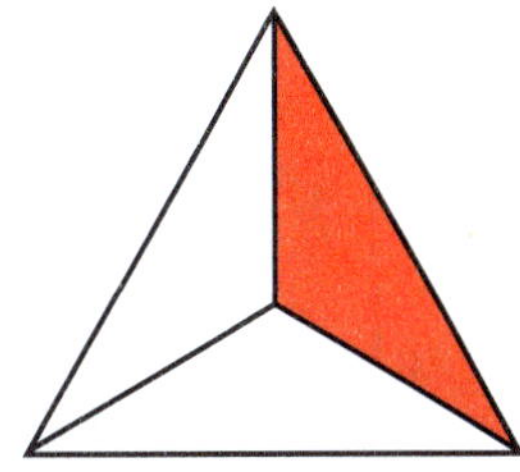 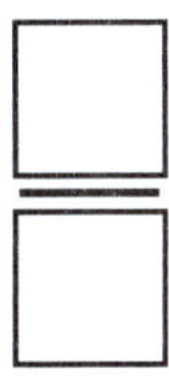

Circle the correct fraction.

1. 

$\frac{3}{4}$ $\frac{1}{4}$ $\frac{2}{3}$

2. 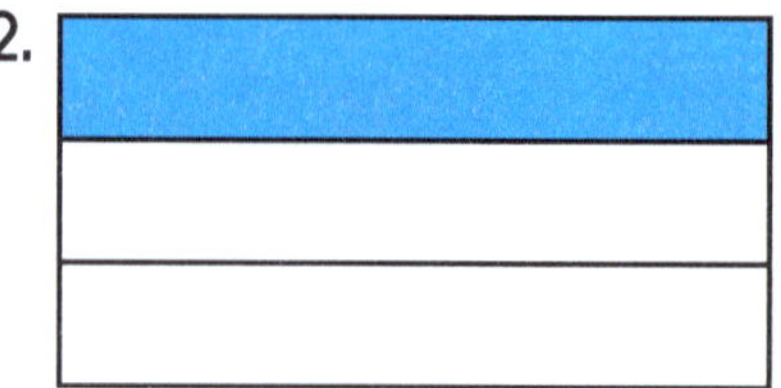

$\frac{2}{3}$ $\frac{1}{2}$ $\frac{1}{3}$

3. 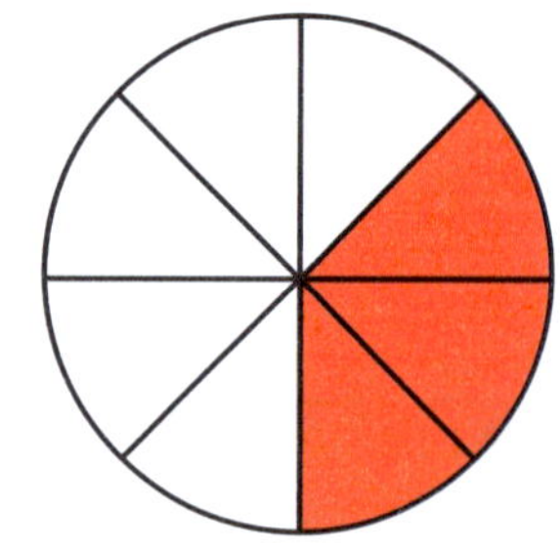

$\frac{1}{8}$ $\frac{7}{8}$ $\frac{3}{8}$

4. 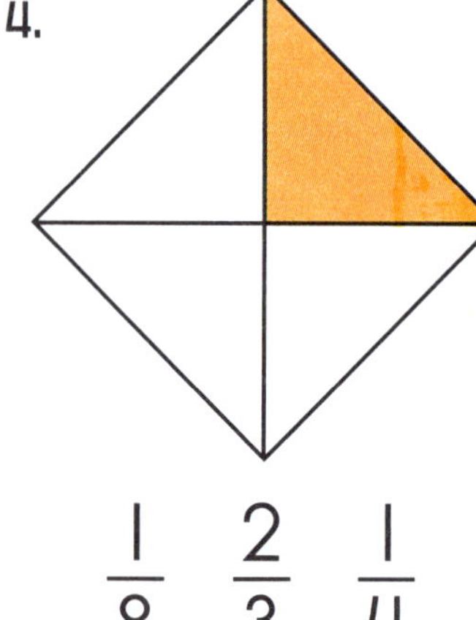

$\frac{1}{8}$ $\frac{2}{3}$ $\frac{1}{4}$

5. 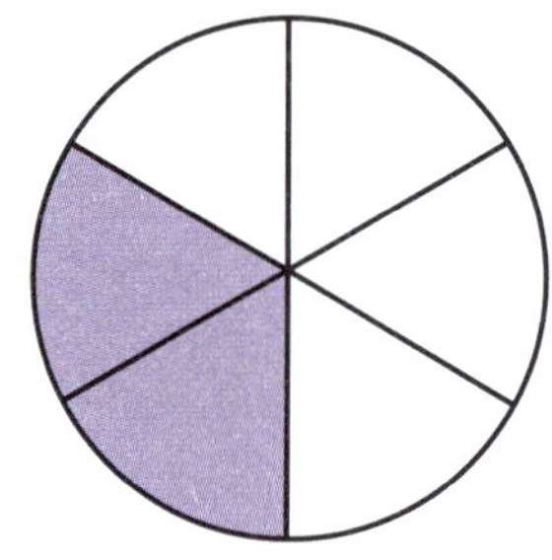

$\frac{1}{6}$ $\frac{1}{2}$ $\frac{2}{6}$

6. 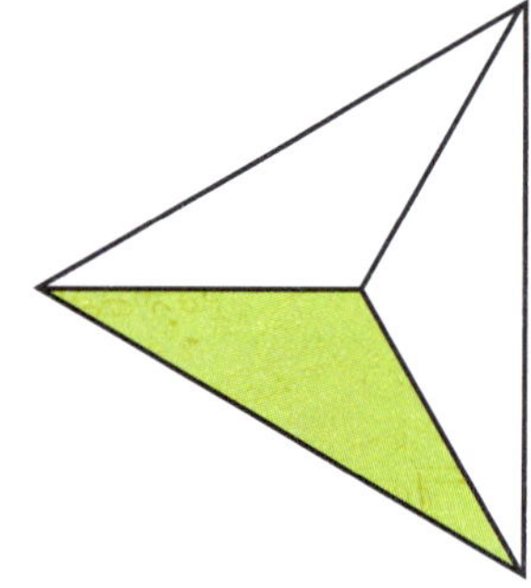

$\frac{1}{4}$ $\frac{1}{3}$ $\frac{1}{2}$

7. 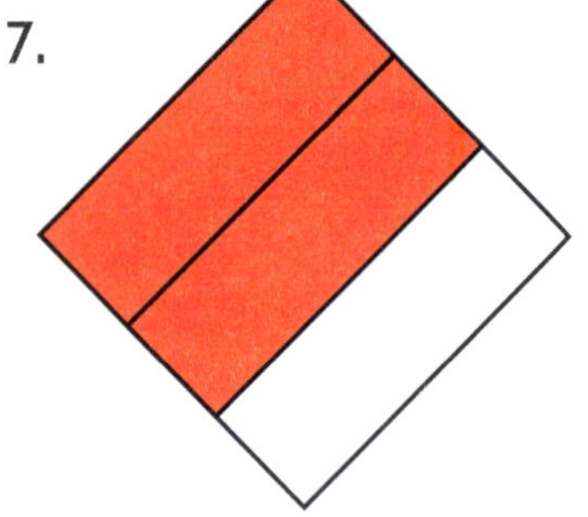

$\frac{1}{3}$ $\frac{2}{3}$ $\frac{1}{2}$

8. 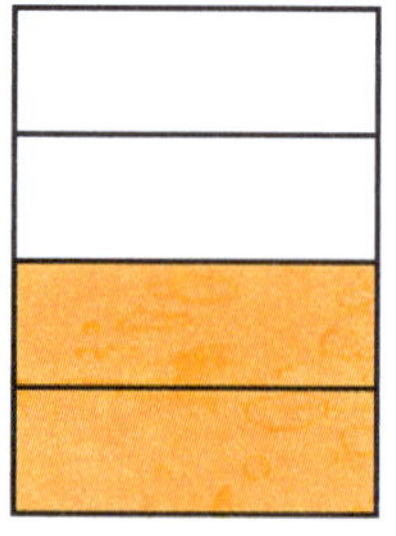

$\frac{3}{4}$ $\frac{1}{4}$ $\frac{2}{4}$

9. 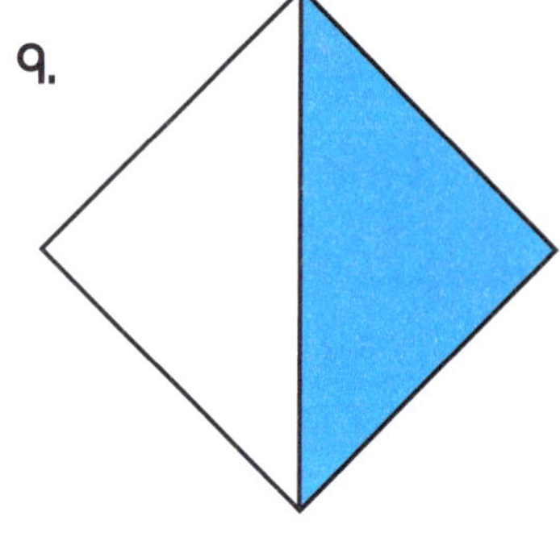

$\frac{1}{3}$ $\frac{1}{2}$ $\frac{2}{4}$

$\frac{2}{3}$ ←parts colored ←equal parts

Color the correct number of parts to show each fraction.

1. $\frac{1}{2}$

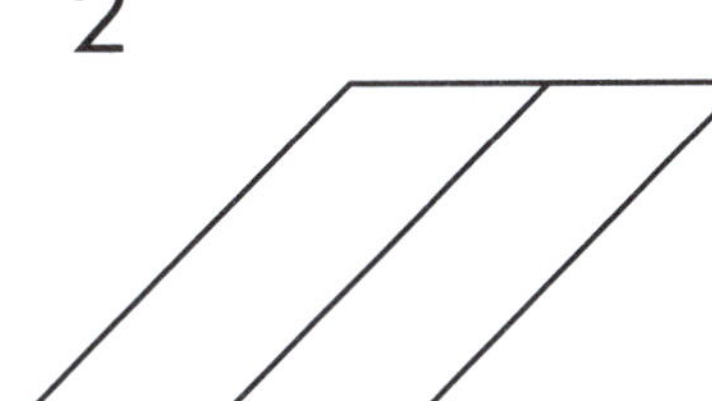

2. $\frac{2}{3}$

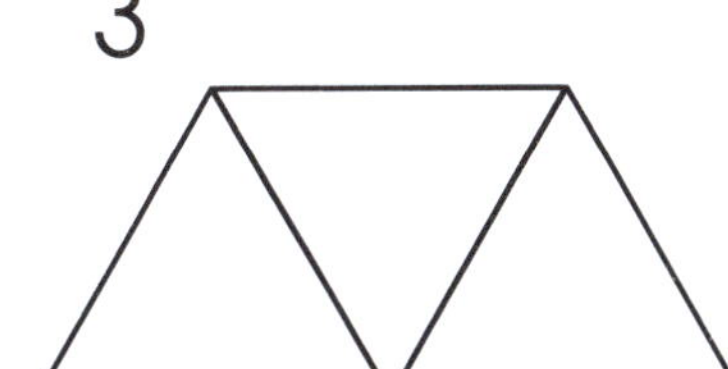

3. $\frac{4}{6}$

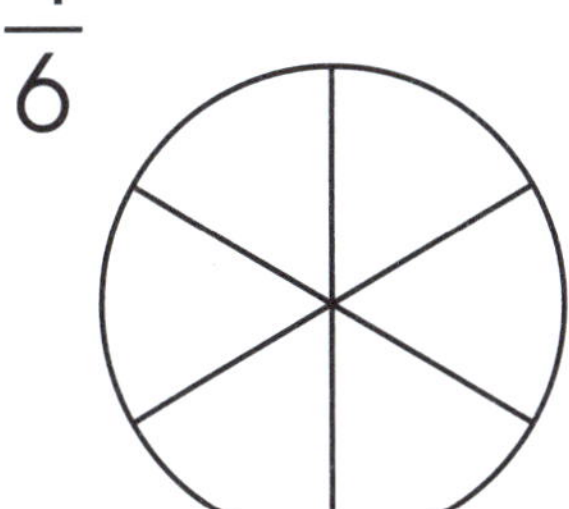

4. $\frac{1}{4}$

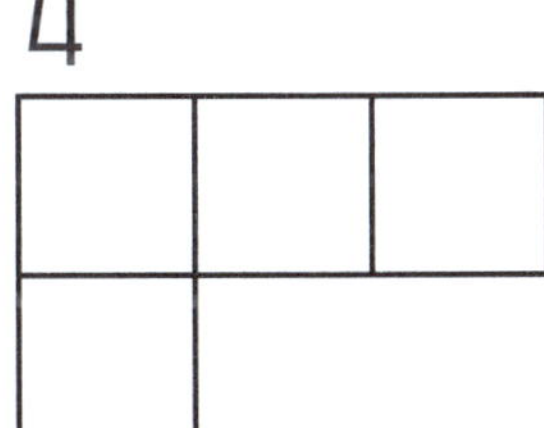

5. $\frac{5}{6}$

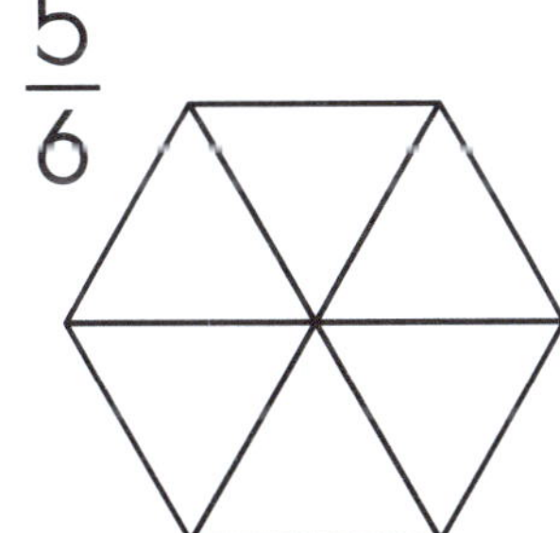

6. $\frac{3}{4}$

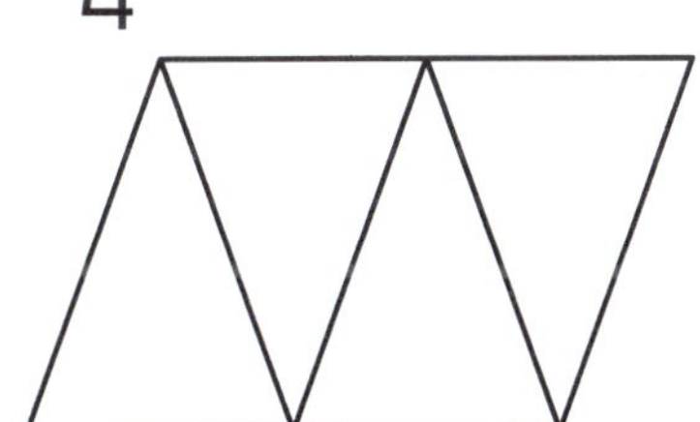

7. $\frac{3}{8}$

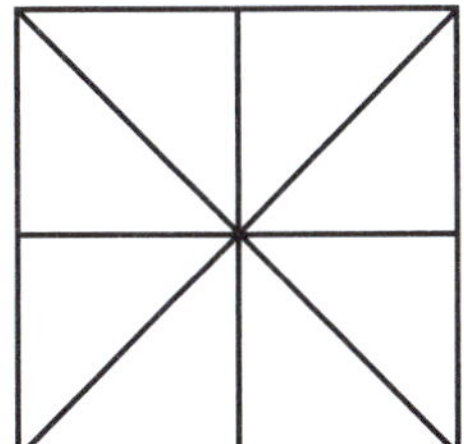

8. $\frac{2}{2}$

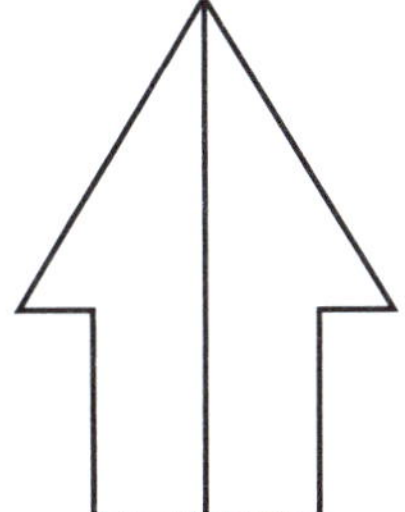

9. $\frac{2}{5}$

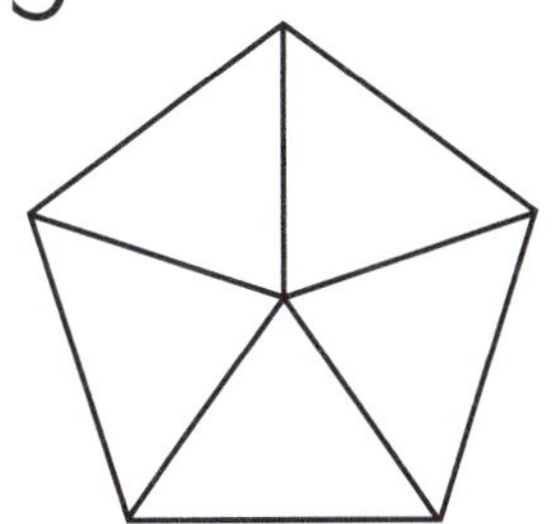

Draw lines in the shape to show all the equal parts.
Then color the number of parts to show the fraction.

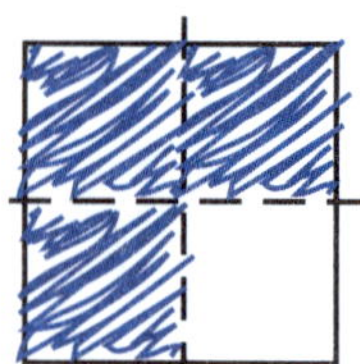

Look at the bottom number.
Draw 4 equal parts.

Look at the top number.
Color 3 of the parts.

Draw a line or lines in the shape to show the number of equal parts.
Then color the correct number of parts to show the fraction.

1. $\frac{1}{4}$ 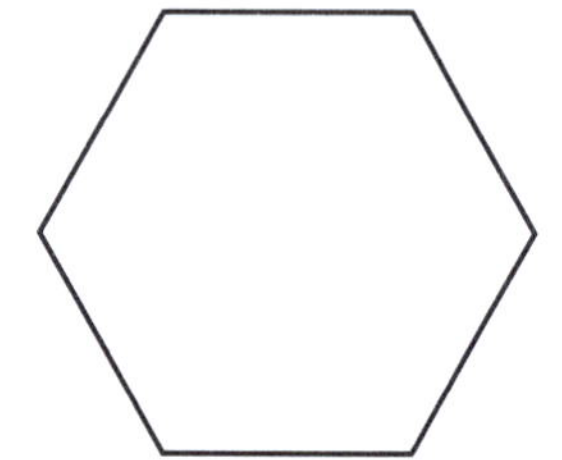

2. $\frac{1}{2}$ 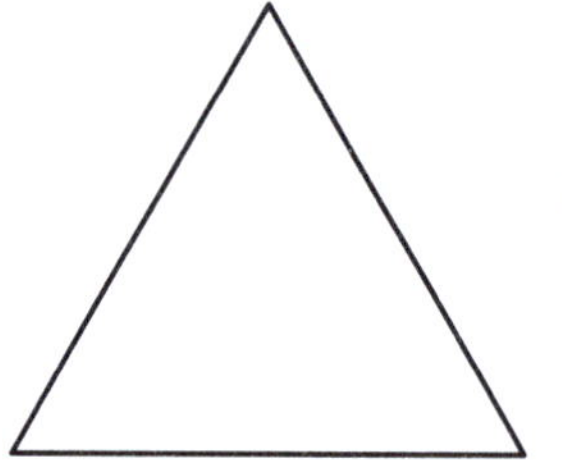

3. $\frac{2}{3}$ 

4. $\frac{1}{6}$

5. $\frac{3}{4}$ 

6. $\frac{2}{4}$ 

7. $\frac{3}{8}$ 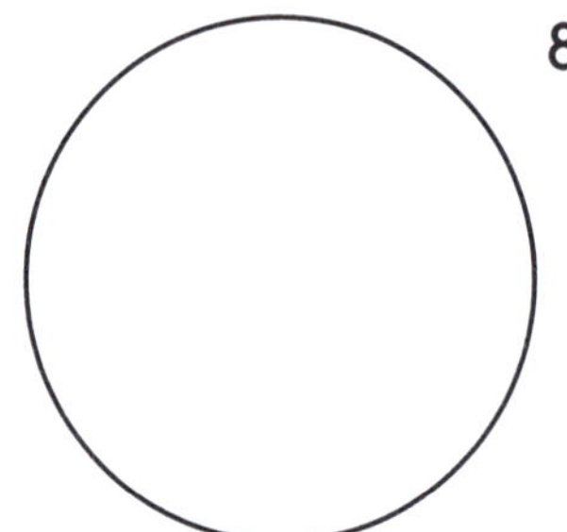

8. $\frac{4}{4}$ 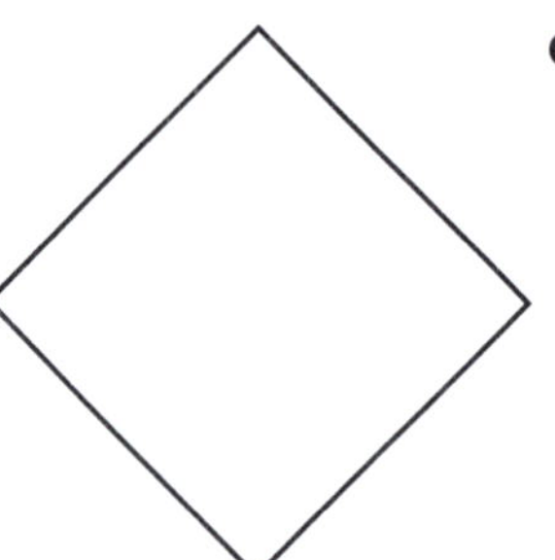

9. $\frac{7}{8}$ 

SHOWING FRACTIONS

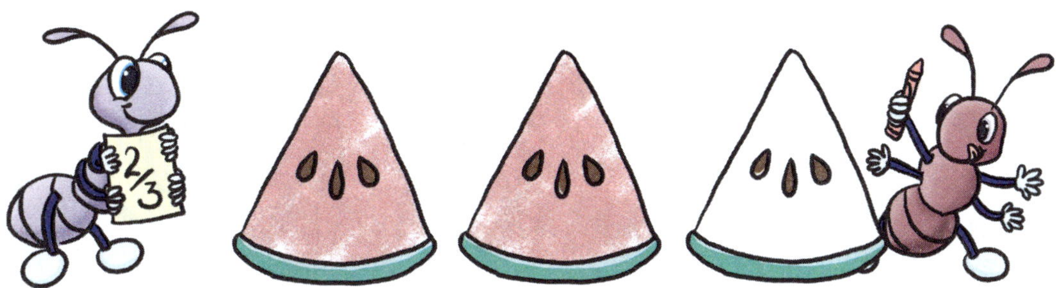

Color the object or objects to show each fraction.

1. $\frac{1}{2}$

2. $\frac{3}{4}$

3. $\frac{2}{3}$

4. $\frac{7}{8}$

5. $\frac{2}{5}$

6. $\frac{1}{4}$

7. $\frac{1}{8}$

8. $\frac{5}{6}$

What fractional part of the group is green?

2 green crayons → 2
3 crayons in all → 3

$\frac{2}{3}$

What part of each group is green? Write the fraction.

1.  $\frac{3}{4}$

2.   $\frac{1}{\square}$

3.  $\frac{\square}{\square}$

4. 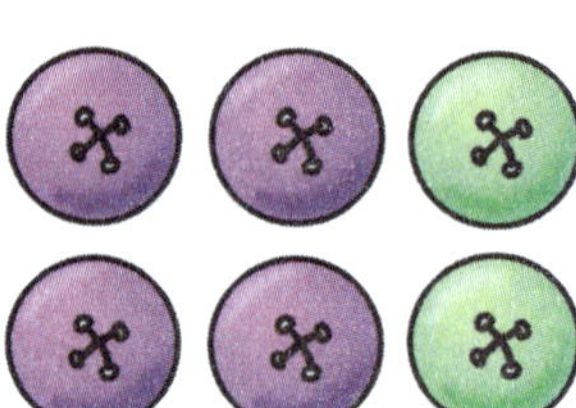 $\frac{\square}{\square}$

5.  $\frac{\square}{\square}$

6.  $\frac{\square}{\square}$

7.  $\frac{\square}{\square}$

8.  $\frac{\square}{\square}$

WORKING WITH PARTS OF GROUPS

The whole group is 4 cows.

$\frac{1}{2}$ $\frac{1}{2}$ Half of the group is 2 cows.

Circle half of the objects in each group.

1. 

2. 

3. 

4. 

5. 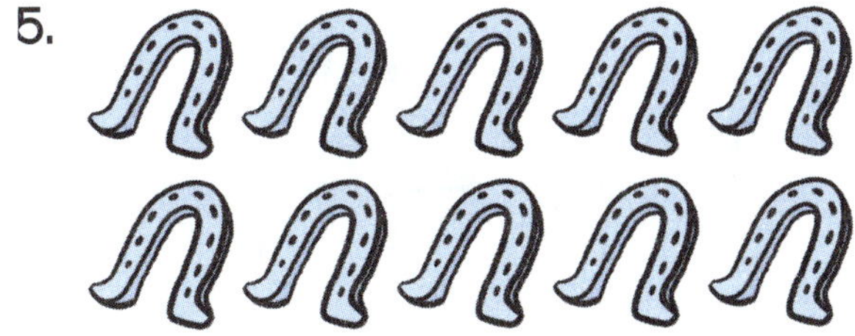

6. 

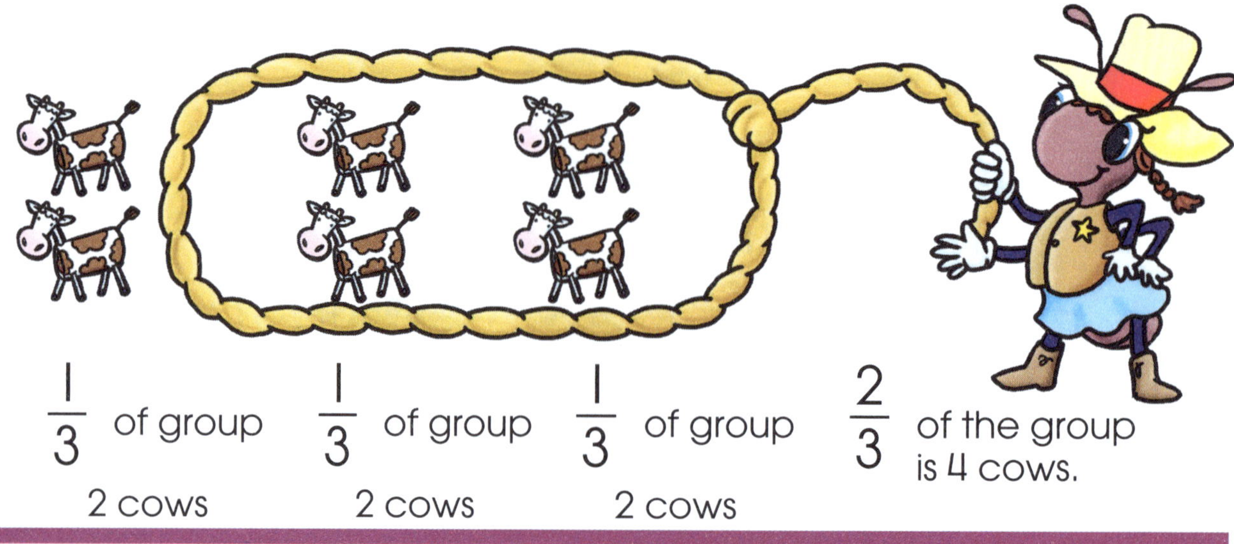

$\frac{1}{3}$ of group
2 cows

$\frac{1}{3}$ of group
2 cows

$\frac{1}{3}$ of group
2 cows

$\frac{2}{3}$ of the group is 4 cows.

Circle the objects to show the fractional part of the group.

1. $\frac{1}{3}$

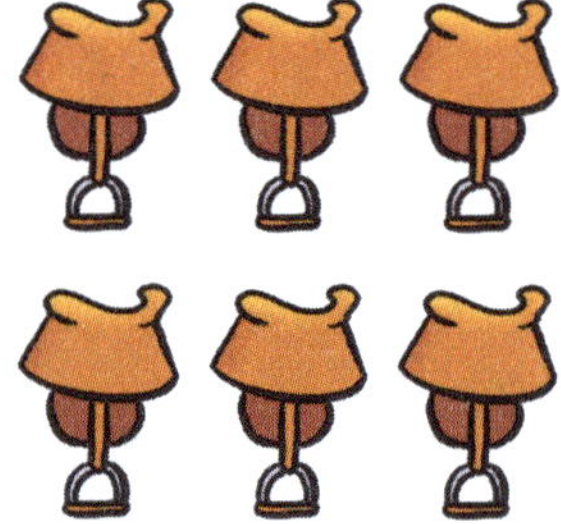

2. $\frac{1}{4}$

3. $\frac{1}{4}$

4. $\frac{2}{3}$

5. $\frac{3}{4}$

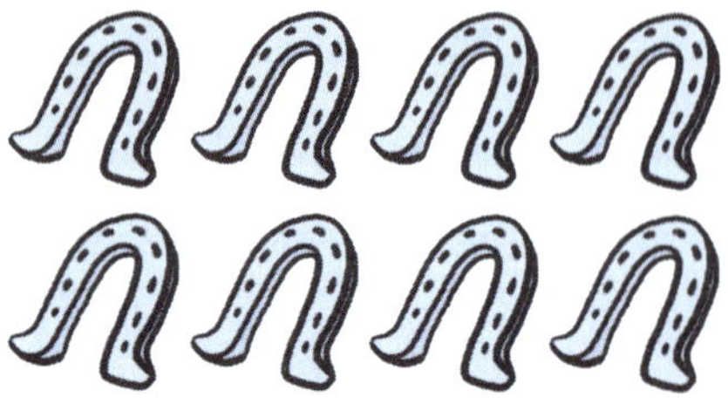

6. $\frac{2}{5}$

Color the fractional parts of the objects in the picture.

1. Color $\frac{1}{2}$ of the shoes

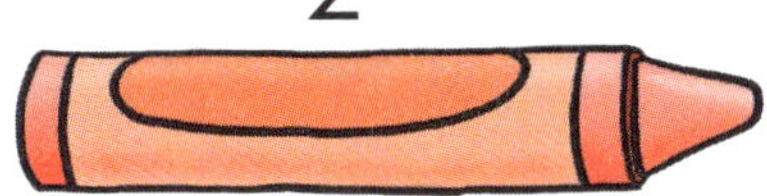

2. Color $\frac{2}{3}$ of the flowers

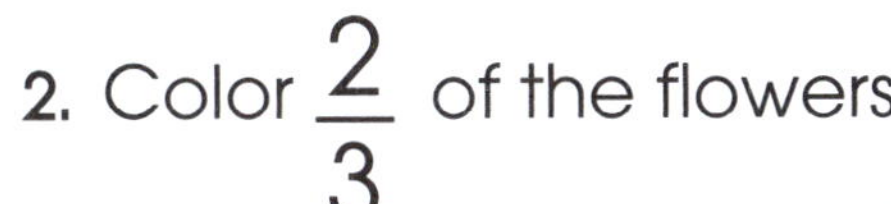

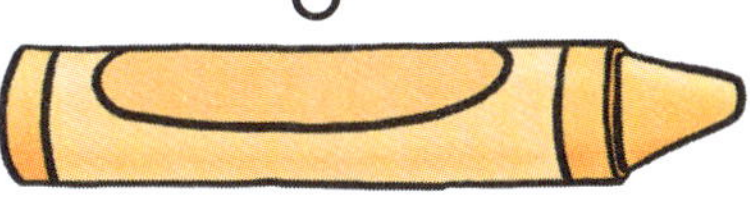

3. Color $\frac{5}{6}$ of the stars

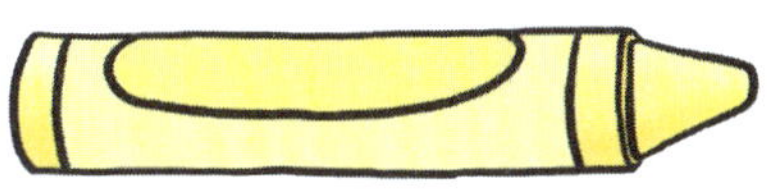

4. Color $\frac{3}{5}$ of the balloons

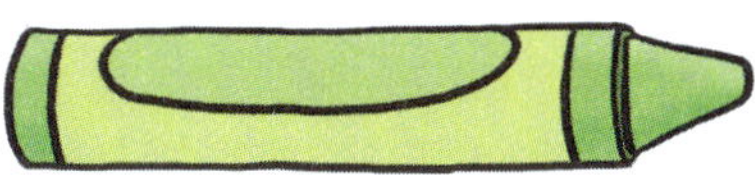

5. Color $\frac{4}{5}$ of the balls

6. Color $\frac{1}{2}$ of the buttons

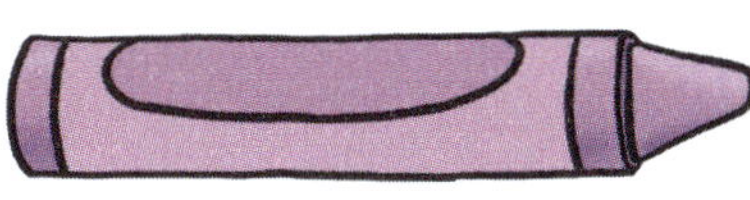

7. Color $\frac{3}{4}$ of the bunnies

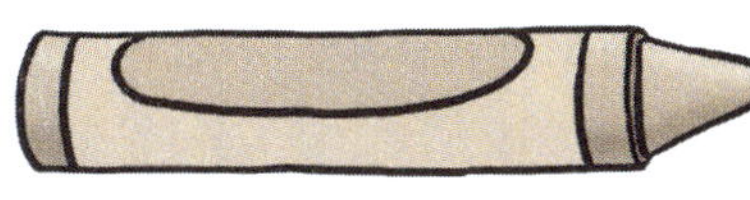

MORE ABOUT FRACTIONS

Color the correct part of each shape or group.
Then write the fraction.

1. Color **one-fifth** of the shape.

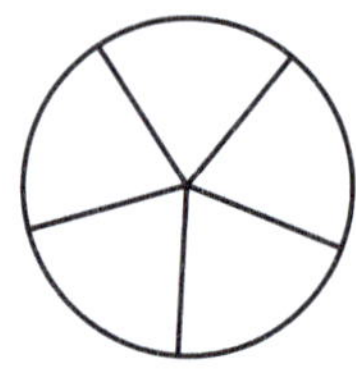
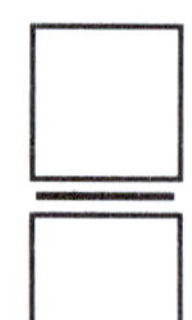

2. Color **one-fourth** of the group.

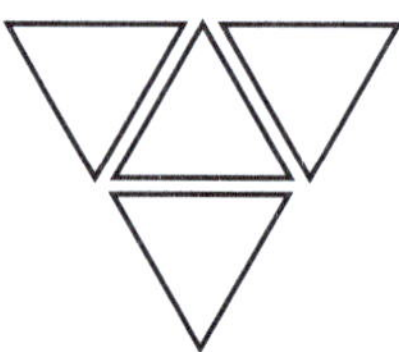
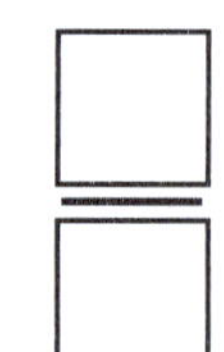

3. Color **two-thirds** of the shape.

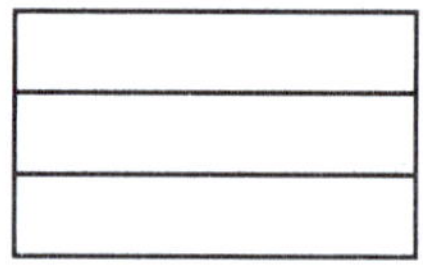

4. Color **three-fifths** of the group.

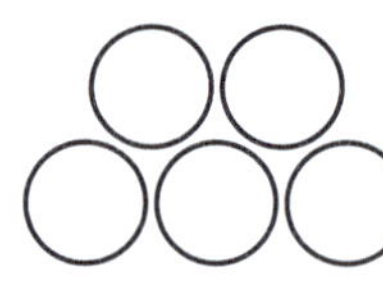

5. Color **three-fourths** of the shape.

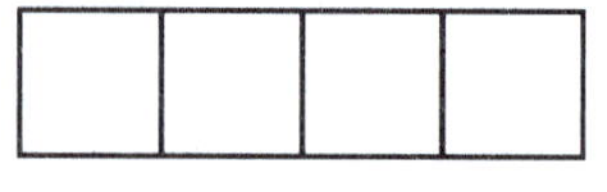
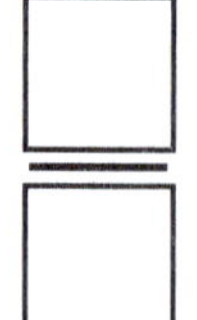

6. Color **five-sixths** of the group.

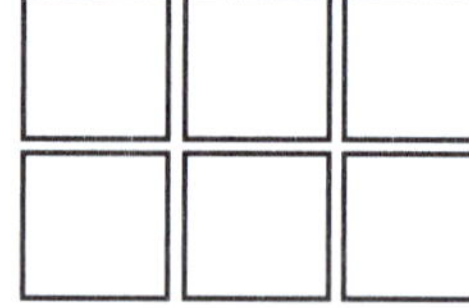
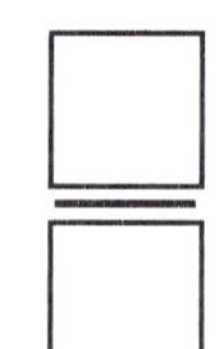

7. Color **one-half** of the shape.

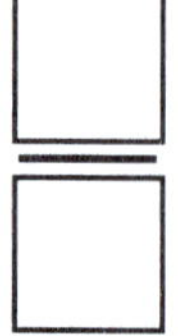

8. Color **five-eighths** of the group.

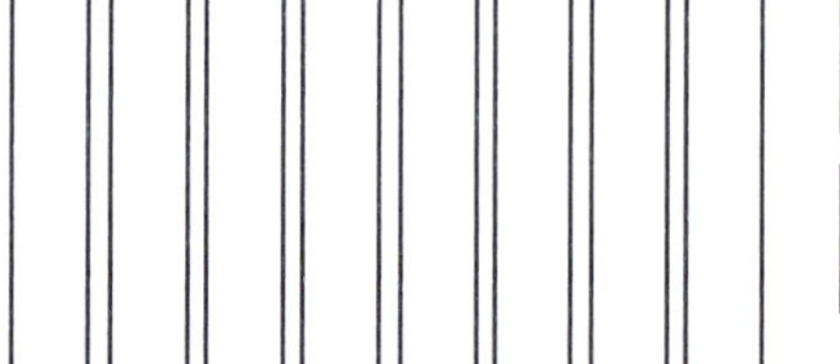

WHAT I LEARNED ABOUT MONEY

1. Count the money. Write the amount on the price tag.

____ ¢ ____ ¢ ____ ¢ ____ ¢ ____ ¢ ____ ¢

2. Count the money. Write the amounts.
   Is there enough money to buy the hamburger? Circle **yes** or **no**.

____ ¢ ____ ¢ ____ ¢ ____ ¢ ____ ¢

yes

no

3. Count the money.
   Write the amount.

____ ¢

4. Circle the coins you need to buy the scissors.

WHAT I LEARNED ABOUT MONEY

Circle the correct answer.

1. Which coin has the same value as this group?

2. Count the money. What is the amount?

51¢ 76¢ 81¢

3. Count the money in groups A and B. Is the money in group A more, less, or equal to the amount in group B?

A.

B.

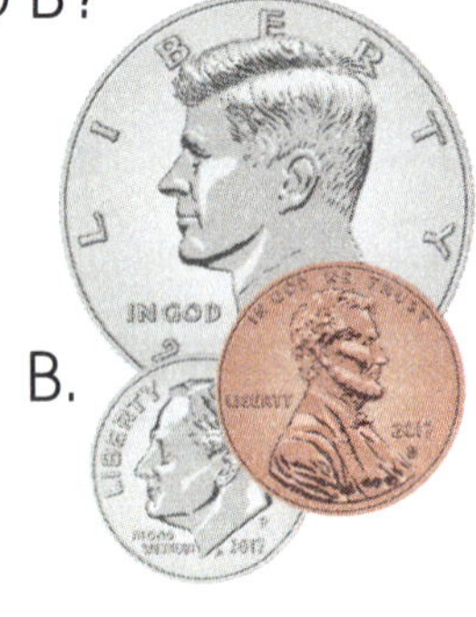

more less equal

4. Which coin is missing to make the amount?

5. What is the total amount for these 2 toys?

59¢ 69¢ 95¢

6. Find the amount of change.

Have Buy Change

$$\begin{array}{r} 35¢ \\ -\ 22¢ \\ \hline \end{array}$$

12¢ 13¢ 17¢

WHAT I LEARNED ABOUT TIME

Write the time in two ways.

1.

_______ o'clock

_______ : _______

2.

Half past _______

_______ : _______

3.

Quarter to _______

_______ : _______

Draw hands on the clock face to show the time.

4.

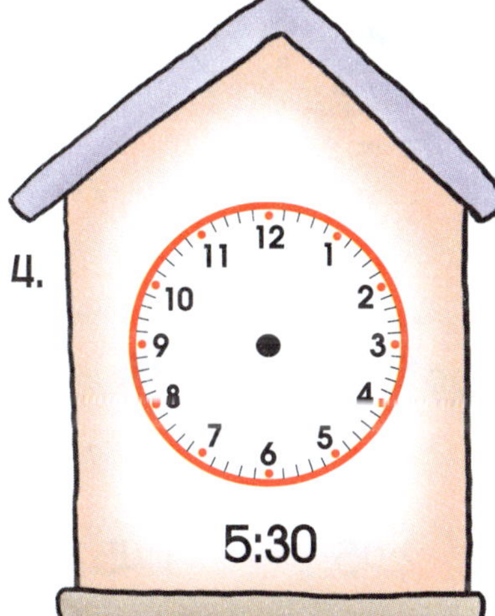

5:30

5.

11:00

6.

7:15

7.

12:20

8.

5:45

9.

1:50

Circle the correct answer.

1. What time is it?

5:00 12:05 12:25

2. What time is it?

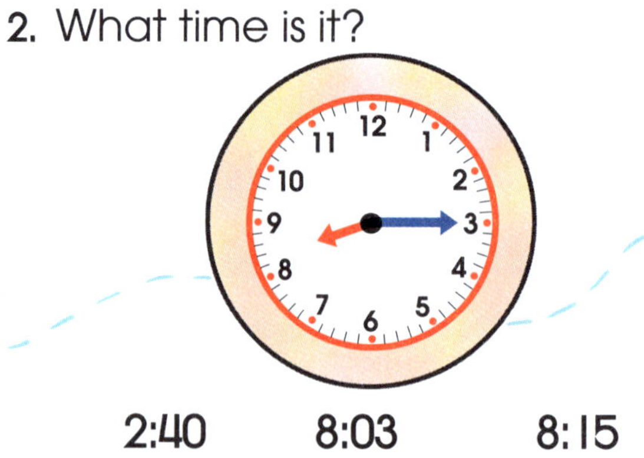

2:40 8:03 8:15

3. What time is it?

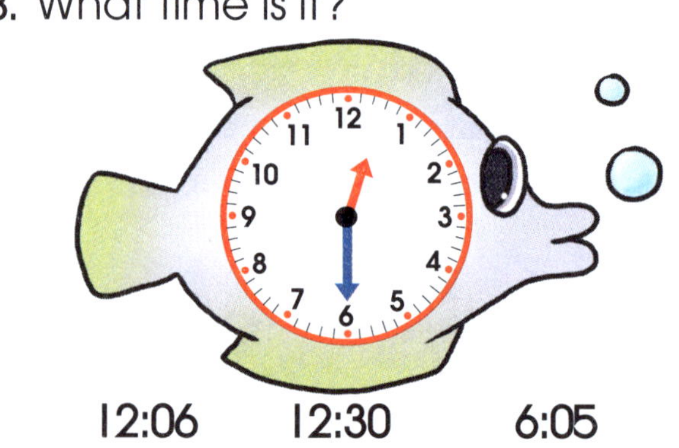

12:06 12:30 6:05

4. What time is it?

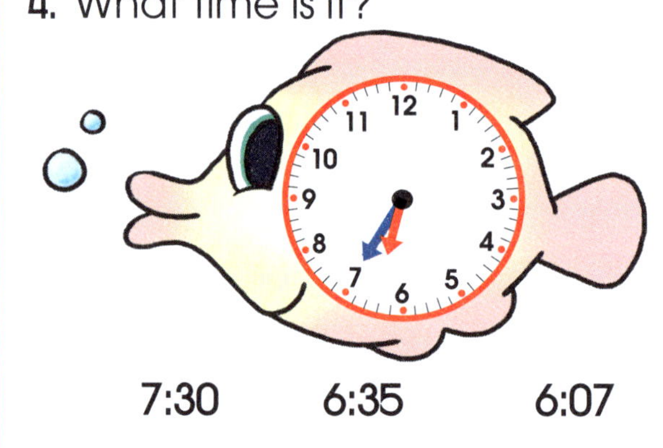

7:30 6:35 6:07

5. What time is the same as **half past 10**?

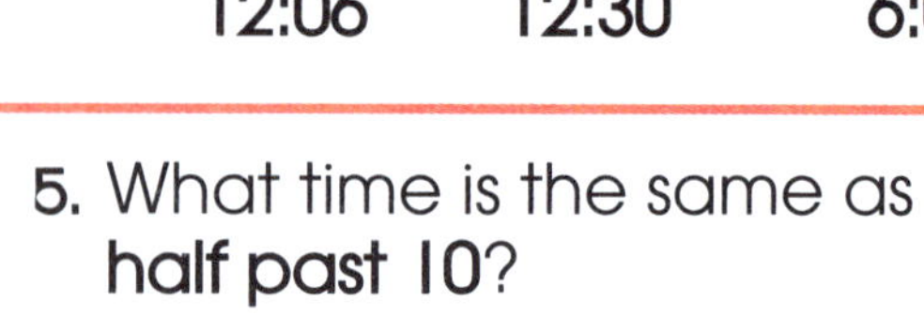

10:15 10:30 10:50

6. What time is the same as **quarter to 2**?

2:15 2:45 1:45

7. What is the ending time?

Start End

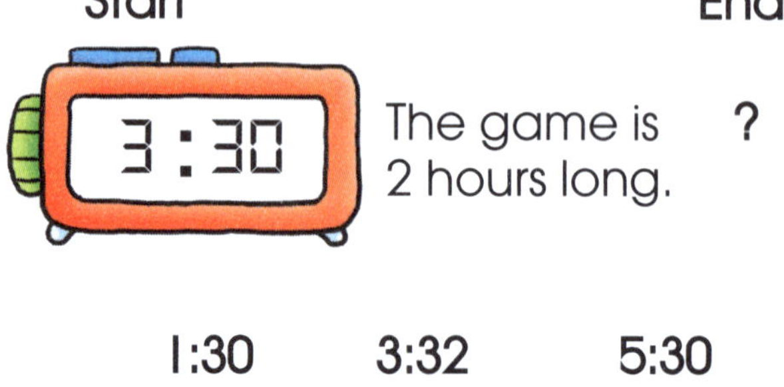

The game is 2 hours long. ?

1:30 3:32 5:30

8. What is the ending time?

Start End

6:30

The movie is 3 hours long. ?

3:30 9:30 8:30

1. Circle the objects with equal parts.

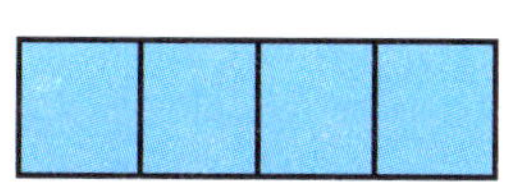

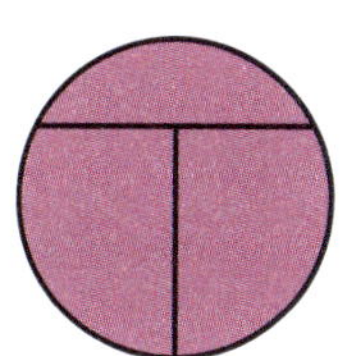
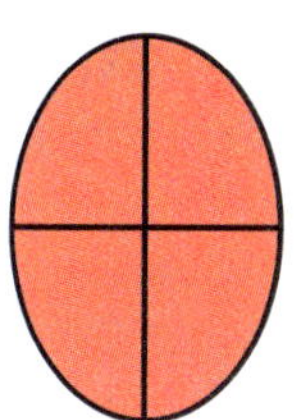

Color the shape or objects to show the fraction.

2. $\frac{1}{3}$

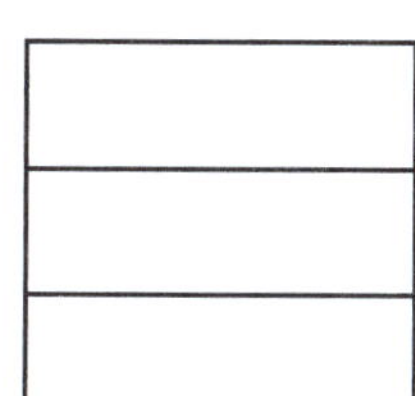

3. $\frac{1}{4}$

4. $\frac{5}{8}$

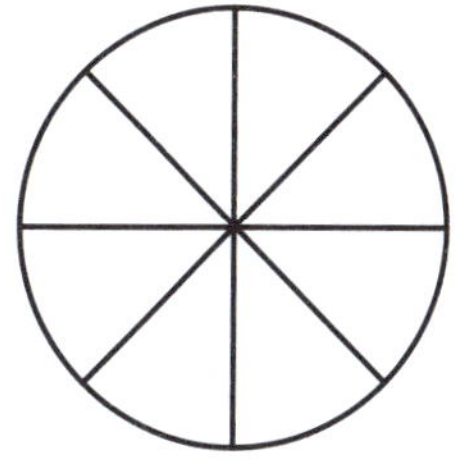

5. $\frac{2}{5}$

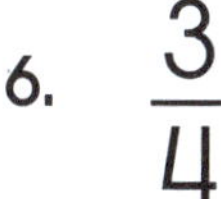

6. $\frac{3}{4}$

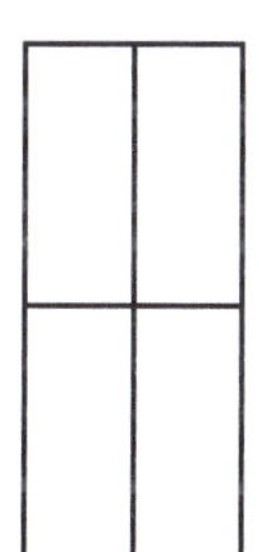

7. $\frac{1}{2}$

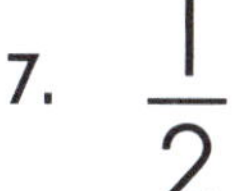
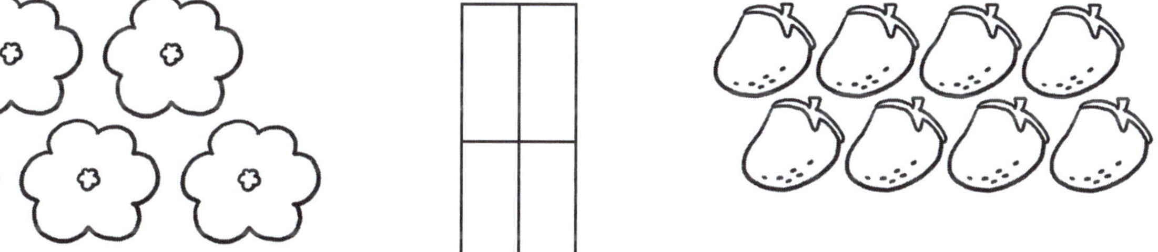

8. $\frac{5}{6}$

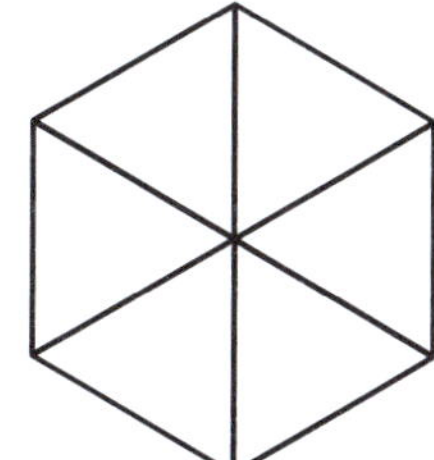

9. $\frac{2}{3}$

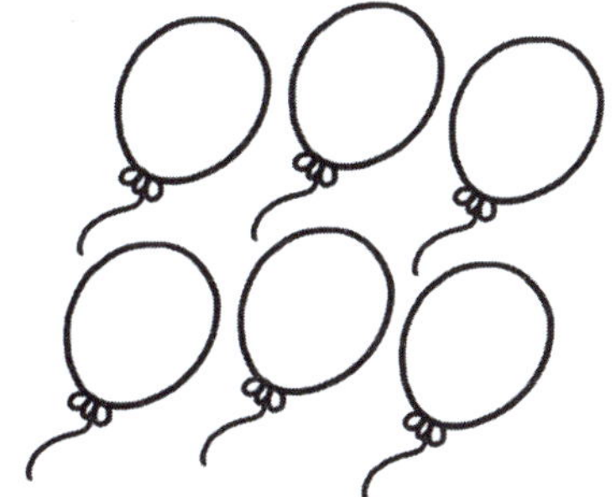

10. $\frac{7}{8}$

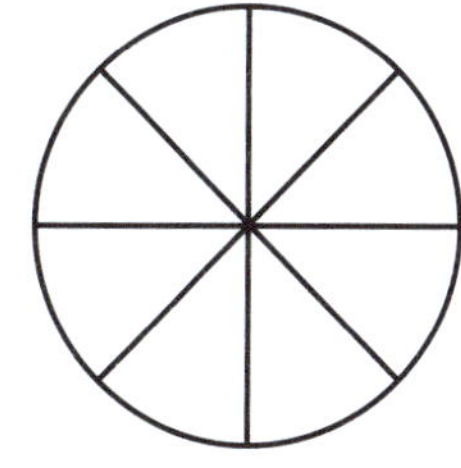

Look at the colored part of each shape or group.
Circle the correct answer.

1.

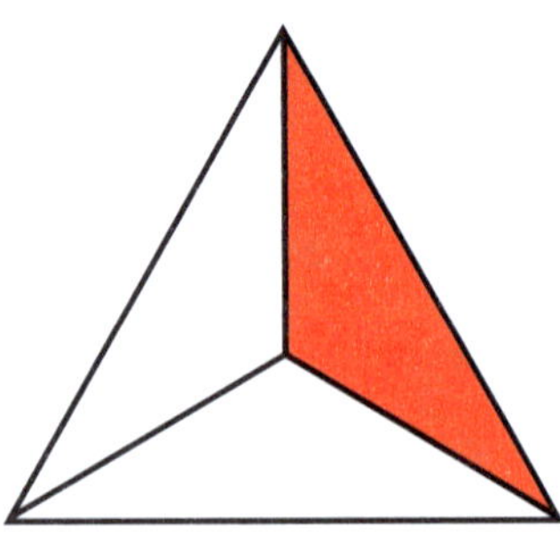

$\frac{1}{2}$ $\frac{1}{3}$ $\frac{1}{4}$

2.

$\frac{1}{3}$ $\frac{1}{4}$ $\frac{1}{5}$

3.

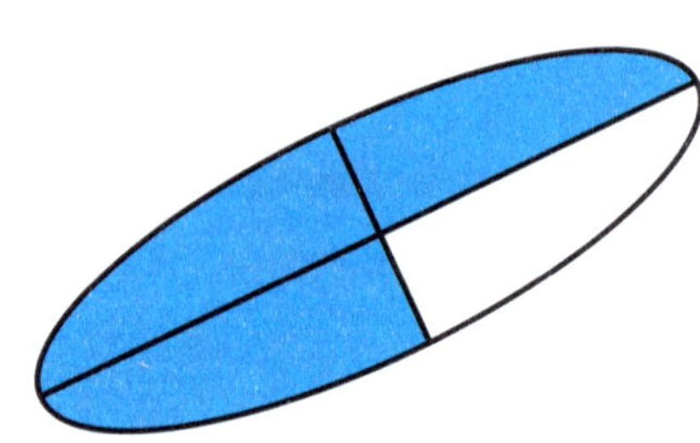

one-third
three-fourths
one-fourth

4.

one-half
one-third
two-thirds

5.

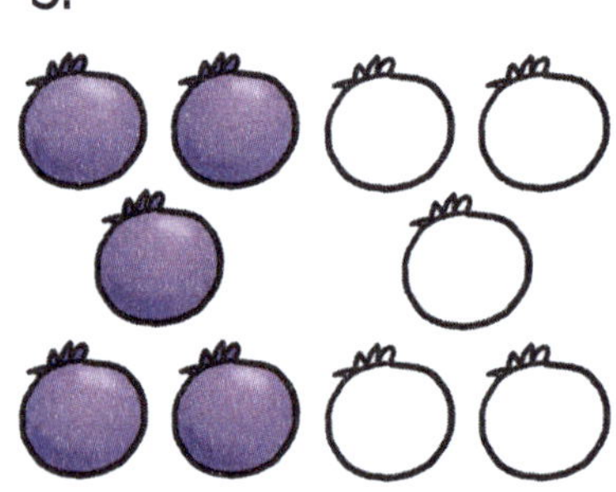

$\frac{1}{2}$ $\frac{1}{5}$ $\frac{5}{8}$

6.

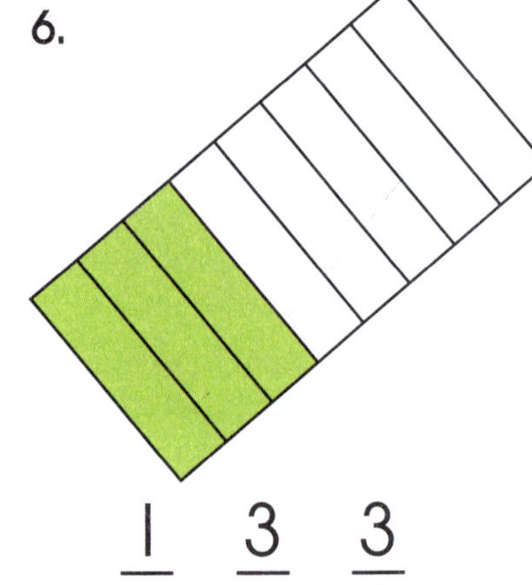

$\frac{1}{3}$ $\frac{3}{5}$ $\frac{3}{8}$

7.

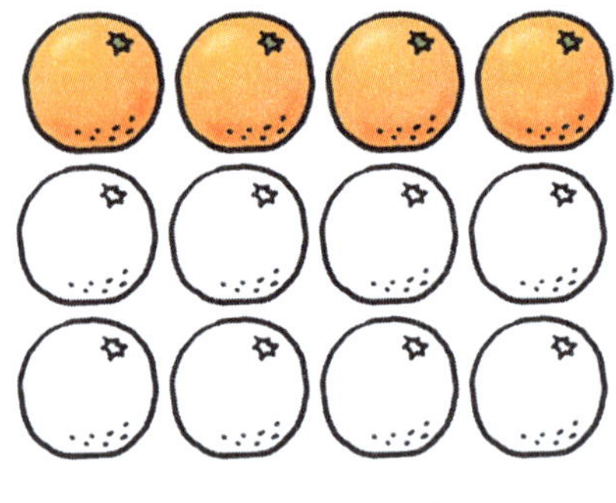

$\frac{1}{3}$ $\frac{1}{4}$ $\frac{1}{12}$

8.

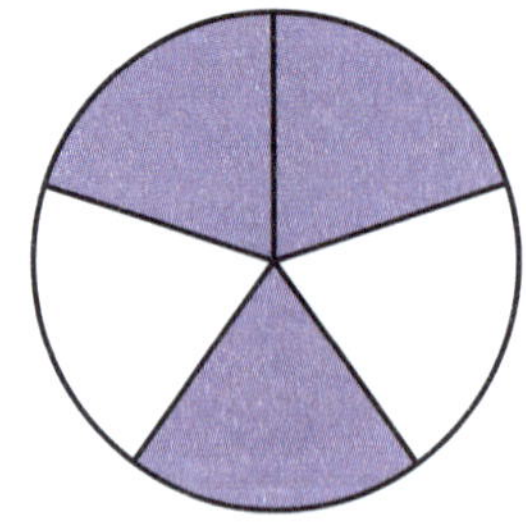

$\frac{2}{3}$ $\frac{2}{5}$ $\frac{3}{5}$

9.

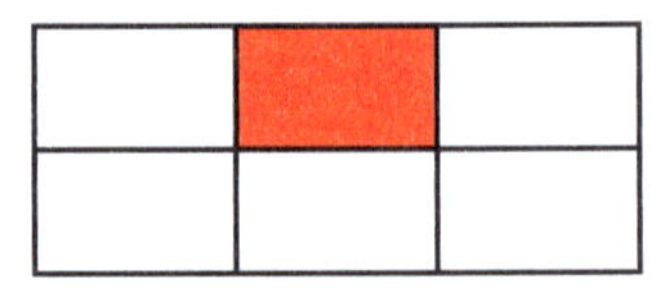

one-third
one-fifth
one-sixth

The answer to an addition problem is called the **sum**.
You can write an **addition number sentence** like this: **2 + 3 = 5**

2 + 3 = 5

Write a **number sentence** about the pictures.

1. + ____ + ____ = ____

2. + ____ + ____ = ____

3. + ____ + ____ = ____

4. + ____ + ____ = ____

5. + ____ + ____ = ____

6. + ____ + ____ = ____

7. + ____ + ____ = ____

You can use a number line to find the **sum** for **4 + 2**.
Start at **4**. Then count on **2** more numbers: **4**, ...**5**, **6**.

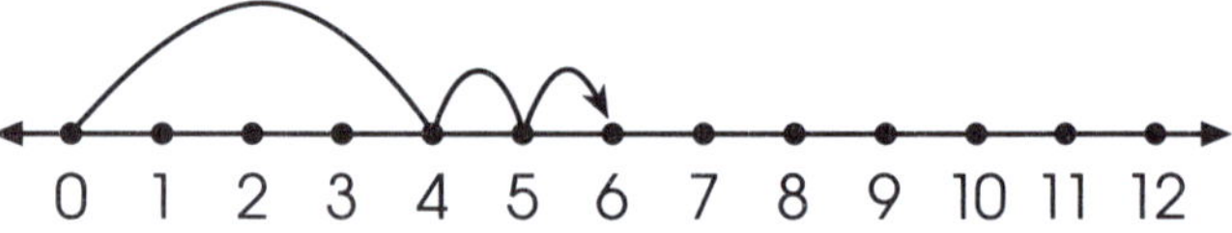

4 + 2 = 6 4 + 2 = 6

Find the **sum**. Use the number line if you need help.

1. 3 + 3 = ____ 2. 1 + 4 = ____ 3. 4 + 2 = ____

4. 5 + 1 = ____ 5. 2 + 3 = ____ 6. 2 + 2 = ____

7. 4 + 1 = ____
8. 2 + 4 = ____
9. 3 + 3 = ____
10. 1 + 1 = ____
11. 1 + 5 = ____

12. 2 + 2 = ____
13. 1 + 2 = ____
14. 4 + 2 = ____
15. 3 + 2 = ____
16. 1 + 3 = ____

The answer to a subtraction problem is called the **difference**.
You can write a **subtraction number sentence** like this: 4 – 2 = 2

Write a **number sentence** about the pictures.

1.   ____ – ____ = ____

2.  ____ – ____ = ____

3. 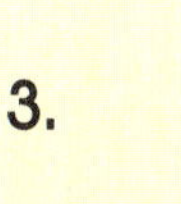  ____ – ____ = ____

4.  ____ – ____ = ____

5.  ____ – ____ = ____

6.  ____ – ____ = ____

7.   ____ – ____ = ____

You can use a number line to find the **difference** for **5 – 2**.
Start at **5**. Then count back **2** numbers: **5**, ...**4**, **3**.

The **difference** of **5 – 2** is **3**.

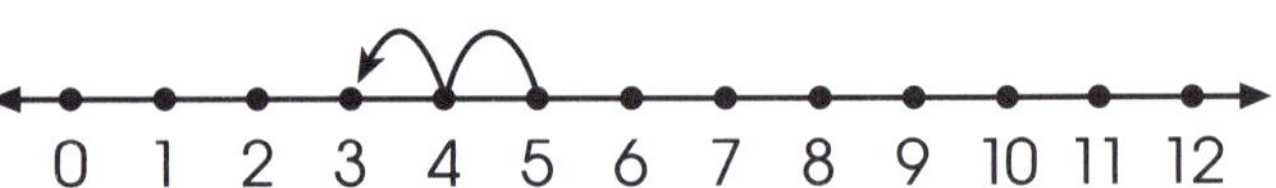

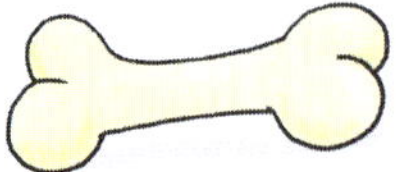

5 – 2 = 3

Find the **difference**. Use the number line if you need help.

1. 6 – 3 = ____
2. 5 – 2 = ____
3. 4 – 2 = ____
4. 3 – 2 = ____
5. 3 – 1 = ____
6. 2 – 1 = ____

7. 5 – 1
8. 6 – 4
9. 5 – 3
10. 6 – 1
11. 5 – 4
12. 4 – 2
13. 6 – 3
14. 6 – 5
15. 5 – 2
16. 4 – 3
17. 3 – 2
18. 6 – 2

ADDING & SUBTRACTING 0 AND 1

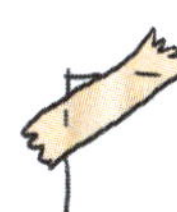

0+0=0		0-0=0	
1+0=1	0+1=1	1-0=1	1-1=0
2+0=2	1+1=2	2-0=2	2-1=1
3+0=3	2+1=3	3-0=3	3-1=2
4+0=4	3+1=4	4-0=4	4-1=3
5+0=5	4+1=5	5-0=5	5-1=4
6+0=6	5+1=6	6-0=6	6-1=5

Find the **sum**.

1. $4 + 0$
2. $2 + 1$
3. $5 + 1$
4. $1 + 4$
5. $2 + 0$
6. $1 + 1$
7. $5 + 0$
8. $0 + 1$
9. $1 + 3$
10. $6 + 0$

Find the **difference**.

11. $3 - 1$
12. $2 - 1$
13. $4 - 1$
14. $3 - 0$
15. $1 - 1$
16. $5 - 0$
17. $6 - 1$
18. $0 - 0$
19. $2 - 0$
20. $4 - 0$

A **fact family** uses the same numbers in its addition and subtraction number sentences.

One fact family of **5** uses the numbers **2**, **3**, and **5**.

Other fact families for **5** might use the numbers **1**, **4**, and **5** or **0**, **5**, and **5**.

$2+3=5$	$1+4=5$	$0+5=5$
$3+2=5$	$4+1=5$	$5+0=5$
$5-2=3$	$5-1=4$	$5-0=5$
$5-3=2$	$5-4=1$	$5-5=0$

Find the **sum(s)** and **difference(s)** for the **fact family**.

1. $1 + 3$　　$3 + 1$　　$4 - 1$　　$4 - 3$

2. $5 + 1$　　$1 + 5$　　$6 - 5$　　$6 - 1$

3. $4 + 0$　　$0 + 4$　　$4 - 4$　　$4 - 0$

4. $3 + 3$　　$6 - 3$

5. $1 + 1$　　$2 - 1$

6. $2 + 2$　　$4 - 2$

Write the **sums** or **differences**.

1. Add **1**

4 5
2 ___
0 ___
5 ___

2. Add **3**

1 ___
3 ___
2 ___
0 ___

3. Add **0**

6 ___
4 ___
1 ___
5 ___

4. Subtract **1**

6 5
3 ___
5 ___
2 ___

5. Subtract **0**

5 ___
2 ___
6 ___
1 ___

6. Subtract **2**

2 ___
3 ___
6 ___
5 ___

7. How many hidden 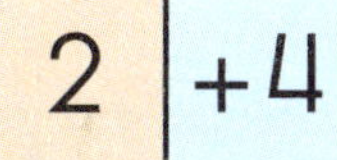 can you find in the picture?
Finish the puzzle to find the answer.

2	+4		−3		−1		+2	=		

5 + 2 = 7

Write a **number sentence** about the pictures.

1. + ____ + ____ = ____

2. + ____ + ____ = ____

3. + ____ + ____ = ____

4. + ____ + ____ = ____

5. + ____ + ____ = ____

6. + ____ + ____ = ____

7. + ____ + ____ = ____

Write a **number sentence** about the pictures.

1. 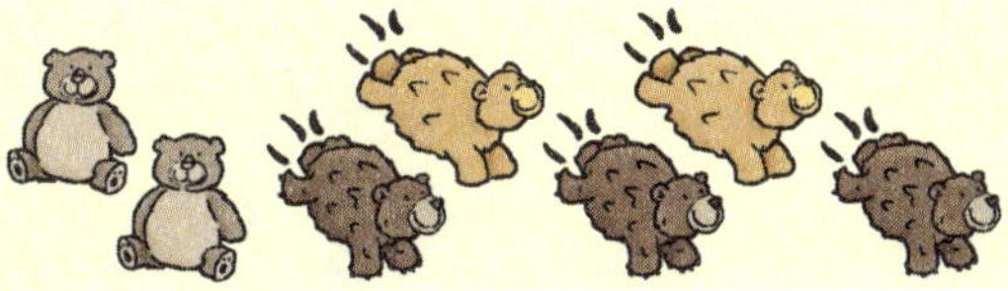 ___ - ___ = ___

2. 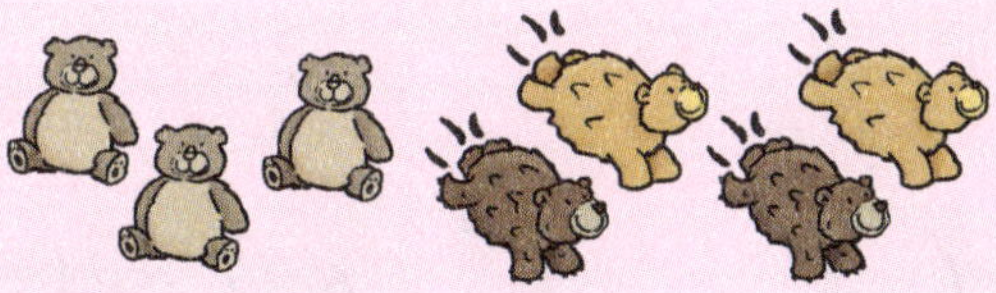 ___ - ___ = ___

3. 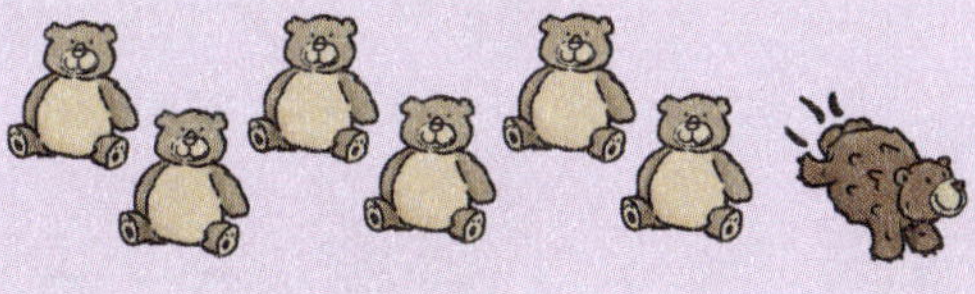 ___ - ___ = ___

4. 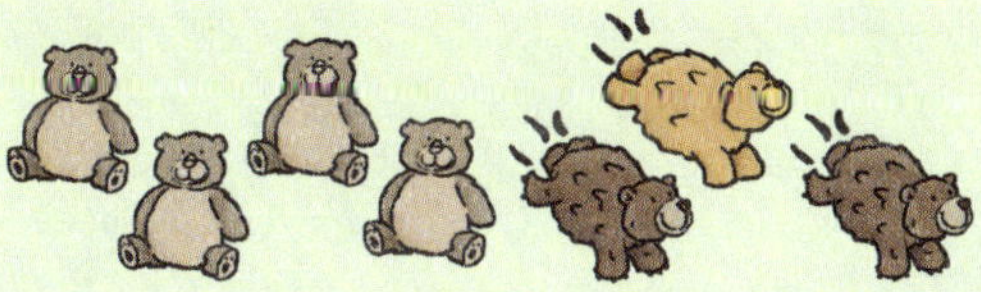 ___ - ___ = ___

5. 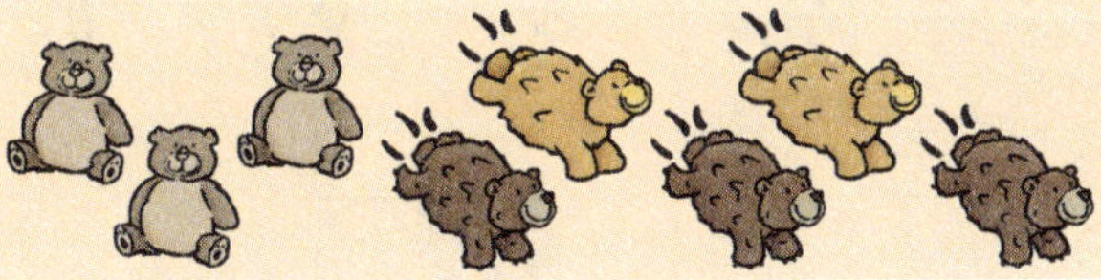 ___ - ___ = ___

6. 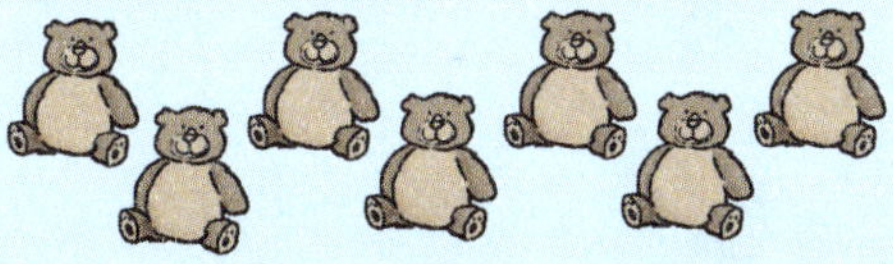 ___ - ___ = ___

7. 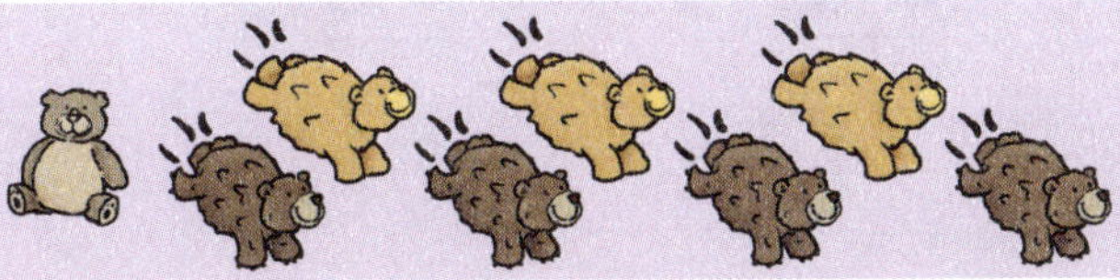 ___ - ___ = ___

Find the **sum** or **difference**. Use the number line if you need help.

1. 4 + 3 = ____
2. 6 + 2 = ____
3. 8 − 4 = ____
4. 8 − 3 = ____
5. 1 + 6 = ____
6. 7 − 4 = ____
7. 2 + 5 = ____
8. 7 + 1 = ____
9. 8 − 2 = ____

10. $\begin{array}{r} 6 \\ +\ 2 \\ \hline \end{array}$
11. $\begin{array}{r} 7 \\ -\ 2 \\ \hline \end{array}$
12. $\begin{array}{r} 0 \\ +\ 7 \\ \hline \end{array}$
13. $\begin{array}{r} 8 \\ -\ 2 \\ \hline \end{array}$
14. $\begin{array}{r} 8 \\ -\ 5 \\ \hline \end{array}$

15. $\begin{array}{r} 7 \\ -\ 5 \\ \hline \end{array}$
16. $\begin{array}{r} 8 \\ -\ 3 \\ \hline \end{array}$
17. $\begin{array}{r} 5 \\ +\ 3 \\ \hline \end{array}$
18. $\begin{array}{r} 7 \\ -\ 3 \\ \hline \end{array}$
19. $\begin{array}{r} 4 \\ +\ 4 \\ \hline \end{array}$

Here is a **fact family** for **8**.
It uses the numbers **3**, **5**, and **8**.

$3 + 5 = 8$ $5 + 3 = 8$ $8 - 3 = 5$ $8 - 5 = 3$

Find the **sum(s)** and **difference(s)** for the **fact family**.

1. $\begin{array}{r} 4 \\ +3 \\ \hline \end{array}$ $\begin{array}{r} 3 \\ +4 \\ \hline \end{array}$ $\begin{array}{r} 7 \\ -4 \\ \hline \end{array}$ $\begin{array}{r} 7 \\ -3 \\ \hline \end{array}$

2. $\begin{array}{r} 4 \\ +4 \\ \hline \end{array}$ $\begin{array}{r} 8 \\ -4 \\ \hline \end{array}$

3. $\begin{array}{r} 2 \\ +5 \\ \hline \end{array}$ $\begin{array}{r} 5 \\ +2 \\ \hline \end{array}$ $\begin{array}{r} 7 \\ -2 \\ \hline \end{array}$ $\begin{array}{r} 7 \\ -5 \\ \hline \end{array}$

4. $\begin{array}{r} 2 \\ +6 \\ \hline \end{array}$ $\begin{array}{r} 6 \\ +2 \\ \hline \end{array}$ $\begin{array}{r} 8 \\ -2 \\ \hline \end{array}$ $\begin{array}{r} 8 \\ -6 \\ \hline \end{array}$

5. $\begin{array}{r} 7 \\ +1 \\ \hline \end{array}$ $\begin{array}{r} 1 \\ +7 \\ \hline \end{array}$ $\begin{array}{r} 8 \\ -7 \\ \hline \end{array}$ $\begin{array}{r} 8 \\ -1 \\ \hline \end{array}$

6. $\begin{array}{r} 0 \\ +8 \\ \hline \end{array}$ $\begin{array}{r} 8 \\ -8 \\ \hline \end{array}$

3 + 6 = 9

Write a **number sentence** about the pictures.

1. ___ + ___ = ___

2. ___ + ___ = ___

3. ___ + ___ = ___

4. ___ + ___ = ___

5. ___ + ___ = ___

6. ___ + ___ = ___

7. ___ + ___ = ___

Write a **number sentence** about the pictures.

1. 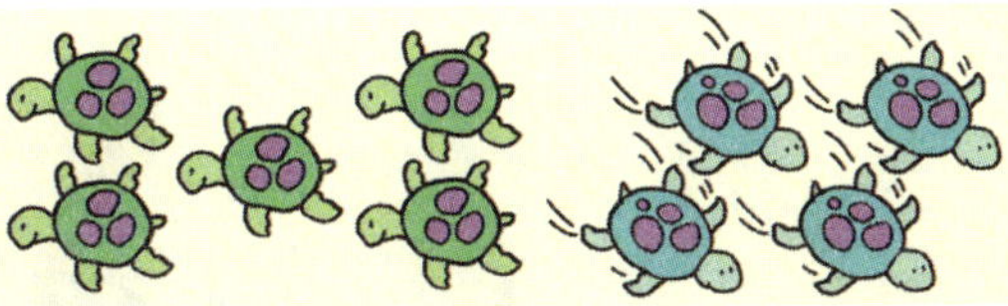 ____ - ____ = ____

2. 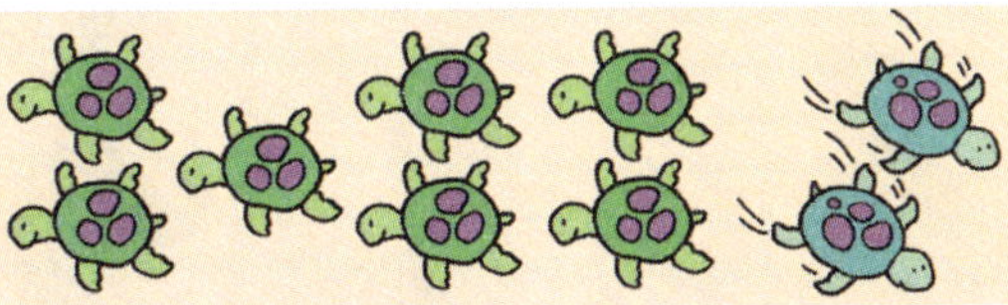 ____ - ____ = ____

3. 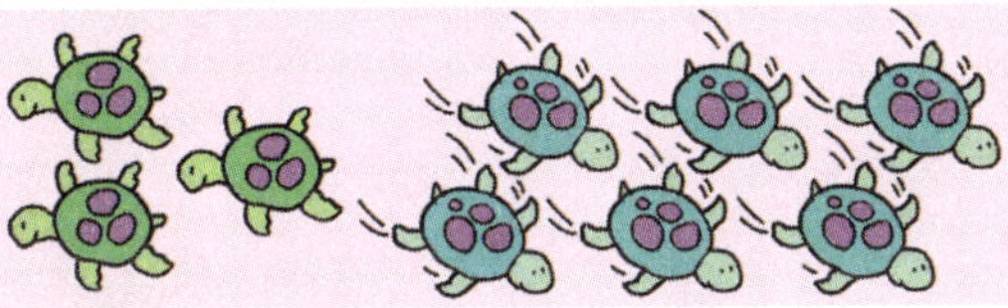 ____ - ____ = ____

4. 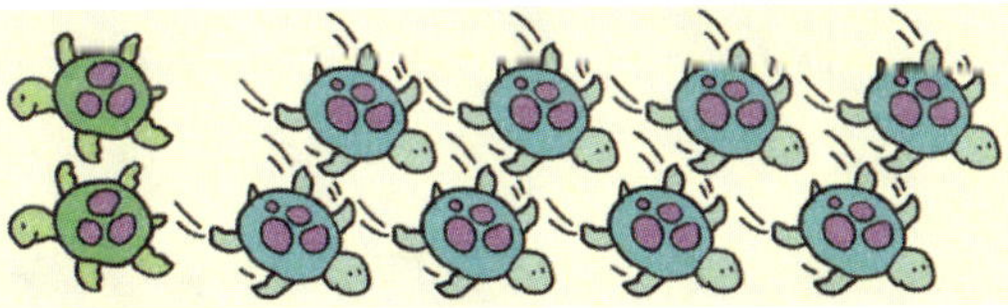 ____ - ____ = ____

5. 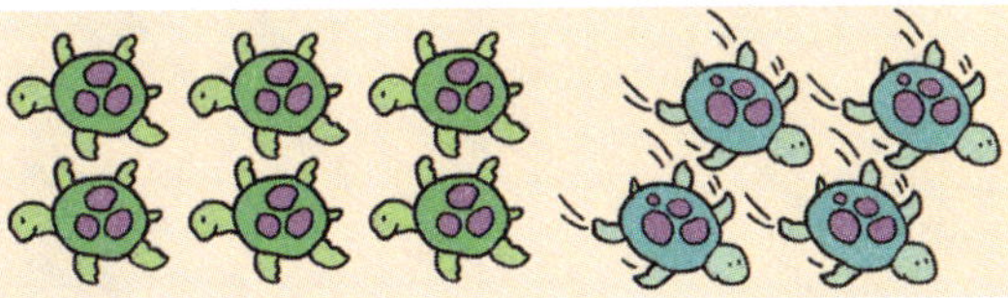 ____ - ____ = ____

6. 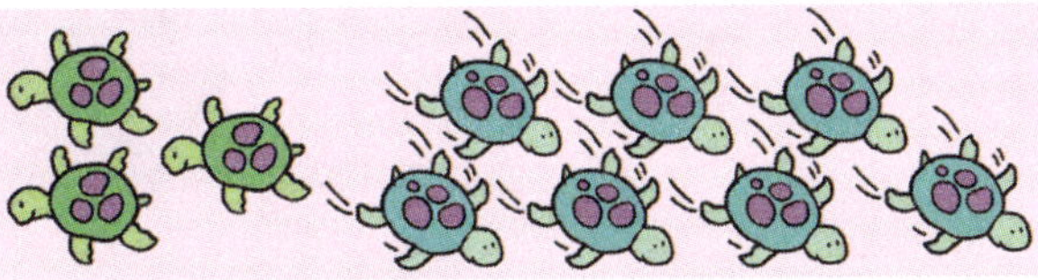 ____ - ____ = ____

7. 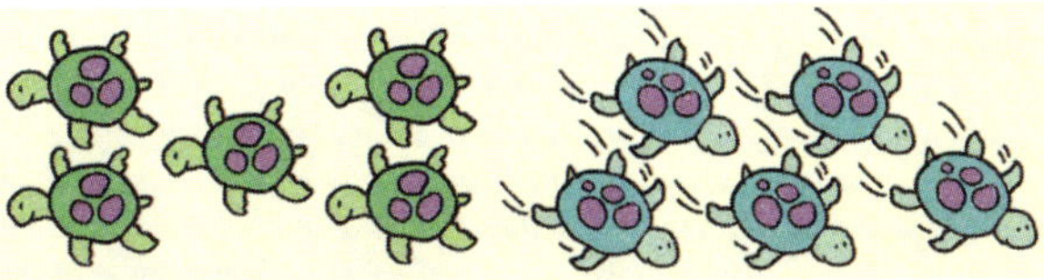 ____ - ____ = ____

Here is a **fact family** for **9**.
It uses the numbers **1**, **8**, and **9**.

$\begin{array}{r} 1 \\ +8 \\ \hline 9 \end{array}$	$\begin{array}{r} 8 \\ +1 \\ \hline 9 \end{array}$	$\begin{array}{r} 9 \\ -1 \\ \hline 8 \end{array}$	$\begin{array}{r} 9 \\ -8 \\ \hline 1 \end{array}$

Find the **sum(s)** and **difference(s)** for the **fact family**.

1. $\begin{array}{r} 6 \\ +3 \\ \hline \end{array}$ $\begin{array}{r} 3 \\ +6 \\ \hline \end{array}$ $\begin{array}{r} 9 \\ -6 \\ \hline \end{array}$ $\begin{array}{r} 9 \\ -3 \\ \hline \end{array}$

2. $\begin{array}{r} 5 \\ +4 \\ \hline \end{array}$ $\begin{array}{r} 4 \\ +5 \\ \hline \end{array}$ $\begin{array}{r} 9 \\ -5 \\ \hline \end{array}$ $\begin{array}{r} 9 \\ -4 \\ \hline \end{array}$

3. $\begin{array}{r} 6 \\ +4 \\ \hline \end{array}$ $\begin{array}{r} 4 \\ +6 \\ \hline \end{array}$ $\begin{array}{r} 10 \\ -6 \\ \hline \end{array}$ $\begin{array}{r} 10 \\ -4 \\ \hline \end{array}$

4. $\begin{array}{r} 7 \\ +3 \\ \hline \end{array}$ $\begin{array}{r} 3 \\ +7 \\ \hline \end{array}$ $\begin{array}{r} 10 \\ -7 \\ \hline \end{array}$ $\begin{array}{r} 10 \\ -3 \\ \hline \end{array}$

5. $\begin{array}{r} 2 \\ +8 \\ \hline \end{array}$ $\begin{array}{r} 8 \\ +2 \\ \hline \end{array}$ $\begin{array}{r} 10 \\ -2 \\ \hline \end{array}$ $\begin{array}{r} 10 \\ -8 \\ \hline \end{array}$

6. $\begin{array}{r} 10 \\ -5 \\ \hline \end{array}$ $\begin{array}{r} 5 \\ +5 \\ \hline \end{array}$

PRACTICE FACTS 9 & 10

Find the **sum** or **difference**. Use the number line if you need help.

1. $9 - 3 =$ ____
2. $4 + 5 =$ ____
3. $9 - 4 =$ ____
4. $5 + 5 =$ ____
5. $9 - 7 =$ ____
6. $10 - 2 =$ ____
7. $4 + 6 =$ ____
8. $10 - 4 =$ ____
9. $7 + 2 =$ ____

10. $\begin{array}{r} 7 \\ +\,3 \\ \hline \end{array}$
11. $\begin{array}{r} 8 \\ +\,2 \\ \hline \end{array}$
12. $\begin{array}{r} 9 \\ -\,0 \\ \hline \end{array}$
13. $\begin{array}{r} 9 \\ -\,6 \\ \hline \end{array}$
14. $\begin{array}{r} 9 \\ -\,2 \\ \hline \end{array}$
15. $\begin{array}{r} 3 \\ +\,7 \\ \hline \end{array}$
16. $\begin{array}{r} 6 \\ +\,4 \\ \hline \end{array}$
17. $\begin{array}{r} 10 \\ -\,5 \\ \hline \end{array}$
18. $\begin{array}{r} 9 \\ -\,1 \\ \hline \end{array}$

Find the **sum** or **difference**. Be careful!

1. $9 - 3 =$ ____ 2. $10 - 7 =$ ____

3. $6 + 4 =$ ____ 4. $2 + 8 =$ ____

5. $5 + 3 =$ ____ 6. $10 - 2 =$ ____

7. $8 - 5 =$ ____ 8. $5 + 4 =$ ____

9. $\begin{array}{r} 0 \\ +4 \\ \hline \end{array}$ 10. $\begin{array}{r} 6 \\ +3 \\ \hline \end{array}$ 11. $\begin{array}{r} 9 \\ -6 \\ \hline \end{array}$

12. $\begin{array}{r} 9 \\ -2 \\ \hline \end{array}$ 13. $\begin{array}{r} 9 \\ -3 \\ \hline \end{array}$ 14. $\begin{array}{r} 5 \\ +2 \\ \hline \end{array}$

15. $\begin{array}{r} 3 \\ +4 \\ \hline \end{array}$ 16. $\begin{array}{r} 10 \\ -8 \\ \hline \end{array}$ 17. $\begin{array}{r} 4 \\ +4 \\ \hline \end{array}$

18. $\begin{array}{r} 7 \\ +3 \\ \hline \end{array}$ 19. $\begin{array}{r} 6 \\ -0 \\ \hline \end{array}$ 20. $\begin{array}{r} 7 \\ +2 \\ \hline \end{array}$

SIGN UP!

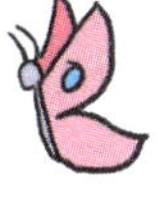

Look at the problem. What's missing?
The problem needs a + or – sign.
Write + or – in the box to make the problem true.

$$\begin{array}{r} 6 \\ \boxed{+}\ 3 \\ \hline 9 \end{array} \qquad \begin{array}{r} 7 \\ \boxed{-}\ 3 \\ \hline 4 \end{array}$$

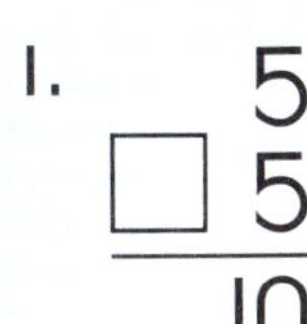

1. $\begin{array}{r} 5 \\ \square\ 5 \\ \hline 10 \end{array}$

2. $\begin{array}{r} 6 \\ \square\ 2 \\ \hline 4 \end{array}$

3. $\begin{array}{r} 5 \\ \square\ 3 \\ \hline 2 \end{array}$

4. $\begin{array}{r} 8 \\ \square\ 2 \\ \hline 10 \end{array}$

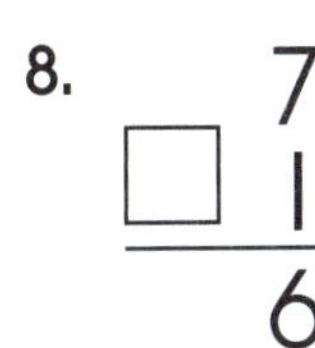

5. $\begin{array}{r} 8 \\ \square\ 5 \\ \hline 3 \end{array}$

6. $\begin{array}{r} 2 \\ \square\ 6 \\ \hline 8 \end{array}$

7. $\begin{array}{r} 6 \\ \square\ 4 \\ \hline 2 \end{array}$

8. $\begin{array}{r} 7 \\ \square\ 1 \\ \hline 6 \end{array}$

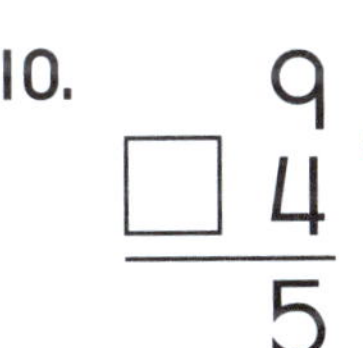

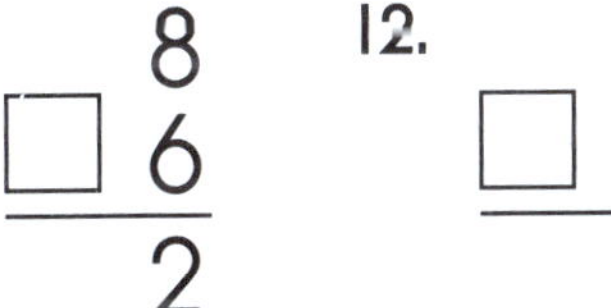

9. $\begin{array}{r} 6 \\ \square\ 3 \\ \hline 9 \end{array}$

10. $\begin{array}{r} 9 \\ \square\ 4 \\ \hline 5 \end{array}$

11. $\begin{array}{r} 8 \\ \square\ 6 \\ \hline 2 \end{array}$

12. $\begin{array}{r} 2 \\ \square\ 5 \\ \hline 7 \end{array}$

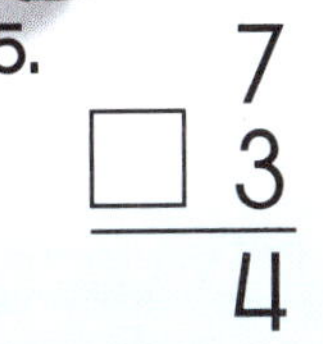

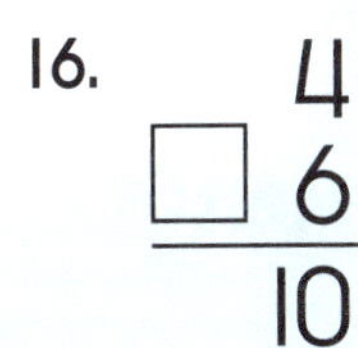

13. $\begin{array}{r} 2 \\ \square\ 6 \\ \hline 8 \end{array}$

14. $\begin{array}{r} 9 \\ \square\ 5 \\ \hline 4 \end{array}$

15. $\begin{array}{r} 7 \\ \square\ 3 \\ \hline 4 \end{array}$

16. $\begin{array}{r} 4 \\ \square\ 6 \\ \hline 10 \end{array}$

Write a **number sentence** about the pictures.

1. 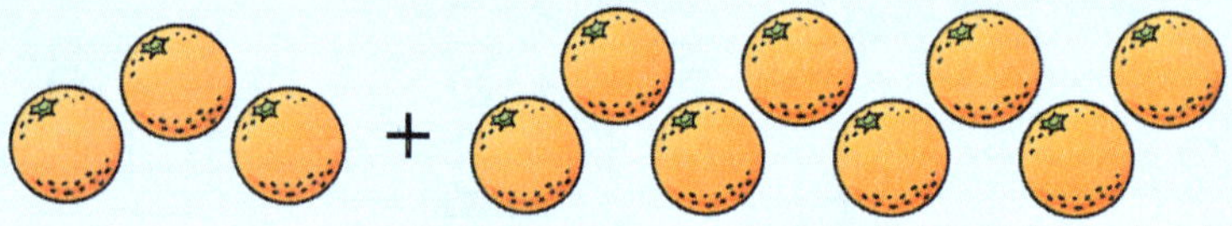 ____ + ____ = ____

2. 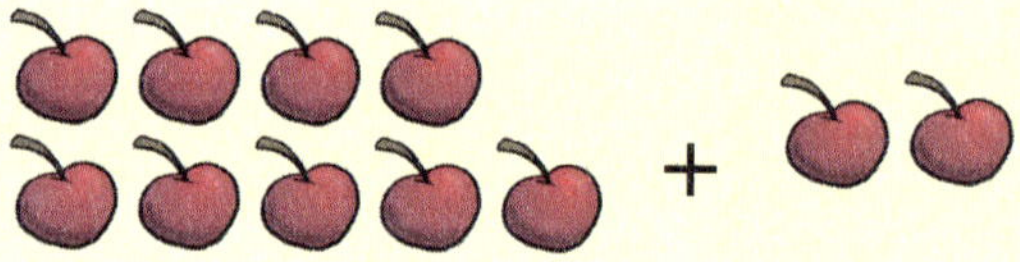 ____ + ____ = ____

3. 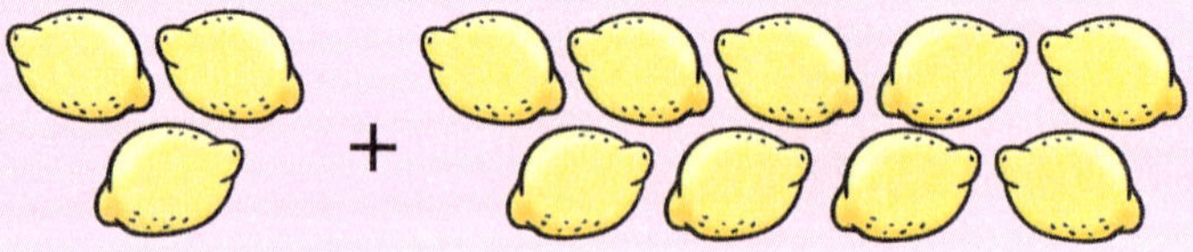 ____ + ____ = ____

4. 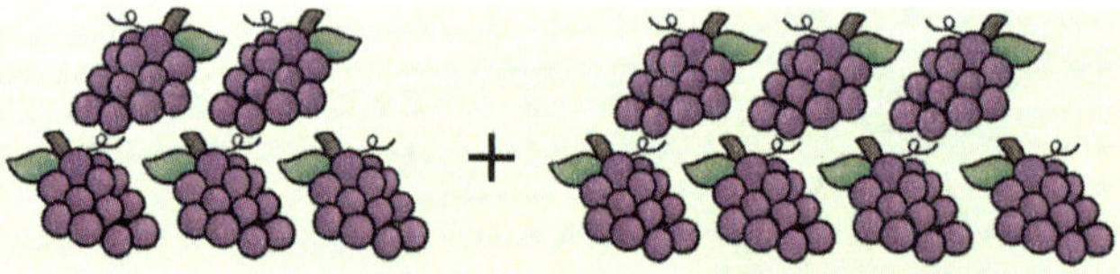 ____ + ____ = ____

5. 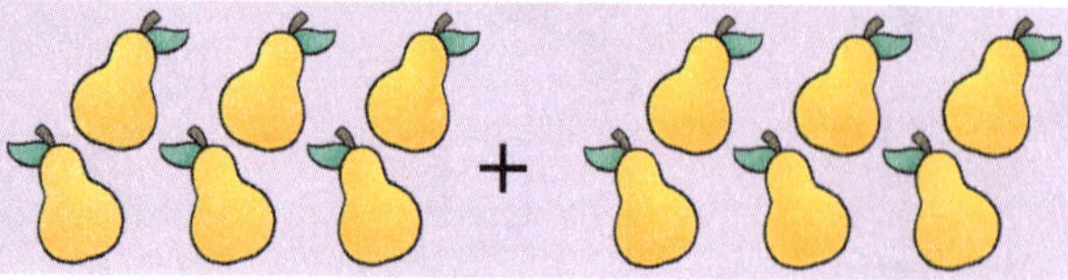 ____ + ____ = ____

6. 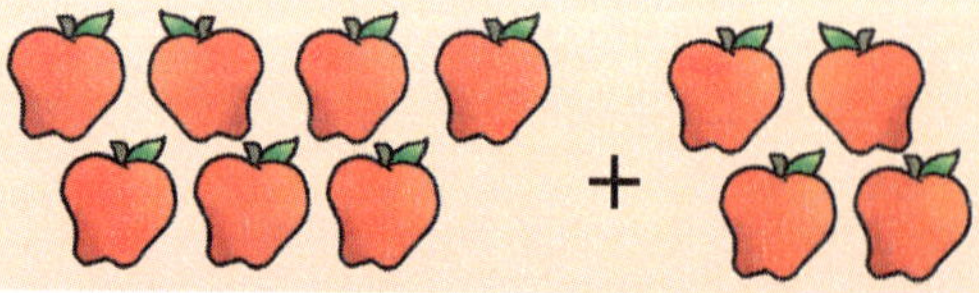 ____ + ____ = ____

ADDITION FACTS 9-12

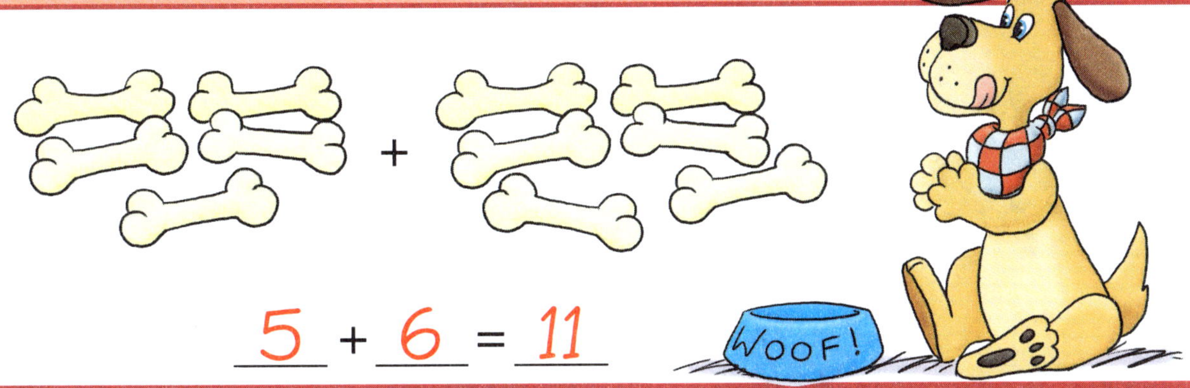

Find the **sum**.

1. $8 + 3 =$ ____
2. $5 + 7 =$ ____
3. $6 + 4 =$ ____
4. $9 + 2 =$ ____
5. $1 + 8 =$ ____
6. $7 + 2 =$ ____
7. $5 + 6 =$ ____
8. $9 + 0 =$ ____
9. $5 + 5 =$ ____
10. $9 + 3$
11. $2 + 8$
12. $7 + 4$
13. $6 + 6$
14. $8 + 4$
15. $9 + 1$
16. $4 + 5$
17. $7 + 3$
18. $8 + 2$
19. $7 + 5$
20. $6 + 3$
21. $4 + 7$

11 - 4 = 7

Write a **number sentence** about the pictures.

1. 

____ - ____ = ____

2. 

____ - ____ = ____

3. 

____ - ____ = ____

4. 

____ - ____ = ____

5. 

____ - ____ = ____

6.

____ - ____ = ____

Find the **difference**.

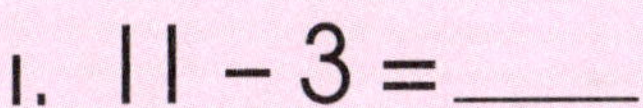

1. $11 - 3 =$ ____ 2. $12 - 9 =$ ____ 3. $11 - 7 =$ ____

4. $12 - 4 =$ ____ 5. $10 - 5 =$ ____ 6. $11 - 2 =$ ____

7. $10 - 7 =$ ____ 8. $12 - 8 =$ ____ 9. $12 - 3 =$ ____

10. $\begin{array}{r} 12 \\ -\ 9 \\ \hline \end{array}$ 11. $\begin{array}{r} 11 \\ -\ 5 \\ \hline \end{array}$ 12. $\begin{array}{r} 9 \\ -\ 7 \\ \hline \end{array}$ 13. $\begin{array}{r} 10 \\ -\ 9 \\ \hline \end{array}$

14. $\begin{array}{r} 11 \\ -\ 4 \\ \hline \end{array}$ 15. $\begin{array}{r} 12 \\ -\ 7 \\ \hline \end{array}$ 16. $\begin{array}{r} 11 \\ -\ 8 \\ \hline \end{array}$ 17. $\begin{array}{r} 10 \\ -\ 4 \\ \hline \end{array}$

18. $\begin{array}{r} 9 \\ -\ 6 \\ \hline \end{array}$ 19. $\begin{array}{r} 11 \\ -\ 6 \\ \hline \end{array}$ 20. $\begin{array}{r} 12 \\ -\ 5 \\ \hline \end{array}$ 21. $\begin{array}{r} 12 \\ -\ 3 \\ \hline \end{array}$

Find the **sum(s)** and **difference(s)** for the **fact family**. Use the number line if you need help.

1. $2 + 9 =$ ___ $9 + 2 =$ ___ $11 - 2 =$ ___ $11 - 9 =$ ___

2. $6 + 6 =$ ___ $12 - 6 =$ ___

3. $4 + 8 =$ ___ $8 + 4 =$ ___ $12 - 4 =$ ___ $12 - 8 =$ ___

4. $5 + 6 =$ ___ $6 + 5 =$ ___ $11 - 5 =$ ___ $11 - 6 =$ ___

5. $4 + 7 =$ ___ $7 + 4 =$ ___ $11 - 4 =$ ___ $11 - 7 =$ ___

6. $3 + 8 =$ ___ $8 + 3 =$ ___ $11 - 3 =$ ___ $11 - 8 =$ ___

7. $9 + 3 =$ ___ $3 + 9 =$ ___ $12 - 9 =$ ___ $12 - 3 =$ ___

8. $5 + 7 =$ ___ $7 + 5 =$ ___ $12 - 5 =$ ___ $12 - 7 =$ ___

Find each **sum** and **difference**.
Circle the clown with the greatest answer.

9	4	12	0	7	5
+ 3	+ 7	− 8	+ 9	− 3	+ 2
12					
− 6	− 6	− 4	+ 2	+ 8	− 4
6					
− 3	+ 5	+ 5	− 7	− 4	− 2
=	=	=	=	=	=
3					

The numbers you add are called **addends**.
You can add three numbers in different ways.

Add the numbers in order:
Add the first two numbers.
4 + 2 = 6

$$\begin{array}{r} 4 \\ 2 \\ +6 \\ \hline 12 \end{array} \quad 4 + 2 = 6$$

Then add the third number.
6 + **6** = 12

Look for a ten:
Look for two numbers with the sum of **10**.
4 + 6 = 10

$$\begin{array}{r} 4 \\ 2 \\ +6 \\ \hline 12 \end{array} \quad 4 + 6 = 10$$

Then add the third number.
10 + **2** = 12

Find the **sums**.

1. $\begin{array}{r} 2 \\ 6 \\ +3 \\ \hline \end{array}$ 2. $\begin{array}{r} 1 \\ 8 \\ +3 \\ \hline \end{array}$ 3. $\begin{array}{r} 9 \\ 1 \\ +2 \\ \hline \end{array}$ 4. $\begin{array}{r} 2 \\ 4 \\ +5 \\ \hline \end{array}$

5. $\begin{array}{r} 4 \\ 7 \\ +1 \\ \hline \end{array}$ 6. $\begin{array}{r} 4 \\ 4 \\ +2 \\ \hline \end{array}$ 7. $\begin{array}{r} 3 \\ 1 \\ +7 \\ \hline \end{array}$ 8. $\begin{array}{r} 5 \\ 5 \\ +2 \\ \hline \end{array}$

9. $\begin{array}{r} 6 \\ 2 \\ +2 \\ \hline \end{array}$ 10. $\begin{array}{r} 4 \\ 4 \\ +4 \\ \hline \end{array}$ 11. $\begin{array}{r} 3 \\ 2 \\ +5 \\ \hline \end{array}$ 12. $\begin{array}{r} 1 \\ 2 \\ +8 \\ \hline \end{array}$

Find each **sum** and **difference**.
Use the code below to solve the riddle.

Riddle:

They are sometimes called "kings."
At the circus, they jump through rings.

8	10	3	2	7
+ 2	− 5	+ 8	+ 6	− 4
− 8	+ 2	− 6	+ 3	+ 9
+ 7	+ 5	− 5	− 4	− 8
=	=	=	=	=
____	____	____	____	____

code

0	1	2	3	4	5	6	7	8	9	10	11	12
O	Z	E	B	S	R	K	N	H	L	F	P	I

Write a **number sentence** about the pictures.

1. 

____ + ____ = ____

2. ____ + ____ = ____

3. ____ + ____ = ____

4. ____ + ____ = ____

5. ____ + ____ = ____

6. ____ + ____ = ____

If you change the order of the **addends**, the **sum** is still the same.

Find the **sum**.

1. 5 + 6 = ____ 6 + 5 = ____
2. 6 + 8 = ____ 8 + 6 = ____
3. 4 + 7 = ____ 7 + 4 = ____
4. 8 + 2 = ____ 2 + 8 = ____
5. 8 + 5 = ____ 5 + 8 = ____
6. 4 + 9 = ____ 9 + 4 = ____
7. 7 + 3 = ____ 3 + 7 = ____
8. 7 + 5 = ____ 5 + 7 = ____
9. 6 + 7 = ____ 7 + 6 = ____
10. 5 + 9 = ____ 9 + 5 = ____
11. 4 + 8 = ____ 8 + 4 = ____
12. 3 + 8 = ____ 8 + 3 = ____
13. 9 + 3 = ____ 3 + 9 = ____
14. 7 + 2 = ____ 2 + 7 = ____

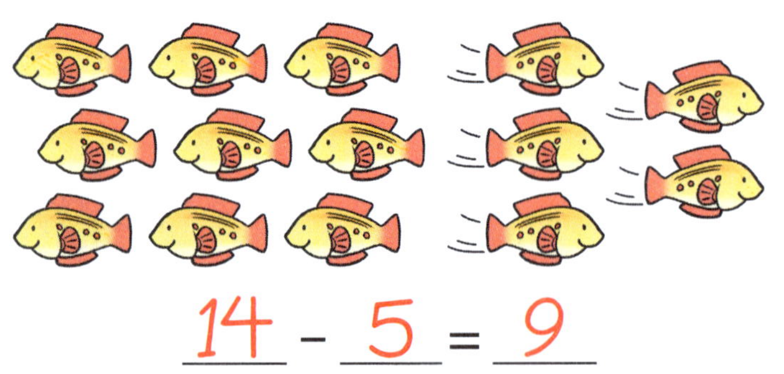

Write a **number sentence** about the pictures.

1. ____ - ____ = ____

2. ____ - ____ = ____

3. ____ - ____ = ____

4. ____ - ____ = ____

5. ____ - ____ = ____

6. ____ - ____ = ____

Find the **missing number** in the problem.
Remember the addition and subtraction facts.

1. $7 + 5 = \square$
2. $14 - 7 = \square$
3. $12 - \square = 7$
4. $14 - 8 = \square$
5. $5 + \square = 13$
6. $5 + 9 = \square$
7. $8 + \square = 12$
8. $4 + 9 = \square$
9. $14 - 9 = \square$

10. $\begin{array}{r} 8 \\ +\ 3 \\ \hline \square \end{array}$
11. $\begin{array}{r} 5 \\ +\ \square \\ \hline 13 \end{array}$
12. $\begin{array}{r} 3 \\ +\ 9 \\ \hline \square \end{array}$
13. $\begin{array}{r} 12 \\ -\ \square \\ \hline 4 \end{array}$
14. $\begin{array}{r} 11 \\ -\ 7 \\ \hline \square \end{array}$
15. $\begin{array}{r} 13 \\ -\ 5 \\ \hline \square \end{array}$
16. $\begin{array}{r} 5 \\ +\ \square \\ \hline 11 \end{array}$
17. $\begin{array}{r} 7 \\ +\ 5 \\ \hline \square \end{array}$
18. $\begin{array}{r} 4 \\ +\ \square \\ \hline 12 \end{array}$
19. $\begin{array}{r} 11 \\ -\ 3 \\ \hline \square \end{array}$

9 + 8 = 17

Write a **number sentence** about the pictures.

1. 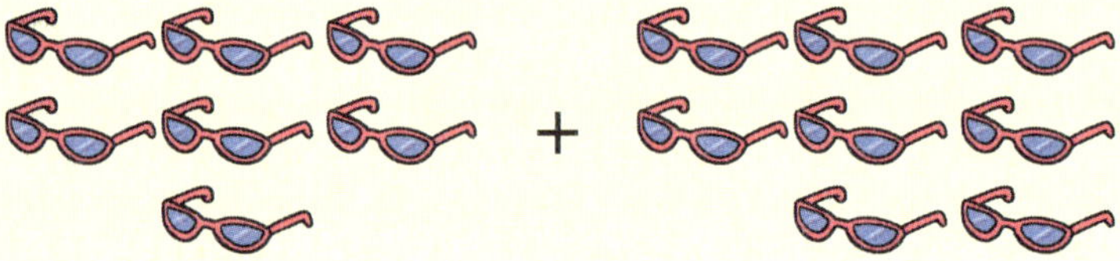 ___ + ___ = ___

2. 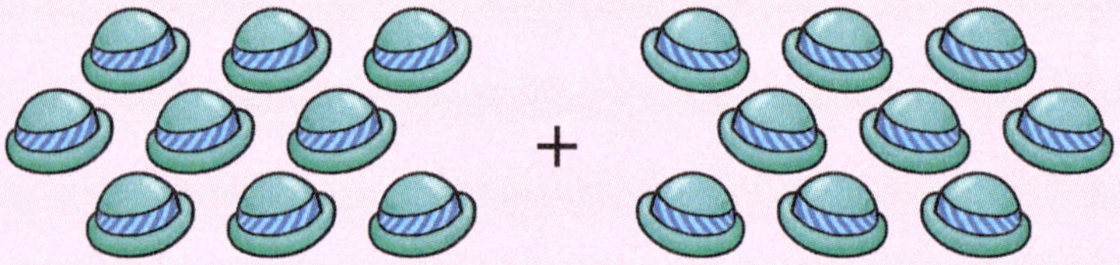 ___ + ___ = ___

3. 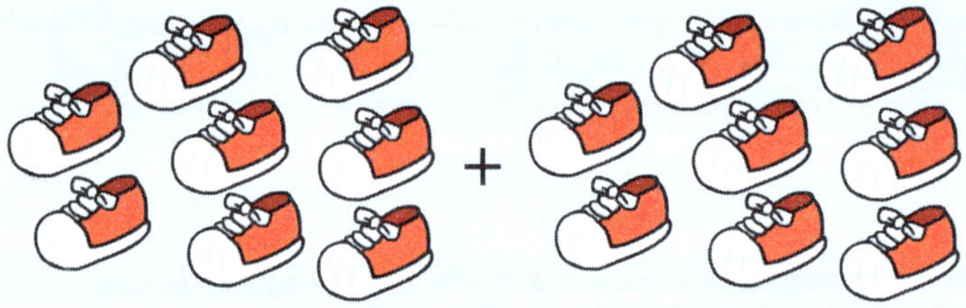 ___ + ___ = ___

4.  ___ + ___ = ___

5. 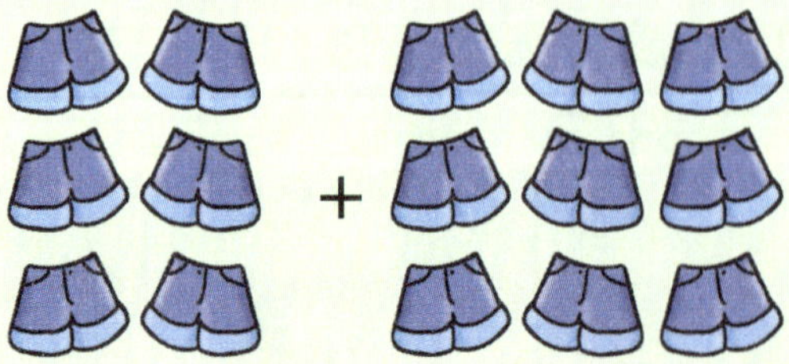 ___ + ___ = ___

ADDITION FACTS 10-18

Circle the pair(s) of **addends** that match the **sum**.

1. **10**
   - 5 + 5
   - 4 + 6
   - 3 + 8
   - 5 + 4

2. **11**
   - 5 + 6
   - 3 + 7
   - 8 + 3
   - 4 + 7

3. **12**
   - 8 + 2
   - 6 + 6
   - 9 + 2
   - 6 + 7

4. **13**
   - 8 + 4
   - 6 + 7
   - 4 + 9
   - 10 + 3

5. **14**
   - 8 + 6
   - 9 + 5
   - 7 + 7
   - 4 + 10

6. **15**
   - 9 + 6
   - 7 + 8
   - 8 + 8
   - 10 + 5

7. **16**
   - 8 + 9
   - 10 + 6
   - 9 + 7
   - 8 + 8

8. **17**
   - 8 + 8
   - 9 + 8
   - 9 + 9
   - 10 + 7

9. **18**
   - 8 + 8
   - 8 + 10
   - 9 + 9
   - 8 + 9

Practice the addition facts.
Write the missing **sums** in the chart.

+	0	1	2	3	4	5	6	7	8	9
0	0			3		5	6		8	
1		2								10
2	2			5				9		
3		4								
4	4			7			10			
5		6								14
6						11				
7	7									
8		9					14			17
9	9			12				16		

Learn the **doubles facts** to make adding easier.

Learn these **doubles facts** so you can say them as fast as you can!

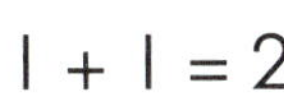

1 + 1 = 2	4 + 4 = 8	7 + 7 = 14
2 + 2 = 4	5 + 5 = 10	8 + 8 = 16
3 + 3 = 6	6 + 6 = 12	9 + 9 = 18

Find the **sum**.

1. 3 + 3 = ____
2. 2 + 2 = ____
3. 5 + 5 = ____
4. 1 + 1 = ____
5. 6 + 6 = ____
6. 8 + 8 = ____
7. 4 + 4 = ____
8. 7 + 7 = ____
9. 9 + 9 = ____
10. 6 + 6 = ____
11. 3 + 3 = ____
12. 2 + 2 = ____
13. 4 + 4 = ____
14. 1 + 1 = ____
15. 7 + 7 = ____

ADDING DOUBLES PLUS 1

A **double plus 1 fact** is a double fact and 1 more.

Learn the **doubles plus 1 facts.** They're easy if you know the doubles facts.

$2 + 2 + 1 = 5$ $2 + 3 = 5$

Find the **sum**.

1. $4 + 5 =$ ____
2. $1 + 2 =$ ____
3. $3 + 4 =$ ____
4. $6 + 7 =$ ____
5. $2 + 3 =$ ____
6. $8 + 9 =$ ____
7. $7 + 8 =$ ____
8. $3 + 4 =$ ____
9. $6 + 7 =$ ____
10. $8 + 9 =$ ____
11. $4 + 5 =$ ____
12. $1 + 2 =$ ____
13. $6 + 7 =$ ____
14. $2 + 3 =$ ____
15. $8 + 9 =$ ____

Add the outer number to the middle number to find the **sums**.

Write a **number sentence** about the pictures.

1. 

 ____ - ____ = ____

2. ____ - ____ = ____

3. ____ - ____ = ____

4. ____ - ____ = ____

5. 

 ____ - ____ = ____

As you've learned, you can use a number line to find **differences**.

13 – 7 = 6

Find the **difference**. Use the number line if you need help.

1. $\begin{array}{r} 14 \\ -\ 8 \\ \hline \end{array}$

2. $\begin{array}{r} 15 \\ -\ 7 \\ \hline \end{array}$

3. $\begin{array}{r} 12 \\ -\ 4 \\ \hline \end{array}$

4. $\begin{array}{r} 15 \\ -\ 9 \\ \hline \end{array}$

5. $\begin{array}{r} 13 \\ -\ 7 \\ \hline \end{array}$

6. $\begin{array}{r} 17 \\ -\ 8 \\ \hline \end{array}$

7. $\begin{array}{r} 14 \\ -\ 7 \\ \hline \end{array}$

8. $\begin{array}{r} 12 \\ -\ 5 \\ \hline \end{array}$

9. $\begin{array}{r} 16 \\ -\ 9 \\ \hline \end{array}$

10. $\begin{array}{r} 13 \\ -\ 4 \\ \hline \end{array}$

11. 13 – 8 = ____

12. 16 – 8 =

13. 14 – 9 = ____

14. 10 – 7 = ____

15. 11 – 5 = ____

16. 11 – 3 = ____

17. 12 – 9 = ____

18. 18 – 9 = ____

19. 11 – 7 = ____

MORE FACT FAMILIES

Find the missing numbers to complete the **fact family**.

1. **12**

5 + 7 = ☐
7 + ☐ = 12
12 − 5 = ☐
12 − 7 = ☐

2. **13**

☐ + 9 = 13
9 + 4 = ☐
13 − ☐ = 9
13 − ☐ = 4

3. **14**

8 + 6 = ☐
6 + ☐ = 14
14 − 8 = ☐
14 − 6 = ☐

4. **15**

8 + ☐ = 15
7 + 8 = ☐
15 − ☐ = 7
15 − ☐ = 8

5. **16**

☐ + 7 = 16
7 + 9 = ☐
16 − 9 = ☐
16 − 7 = ☐

6. **17**

8 + ☐ = 17
9 + 8 = ☐
17 − ☐ = 9
17 − ☐ = 8

Think of addition doubles facts to find **subtraction doubles facts.**

$12 - 6 = 6$

$6 + 6 = 12$

$12 - 6 = 6$

Think of addition doubles plus 1 facts to find **subtraction doubles plus 1 facts.**

$13 - 6 = 7$

$6 + 6 + 1 = 13$

$13 - 6 = 6 + 1$

Find the **difference.**

1. $14 - 7$
2. $12 - 6$
3. $10 - 5$
4. $16 - 8$
5. $18 - 9$

6. $15 - 7$
7. $13 - 6$
8. $11 - 5$
9. 17 8
10. $17 - 9$

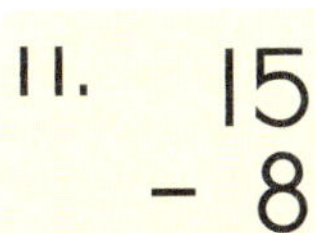

11. $15 - 8$
12. $13 - 7$
13. $11 - 6$

Find the **missing number** in the problem.
Remember the addition and subtraction facts.

1. 7 + 3 = ☐
2. 5 + 6 = ☐
3. 8 + 9 = ☐
4. 12 – 8 = ☐
5. 18 – 9 = ☐
6. 15 – 8 = ☐
7. 8 + ☐ = 9
8. 11 – ☐ = 2
9. 5 + ☐ = 14
10. 13 – 8 = ☐
11. 14 – 8 = ☐
12. 13 – 7 = ☐

Write the **sums** or **differences**.

13. Subtract **5**	14. Add **6**	15. Subtract **7**	16. Add **8**
10 ____	8 ____	14 ____	6 ____
13 ____	5 ____	15 ____	8 ____
11 ____	9 ____	11 ____	7 ____
14 ____	7 ____	9 ____	9 ____

Write each **sum** and **difference**.
Circle the flamingo with the greatest answer.

8	17	10	15	7	6
+ 7	− 9	− 2	− 6	+ 8	+ 3
− 9	− 5	− 8	+ 4	− 6	+ 5
+ 7	+ 9	+ 7	− 9	+ 9	− 6
=	=	=	=	=	=

1. Add the **ones**.

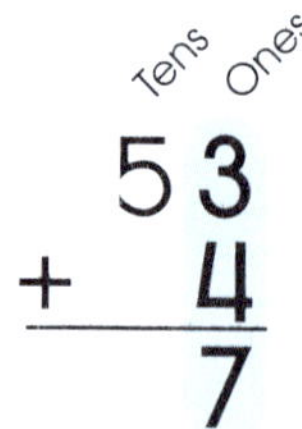

2. Add the **tens**.

Add the **ones**.
Then add the **tens**.

1. 63 + 4	2. 91 + 8	3. 50 + 5
4. 78 + 1	5. 25 + 3	6. 83 + 6
7. 45 + 34	8. 27 + 70	9. 44 + 42
10. 32 + 66	11. 46 + 53	12. 37 + 32

Solve the riddle.
Remember: Add the **ones** and then the **tens**.

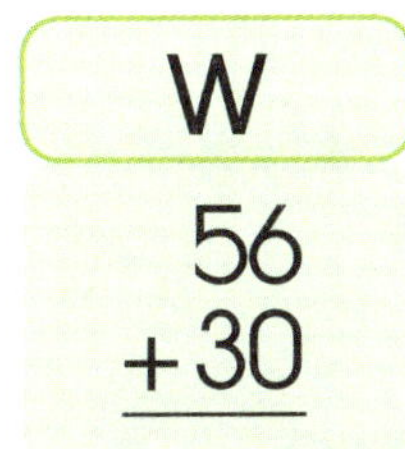

Riddle:
What animal can fit an elephant on its tongue?

1. W
$$\begin{array}{r} 56 \\ +30 \\ \hline \end{array}$$

2. C
$$\begin{array}{r} 71 \\ +25 \\ \hline \end{array}$$

3. T
$$\begin{array}{r} 43 \\ +35 \\ \hline \end{array}$$

4. W
$$\begin{array}{r} 20 \\ +74 \\ \hline \end{array}$$

5. A
$$\begin{array}{r} 81 \\ +14 \\ \hline \end{array}$$

6. J
$$\begin{array}{r} 90 \\ +\ 7 \\ \hline \end{array}$$

7. R
$$\begin{array}{r} 85 \\ +14 \\ \hline \end{array}$$

8. G
$$\begin{array}{r} 34 \\ +30 \\ \hline \end{array}$$

9. U
$$\begin{array}{r} 20 \\ +61 \\ \hline \end{array}$$

10. E
$$\begin{array}{r} 17 \\ +42 \\ \hline \end{array}$$

11. H
$$\begin{array}{r} 55 \\ +11 \\ \hline \end{array}$$

12. L
$$\begin{array}{r} 62 \\ +\ 6 \\ \hline \end{array}$$

13. W
$$\begin{array}{r} 47 \\ +30 \\ \hline \end{array}$$

14. L
$$\begin{array}{r} 21 \\ +\ 4 \\ \hline \end{array}$$

15. E
$$\begin{array}{r} 40 \\ +30 \\ \hline \end{array}$$

16. B
$$\begin{array}{r} 26 \\ +23 \\ \hline \end{array}$$

The ___ ___ ___ ___ ___ ___ ___ ___ ___
49 25 81 70 94 66 95 68 59

1. Subtract the **ones**.

	Tens	Ones
	4	9
−		5
		4

2. Subtract the **tens**.

	Tens	Ones
	4	9
−		5
	4	4

Subtract the **ones**.
Then **subtract** the **tens**.

1. 57 − 2	2. 45 − 3	3. 69 − 7
4. 78 − 5	5. 24 − 3	6. 98 − 6
7. 47 − 22	8. 66 − 43	9. 89 − 26
10. 59 − 23	11. 76 − 34	12. 99 − 47

Remember: **Subtract** the **ones** and then the **tens**.

1. 58 − 36 = ____
2. 77 − 30 = ____
3. 45 − 24 = ____
4. 26 − 5 = ____
5. 86 − 3 = ____
6. 38 − 17 = ____
7. 67 − 21 = ____
8. 53 − 30 = ____
9. 99 − 65 = ____
10. 85 − 45 = ____
11. 78 − 4 = ____
12. 37 − 30 = ____
13. 48 − 25 = ____
14. 59 − 30 = ____
15. 76 − 24 = ____
16. 87 − 3 = ____

Find each **sum** and **difference**.
Connect the dots from the **least** number to the **greatest** number.
Then color the picture.

Help the lion cub find its mother.
Find each **missing number** to finish the puzzle and get the lion cub home.

		3 1 + 7 ☐	9 2 + 1 ☐	2 4 + 5 ☐	50 + 8 ☐
6 − 4 ☐		4 7 + 1 ☐			44 + 34 ☐
5 + ☐ 8		5 2 + 3 ☐		38 − 5 ☐	29 − 2 ☐
8 + ☐ 12		12 − 7 ☐		69 + 20 ☐	
7 + ☐ 11	12 − 8 ☐	5 + ☐ 11		59 − 3 ☐	13 + ☐ 15
					5 + ☐ 12

1. Add the **ones**.
6 + 6 = 12
Regroup 12 ones
as **1** ten and **2** ones.

Tens	Ones
1	
3	6
+	6
	2

2. Add the **tens**.
3 + 1 = **4** tens

Tens	Ones
1	
3	6
+	6
4	2

Add. Regroup as needed.

1. $58 + 4$
2. $24 + 7$

3. $36 + 4$
4. $75 + 6$

5. $48 + 34$
6. $62 + 18$

7. $78 + 7$
8. $59 + 24$

9. $67 + 18$
10. $56 + 24$
11. $29 + 58$
12. $45 + 35$

13. $76 + 18$
14. $54 + 27$

15. $43 + 49$
16. $87 + 8$

Add. Regroup as needed.

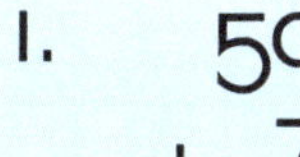

1. $\begin{array}{r} 59 \\ +\ 7 \\ \hline \end{array}$	2. $\begin{array}{r} 74 \\ +15 \\ \hline \end{array}$	3. $\begin{array}{r} 85 \\ +\ 7 \\ \hline \end{array}$	4. $\begin{array}{r} 76 \\ +12 \\ \hline \end{array}$
5. $\begin{array}{r} 70 \\ +19 \\ \hline \end{array}$	6. $\begin{array}{r} 66 \\ +23 \\ \hline \end{array}$	7. $\begin{array}{r} 48 \\ +23 \\ \hline \end{array}$	8. $\begin{array}{r} 27 \\ +\ 8 \\ \hline \end{array}$
9. $\begin{array}{r} 88 \\ +\ 7 \\ \hline \end{array}$	10. $\begin{array}{r} 40 \\ +28 \\ \hline \end{array}$	11. $\begin{array}{r} 75 \\ +17 \\ \hline \end{array}$	12. $\begin{array}{r} 29 \\ +65 \\ \hline \end{array}$

How many miles can these animals swim in an hour?

13. $\begin{array}{r} 32 \\ +18 \\ \hline \end{array}$	14. $\begin{array}{r} 16 \\ +\ 9 \\ \hline \end{array}$	15. $\begin{array}{r} 31 \\ +\ 9 \\ \hline \end{array}$	16. $\begin{array}{r} 37 \\ +28 \\ \hline \end{array}$	17. $\begin{array}{r} 12 \\ +\ 8 \\ \hline \end{array}$
_____ miles	_____ miles	_____ miles	_____ miles	_____ miles

1. Subtract the **ones**.
4 – 6 cannot be done!
You must **regroup**.

	Tens	Ones
	5	4
–	1	6
		?

54 is 5 tens and 4 ones.
Regroup as **4** tens and **14** ones.
14 – 6 = **8** ones

	Tens	Ones
	4	14
	~~5~~	~~4~~
–	1	6
		8

2. Subtract the **tens**.
4 – 1 = **3** tens

	Tens	Ones
	4	14
	~~5~~	~~4~~
–	1	6
	3	8

Subtract. Regroup as needed.

1. 57 – 9 =
2. 24 – 10 =
3. 36 – 17 =
4. 82 – 66 =
5. 75 – 23 =
6. 43 – 18 =
7. 61 – 56 =
8. 40 – 27 =
9. 94 – 58 =
10. 38 – 9 =
11. 88 – 78 =
12. 55 – 27 =
13. 18 – 6 =
14. 44 – 17 =
15. 70 – 35 =
16. 39 – 19 =

Subtract. Regroup as needed.

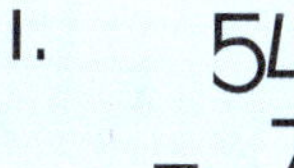

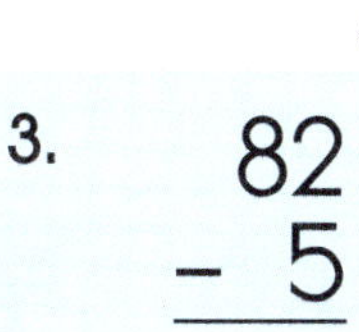

1. $\begin{array}{r} 54 \\ -\ 7 \\ \hline \end{array}$

2. $\begin{array}{r} 67 \\ -\ 8 \\ \hline \end{array}$

3. $\begin{array}{r} 82 \\ -\ 5 \\ \hline \end{array}$

4. $\begin{array}{r} 40 \\ -\ 6 \\ \hline \end{array}$

5. $\begin{array}{r} 22 \\ -\ 4 \\ \hline \end{array}$

6. $\begin{array}{r} 95 \\ -\ 7 \\ \hline \end{array}$

7. $\begin{array}{r} 73 \\ -\ 8 \\ \hline \end{array}$

8. $\begin{array}{r} 36 \\ -\ 7 \\ \hline \end{array}$

9. $\begin{array}{r} 48 \\ -29 \\ \hline \end{array}$

10. $\begin{array}{r} 50 \\ -25 \\ \hline \end{array}$

11. $\begin{array}{r} 26 \\ -17 \\ \hline \end{array}$

12. $\begin{array}{r} 34 \\ -25 \\ \hline \end{array}$

Which animal is the longest? Circle the answer.

13. $\begin{array}{r} 85 \\ -45 \\ \hline \end{array}$ _____ feet

14. $\begin{array}{r} 36 \\ -27 \\ \hline \end{array}$ _____ feet

15. $\begin{array}{r} 30 \\ -29 \\ \hline \end{array}$ _____ foot

16. $\begin{array}{r} 59 \\ -19 \\ \hline \end{array}$ _____ feet

17. $\begin{array}{r} 76 \\ -58 \\ \hline \end{array}$ _____ feet

Find the **sum** or **difference**. Regroup as needed.

1.	2.	3.	4.
45 + 35	89 − 62	36 − 18	72 + 18

5.	6.	7.	8.
50 − 25	65 + 28	91 + 8	25 + 25

9.	10.	11.	12.
32 + 48	49 + 37	74 − 28	19 − 17

13.	14.	15.	16.
88 − 66	36 + 36	67 − 18	91 − 19

Find the **sum** or **difference**.
Regroup as needed.
Write the answers in the puzzle.

1.			2.	3.		4.
		5.		6.		
	7.				8.	
9.			10.			11.
12.					13.	

Across

1. $\begin{array}{r} 53 \\ -26 \\ \hline \end{array}$

2. $\begin{array}{r} 35 \\ +49 \\ \hline \end{array}$

4. $\begin{array}{r} 75 \\ -70 \\ \hline \end{array}$

6. $\begin{array}{r} 72 \\ -65 \\ \hline \end{array}$

7. $\begin{array}{r} 45 \\ +32 \\ \hline \end{array}$

8. $\begin{array}{r} 90 \\ -86 \\ \hline \end{array}$

10. $\begin{array}{r} 36 \\ +36 \\ \hline \end{array}$

12. $\begin{array}{r} 86 \\ -49 \\ \hline \end{array}$

13. $\begin{array}{r} 56 \\ -23 \\ \hline \end{array}$

Down

1. $\begin{array}{r} 60 \\ -35 \\ \hline \end{array}$

3. $\begin{array}{r} 28 \\ +19 \\ \hline \end{array}$

4. $\begin{array}{r} 25 \\ +28 \\ \hline \end{array}$

5. $\begin{array}{r} 66 \\ -29 \\ \hline \end{array}$

9. $\begin{array}{r} 43 \\ +50 \\ \hline \end{array}$

10. $\begin{array}{r} 53 \\ +17 \\ \hline \end{array}$

11. $\begin{array}{r} 47 \\ +16 \\ \hline \end{array}$

Adding without regrouping:

1. Add the **ones**.
   4 + 3 = **7** ones

2. Add the **tens**.
   3 + 5 = **8** tens

3. Add the **hundreds**.
   5 + 2 = **7** hundreds

Hundreds	Tens	Ones
5	3	4
+2	5	3
7	8	7

Adding with regrouping:

1. Add the **ones**.
   7 + 5 = **12** ones
   Regroup 12 ones as **1** ten and **2** ones.

2. Add the **tens**.
   1 + 2 + 5 = **8** tens

3. Add the **hundreds**.
   6 + 1 = **7** hundreds

Hundreds	Tens	Ones
	1	
6	2	7
+1	5	5
7	8	2

Add. Regroup as needed.

1. 547 + 345

2. 136 + 546

3. 481 + 209

4. 628 + 167

5. 287 + 707

6. 345 + 248

7. 407 + 486

8. 524 + 127

9. 753 + 118

When adding greater numbers, you may have to regroup more than once.

1. Add the **ones**.
   8 + 5 = **13** ones
   Regroup 13 ones as **1** ten and **3** ones.

2. Add the **tens**.
   1 + 6 + 7 = **14** tens
   Regroup 14 tens as **1** hundred and **4** tens.

3. Add the **hundreds**.
   1 + 5 + 2 = **8** hundreds

Hundreds	Tens	Ones
1	1	
5	6	8
+2	7	5
8	4	3

Add. Regroup as needed.

1. 584 + 372
2. 240 + 495
3. 798 + 114

4. 591 + 147
5. 278 + 243
6. 632 + 287

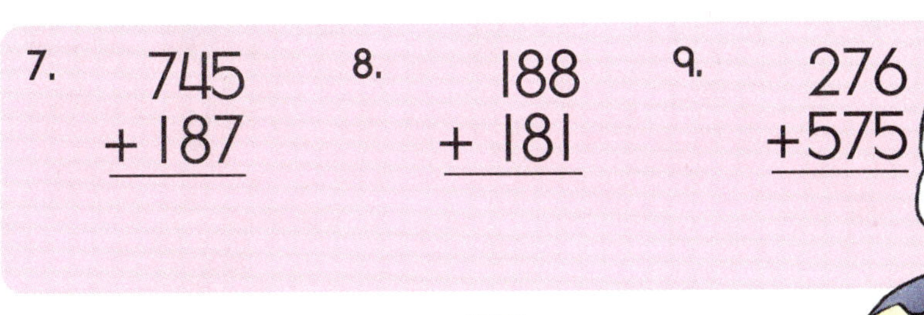

7. 745 + 187
8. 188 + 181
9. 276 + 575

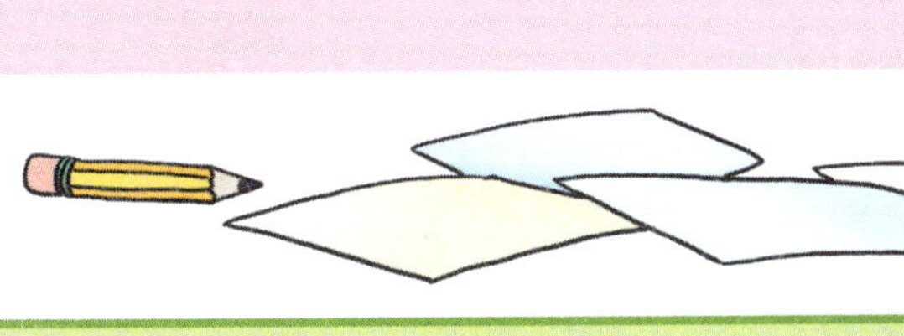

1. Subtract the **ones**.
   5 – 8 cannot be done!
   Regroup 7 tens 5 ones
   as **6** tens **15** ones.
   15 – 8 = **7** ones

2. Subtract the **tens**.
   6 – 2 = **4** tens

3. Subtract the **hundreds**.
   5 – 2 = **3** hundreds

Hundreds	Tens	Ones
	6	15
5	~~7~~	~~5~~
– 2	2	8
3	4	7

Subtract. Regroup as needed.

1. $\begin{array}{r} 574 \\ -458 \\ \hline \end{array}$
2. $\begin{array}{r} 356 \\ -149 \\ \hline \end{array}$
3. $\begin{array}{r} 825 \\ -207 \\ \hline \end{array}$
4. $\begin{array}{r} 756 \\ -348 \\ \hline \end{array}$
5. $\begin{array}{r} 473 \\ -158 \\ \hline \end{array}$
6. $\begin{array}{r} 392 \\ -347 \\ \hline \end{array}$
7. $\begin{array}{r} 864 \\ -508 \\ \hline \end{array}$
8. $\begin{array}{r} 615 \\ -208 \\ \hline \end{array}$
9. $\begin{array}{r} 973 \\ -755 \\ \hline \end{array}$

Find the **sum** or **difference**. Regroup as needed.

1. $\begin{array}{r} 585 \\ -\ 269 \\ \hline \end{array}$

2. $\begin{array}{r} 274 \\ +\ 234 \\ \hline \end{array}$

3. $\begin{array}{r} 108 \\ +\ 544 \\ \hline \end{array}$

4. $\begin{array}{r} 922 \\ -\ 108 \\ \hline \end{array}$

5. $\begin{array}{r} 184 \\ +\ 507 \\ \hline \end{array}$

6. $\begin{array}{r} 355 \\ -\ 118 \\ \hline \end{array}$

7. $\begin{array}{r} 571 \\ +\ 262 \\ \hline \end{array}$

8. $\begin{array}{r} 963 \\ -\ 125 \\ \hline \end{array}$

9. $\begin{array}{r} 456 \\ +\ 138 \\ \hline \end{array}$

10. $\begin{array}{r} 222 \\ -\ 115 \\ \hline \end{array}$

11. $\begin{array}{r} 753 \\ +\ 156 \\ \hline \end{array}$

12. $\begin{array}{r} 151 \\ -\ 138 \\ \hline \end{array}$

Check the facts in each set.
Which seal has the most correct answers? ____________________

Cross out the incorrect answers and write the correct answers.

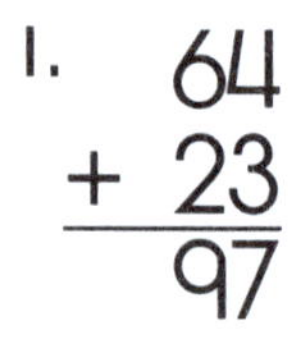

1. $\begin{array}{r} 64 \\ +\ 23 \\ \hline 97 \end{array}$
2. $\begin{array}{r} 36 \\ +\ 27 \\ \hline 63 \end{array}$
3. $\begin{array}{r} 387 \\ +116 \\ \hline 493 \end{array}$
4. $\begin{array}{r} 84 \\ -\ 36 \\ \hline 98 \end{array}$
5. $\begin{array}{r} 73 \\ -\ 27 \\ \hline 46 \end{array}$
6. $\begin{array}{r} 460 \\ -129 \\ \hline 342 \end{array}$

7. $\begin{array}{r} 39 \\ +\ 25 \\ \hline 64 \end{array}$
8. $\begin{array}{r} 47 \\ +\ 35 \\ \hline 82 \end{array}$
9. $\begin{array}{r} 392 \\ +138 \\ \hline 530 \end{array}$
10. $\begin{array}{r} 79 \\ -\ 34 \\ \hline 35 \end{array}$
11. $\begin{array}{r} 83 \\ -\ 36 \\ \hline 47 \end{array}$
12. $\begin{array}{r} 467 \\ -138 \\ \hline 329 \end{array}$

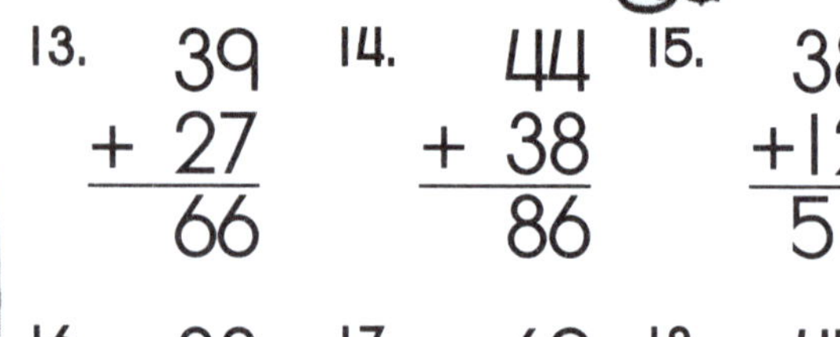

13. $\begin{array}{r} 39 \\ +\ 27 \\ \hline 66 \end{array}$
14. $\begin{array}{r} 44 \\ +\ 38 \\ \hline 86 \end{array}$
15. $\begin{array}{r} 384 \\ +127 \\ \hline 511 \end{array}$
16. $\begin{array}{r} 88 \\ -\ 39 \\ \hline 49 \end{array}$
17. $\begin{array}{r} 60 \\ -\ 27 \\ \hline 33 \end{array}$
18. $\begin{array}{r} 452 \\ -137 \\ \hline 325 \end{array}$

ADDITION & SUBTRACTION REVIEW

Recall basic facts.

1. 9 + 5 = ____
2. 6 + 0 = ____
3. 7 + 9 = ____
4. 4 + 7 = ____
5. 17 − 8 = ____
6. 13 − 5 = ____
7. 15 − 9 = ____
8. 10 − 4 = ____
9. 8 + 8 = ____
10. 14 − 6 = ____
11. 9 + 9 = ____
12. 11 − 2 = ____

Find the **sum**. Regroup as needed.

13. $\begin{array}{r} 43 \\ +25 \\ \hline \end{array}$
14. $\begin{array}{r} 50 \\ +30 \\ \hline \end{array}$
15. $\begin{array}{r} 74 \\ +\ 5 \\ \hline \end{array}$
16. $\begin{array}{r} 26 \\ +52 \\ \hline \end{array}$
17. $\begin{array}{r} 38 \\ +25 \\ \hline \end{array}$
18. $\begin{array}{r} 57 \\ +\ 9 \\ \hline \end{array}$
19. $\begin{array}{r} 66 \\ +17 \\ \hline \end{array}$
20. $\begin{array}{r} 28 \\ +32 \\ \hline \end{array}$

Find the **difference**. Regroup as needed.

21. $\begin{array}{r} 76 \\ -45 \\ \hline \end{array}$
22. $\begin{array}{r} 93 \\ -40 \\ \hline \end{array}$
23. $\begin{array}{r} 59 \\ -29 \\ \hline \end{array}$
24. $\begin{array}{r} 27 \\ -\ 7 \\ \hline \end{array}$
25. $\begin{array}{r} 35 \\ -\ 7 \\ \hline \end{array}$
26. $\begin{array}{r} 54 \\ -29 \\ \hline \end{array}$
27. $\begin{array}{r} 75 \\ -68 \\ \hline \end{array}$
28. $\begin{array}{r} 60 \\ -24 \\ \hline \end{array}$

Find the **sum** or **difference**. Regroup as needed.

29. $\begin{array}{r} 342 \\ +236 \\ \hline \end{array}$
30. $\begin{array}{r} 536 \\ +125 \\ \hline \end{array}$
31. $\begin{array}{r} 456 \\ -327 \\ \hline \end{array}$
32. $\begin{array}{r} 745 \\ -129 \\ \hline \end{array}$

Follow the path of the numbers 1–20 in order. Start at 1.

Count on. Write the missing numbers.

1. 6, ____, ____, ____, ____, ____, ____

2. 10, ____, ____, ____, ____, ____, ____

3. 14, ____, ____, ____, ____, ____, ____

BEFORE, BETWEEN & AFTER

Which number comes **before**?

1. ____ 6 7	2. ____ 10 11	3. ____ 14 15
4. ____ 11 12	5. ____ 18 19	6. ____ 1 2

Which number belongs **between**?

7. 4 ____ 6	8. 11 ____ 13	9. 16 ____ 18
10. 0 ____ 2	11. 17 ____ 19	12. 13 ____ 15

Which number comes **after**?

13. 3 4 ____	14. 15 16 ____	15. 18 19 ____
16. 6 7 ____	17. 17 18 ____	18. 8 9 ____

Greater means more than.
Less means not as many.

Circle the number that is **greater**.

1.	5	8	2.	14	12	3.	19	9
4.	10	0	5.	2	12	6.	13	18
7.	13	3	8.	4	15	9.	20	12

Circle the number that is **less**.

10.	7	9	11.	11	8	12.	20	2
13.	15	11	14.	13	18	15.	0	3
16.	19	9	17.	17	19	18.	12	20

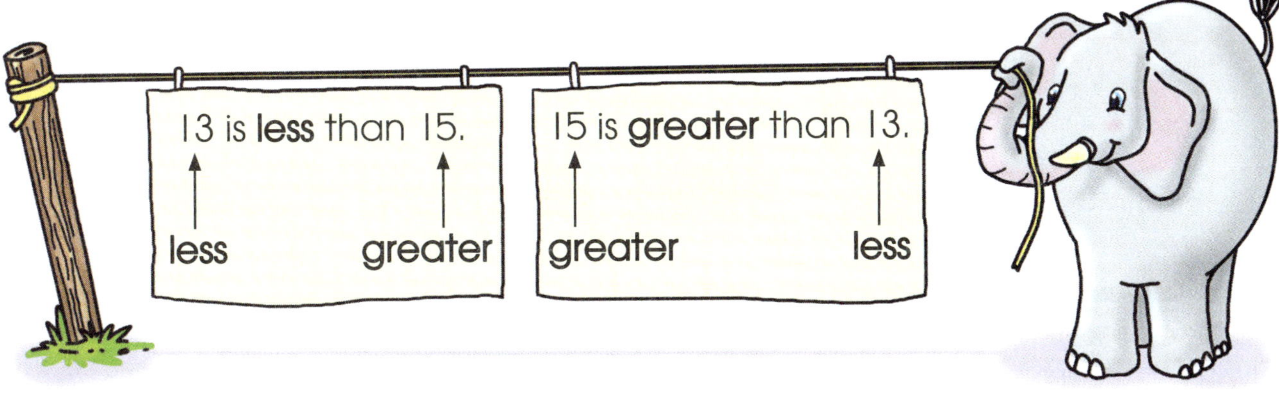

Write the word **greater** or **less** in the blank.

1. 5 is ____________ than 7.
2. 8 is ____________ than 6.
3. 11 is ____________ than 10.
4. 12 is ____________ than 15.
5. 18 is ____________ than 10.
6. 13 is ____________ than 11.
7. 7 is ____________ than 17.
8. 14 is ____________ than 19.
9. 2 is ____________ than 20.
10. 13 is ____________ than 3.

Write the correct number in the blank.

11. ____________ is greater than 5 and less than 7.
12. ____________ is less than 10 and greater than 8.
13. Your choice: 7 is less than ____________ and greater than ____________.

$3 + 4 = $ 7

Look at the picture. Read the number sentence.
Write the **sum**.

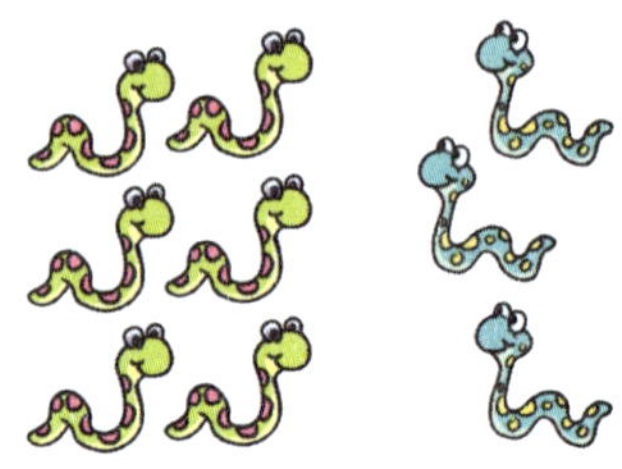

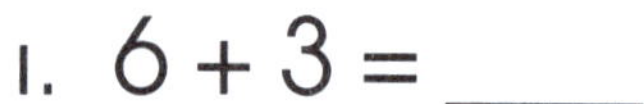

1. $6 + 3 = $ ____
2. $2 + 5 = $ ____
3. $8 + 0 = $ ____

4. $4 + 4 = $ ____
5. $5 + 4 = $ ____
6. $5 + 5 = $ ____

7. $7 + 2 = $ ____
8. $6 + 4 = $ ____

9. $8 + 2 = $ ____

10. 

How many butterflies are there **in all**? 9 10 11

Write the number sentence.

____

11 − 4 = 7

Look at the picture. Read the number sentence.
Write the **difference**.

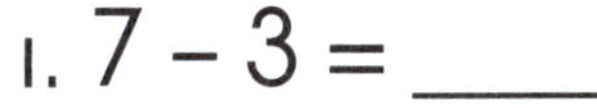

1. 7 − 3 = ____ 2. 10 − 4 = ____ 3. 10 − 8 = ____

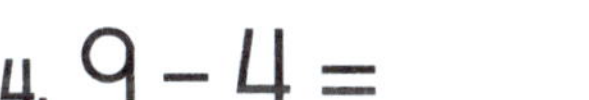

4. 9 − 4 = ____ 5. 9 − 7 = ____ 6. 8 − 2 = ____

7. 7 − 4 = ____ 8. 10 − 5 = ____ 9. 8 − 3 = ____

10. How many **more** ducks than owls are there? 4 5 6

Write the number sentence.

____

As you've learned, a **fact family** uses the same numbers in its addition and subtraction problems.

Write the missing numbers to complete the **fact family**.

1. $5 + 7 = \square$ $\quad 7 + 5 = \square$ $\quad 12 - 5 = \square$ $\quad 12 - 7 = \square$

2. $5 + 5 = \square$ $\quad 10 - 5 = \square$

3. $\square + 6 = 9$ $\quad 6 + 3 = \square$ $\quad 9 - \square = 3$ $\quad 9 - 3 = \square$

4. $6 + \square = 12$ $\quad \square - 6 = 6$

5. $6 + 5 = \square$ $\quad \square + 6 = 11$ $\quad 11 - \square = 6$ $\quad 11 - \square = 5$

6. $7 + \square = 11$ $\quad 4 + 7 = \square$ $\quad 11 - \square = 4$ $\quad \square - 4 = 7$

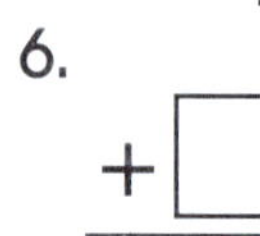

All of the number sentences in a **fact family** use the same numbers.

8, 7, 15

8 + 7 = 15

7 + 8 = 15

15 - 7 = 8

15 - 8 = 7

Complete the **fact family**.

1. 5, 9, 14

5 + ____ = ____

9 + ____ = ____

14 - ____ = ____

____ - ____ = 5

2. 9, 6, 15

____ + ____ = ____

____ + ____ = ____

____ - ____ = ____

____ - ____ = ____

3. 7, 6, 13

____ + ____ = ____

____ + ____ = ____

____ - ____ = ____

____ - ____ = ____

4. 8, 9, 17

____ + ____ = ____

____ + ____ = ____

____ - ____ = ____

____ - ____ = ____

5. 8, 6, 14

____ + ____ = ____

____ + ____ = ____

____ - ____ = ____

____ - ____ = ____

6. 7, 9, 16

____ + ____ = ____

____ + ____ = ____

____ - ____ = ____

____ - ____ = ____

WHICH NUMBER IS MISSING?

Find the missing number. Use the number line if you need help.

0 1 2 3 4 5 6 7 8 9 10

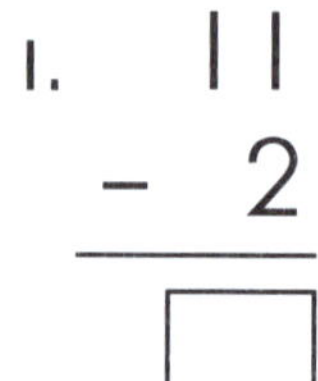

1. 11 − 2 = □
2. 7 − 4 = □
3. 12 − □ = 8
4. 11 − 7 = □
5. 9 − 5 = □
6. □ − 2 = 5
7. 12 − 7 = □
8. 10 − 3 = □
9. 10 − 8 = □
10. 11 − 3 = □
11. 11 − 8 = □
12. 9 − 3 = □
13. 8 − □ = 5
14. 7 − □ = 4
15. □ − 6 = 4
16. □ − 5 = 5

Find the missing numbers.

1.
$$\begin{array}{r} 6 \\ + \square \\ \hline 10 \end{array} \qquad \begin{array}{r} 10 \\ - 6 \\ \hline \square \end{array}$$

2.
$$\begin{array}{r} 14 \\ - 8 \\ \hline \square \end{array} \qquad \begin{array}{r} \square \\ + 8 \\ \hline 14 \end{array}$$

3.
$$\begin{array}{r} 3 \\ + \square \\ \hline 12 \end{array} \qquad \begin{array}{r} 12 \\ - \square \\ \hline 9 \end{array}$$

4.
$$\begin{array}{r} 7 \\ + \square \\ \hline 13 \end{array} \qquad \begin{array}{r} 13 \\ - \square \\ \hline 6 \end{array}$$

5.
$$\begin{array}{r} 15 \\ - 8 \\ \hline \square \end{array} \qquad \begin{array}{r} \square \\ + 7 \\ \hline 15 \end{array}$$

6.
$$\begin{array}{r} 9 \\ + \square \\ \hline 18 \end{array} \qquad \begin{array}{r} 18 \\ - \square \\ \hline 9 \end{array}$$

7. $4 + \square = 11$

$11 - 4 = \square$

8. $7 + \square = 14$

$14 - \square = 7$

9. $6 + \square = 15$

$15 - 9 = \square$

10. $6 + \square = 12$

$12 - \square = 6$

11. $8 + \square = 17$

$17 - \square = 9$

12. $13 - 8 = \square$

$5 + \square = 13$

Solve this riddle:
Which animal would you like to hire to work in an office?
Add and **subtract** to find the answer.

A	E	T
6 + 7 = ____	3 + 9 = ____	14 – 7 = ____
S	**A**	**R**
16 – 8 = ____	5 + 8 = ____	18 – 9 = ____
E	**R**	**R**
4 + 8 = ____	17 – 8 = ____	15 – 6 = ____
S	**Y**	**C**
15 – 7 = ____	8 + 6 = ____	9 + 6 = ____
D	**B**	**I**
7 + 9 = ____	9 + 8 = ____	14 – 9 = ____

The ____ ____ ____ ____ ____ ____ ____ ____ ____
8 12 15 9 12 7 13 9 14

____ ____ ____ ____
17 5 9 16

Check the facts.
Which set has **more** correct answers? _____

Cross out the seven incorrect answers.
Write the correct answers.

$$\begin{array}{r} 7 \\ +\ 8 \\ \hline 15 \end{array} \qquad \begin{array}{r} 7 \\ +\ 5 \\ \hline 12 \end{array}$$

$$\begin{array}{r} 12 \\ -\ 6 \\ \hline 6 \end{array} \qquad \begin{array}{r} 15 \\ -\ 6 \\ \hline 8 \end{array}$$

$$\begin{array}{r} 9 \\ +\ 6 \\ \hline 14 \end{array} \qquad \begin{array}{r} 9 \\ +\ 4 \\ \hline 13 \end{array}$$

$$\begin{array}{r} 18 \\ -\ 9 \\ \hline 9 \end{array} \qquad \begin{array}{r} 17 \\ -\ 8 \\ \hline 8 \end{array}$$

$$\begin{array}{r} 5 \\ +\ 8 \\ \hline 13 \end{array} \qquad \begin{array}{r} 9 \\ +\ 7 \\ \hline 14 \end{array}$$

$$\begin{array}{r} 14 \\ -\ 7 \\ \hline 6 \end{array} \qquad \begin{array}{r} 15 \\ -\ 7 \\ \hline 8 \end{array}$$

$$\begin{array}{r} 4 \\ +\ 8 \\ \hline 12 \end{array} \qquad \begin{array}{r} 8 \\ +\ 6 \\ \hline 13 \end{array}$$

$$\begin{array}{r} 17 \\ -\ 9 \\ \hline 7 \end{array} \qquad \begin{array}{r} 15 \\ -\ 6 \\ \hline 9 \end{array}$$

$$\begin{array}{r} 7 \\ 6 \\ +\ 3 \\ \hline 16 \end{array}$$

You can add numbers in any order.
Look for tens to make the adding easier.

7 + 3 = 10

Then 10 + 6 = 16.

It's easy!

Find the **sum**.

1. $\begin{array}{r} 4 \\ 3 \\ +\ 6 \\ \hline \end{array}$

2. $\begin{array}{r} 2 \\ 7 \\ +\ 8 \\ \hline \end{array}$

3. $\begin{array}{r} 5 \\ 6 \\ +\ 5 \\ \hline \end{array}$

4. $\begin{array}{r} 9 \\ 4 \\ +\ 1 \\ \hline \end{array}$

5. $\begin{array}{r} 3 \\ 8 \\ +\ 0 \\ \hline \end{array}$

6. $\begin{array}{r} 6 \\ 8 \\ +\ 4 \\ \hline \end{array}$

7. $\begin{array}{r} 2 \\ 3 \\ +\ 9 \\ \hline \end{array}$

8. $\begin{array}{r} 7 \\ 1 \\ +\ 7 \\ \hline \end{array}$

9. $\begin{array}{r} 6 \\ 2 \\ 5 \\ +\ 4 \\ \hline \end{array}$

10. $\begin{array}{r} 7 \\ 2 \\ 0 \\ +\ 3 \\ \hline \end{array}$

11. $\begin{array}{r} 3 \\ 4 \\ 5 \\ +\ 6 \\ \hline \end{array}$

12. $\begin{array}{r} 4 \\ 4 \\ 4 \\ +\ 4 \\ \hline \end{array}$

13. 6 + 7 + 4 = ____

14. 7 + 2 + 3 = ____

15. 8 + 5 + 2 = ____

16. 9 + 0 + 9 = ____

17. 6 + 7 + 2 + 3 = ____

18. 4 + 5 + 6 + 5 = ____

Find each **sum** or **difference**.

Solve the problems to fill in the puzzle.

Across

1. $3 + 8 =$ 11
3. $6 + 0 =$ ______
4. $5 + 6 =$ ______
5. $7 + 7 =$ ______
7. $16 - 7 =$ ______
9. $14 - 8 =$ ______
10. $9 + 9 =$ ______
11. $2 + 3 + 4 + 5 =$ ______
12. $8 + 8 =$ ______
13. $5 + 5 + 2 + 5 =$ ______
14. $10 - 0 =$ ______
15. $11 - 4 =$ ______

Down

2. $7 + 9 =$ ______
4. $5 + 9 =$ ______
5. $6 + 4 + 3 =$ ______
6. $4 + 3 + 9 =$ ______
8. $3 + 8 + 7 =$ ______
10. $8 + 8 =$ ______
11. $9 + 8 =$ ______
12. $4 + 6 =$ ______

number

6 tens 5 ones = 65

Circle the groups of ten. Write the number of **tens** and **ones**. Then write the number.

1. 

number

_____ tens _____ ones = _____

2.

number

_____ tens _____ ones = _____

3.

number

_____ tens _____ ones = _____

4. 

number

_____ tens _____ ones = _____

5. 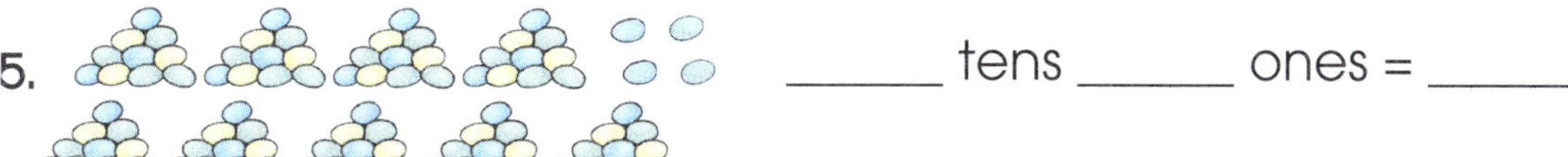

number

_____ tens _____ ones = _____

Circle the objects in groups of ten. Write the number of **tens** and **ones**. Then write how many there are in all.

1.

______ tens ______ ones

How many? ______

2.

______ tens ______ ones

How many? ______

3.

______ tens ______ ones

How many? ______

4.

______ tens ______ ones

How many? ______

5.

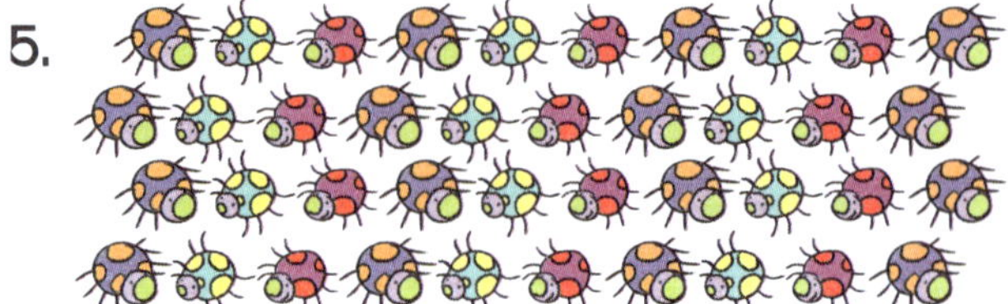

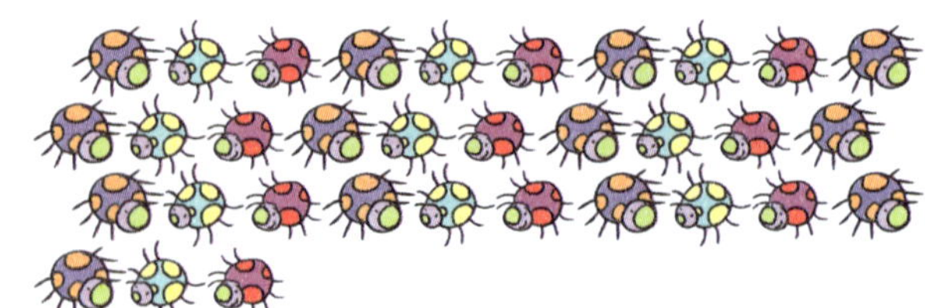

______ tens ______ ones

How many? ______

1	one	11	eleven
2	two	12	twelve
3	three	13	thirteen
4	four	14	fourteen
5	five	15	fifteen
6	six	16	sixteen
7	seven	17	seventeen
8	eight	18	eighteen
9	nine	19	nineteen
10	ten		

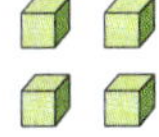

1 tens 4 ones

Number: 14

Number name: fourteen

Write the number.

1. seven ________
2. ten ________
3. eight ________
4. fifteen ________
5. eleven ________
6. eighteen ________

Write the number or number name.

7. 13 ones ________
8. 1 ten 4 ones ________
9. 1 ten 9 ones ________
10. 12 ________
11. 16 ________
12. 17 ________

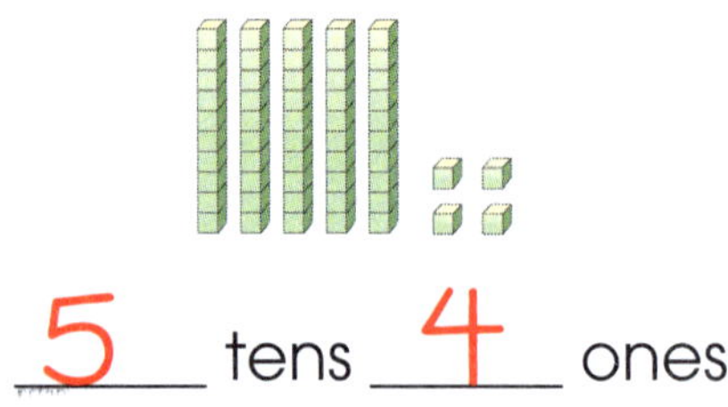

5 tens 4 ones

Number: 54

Number name:

fifty-four

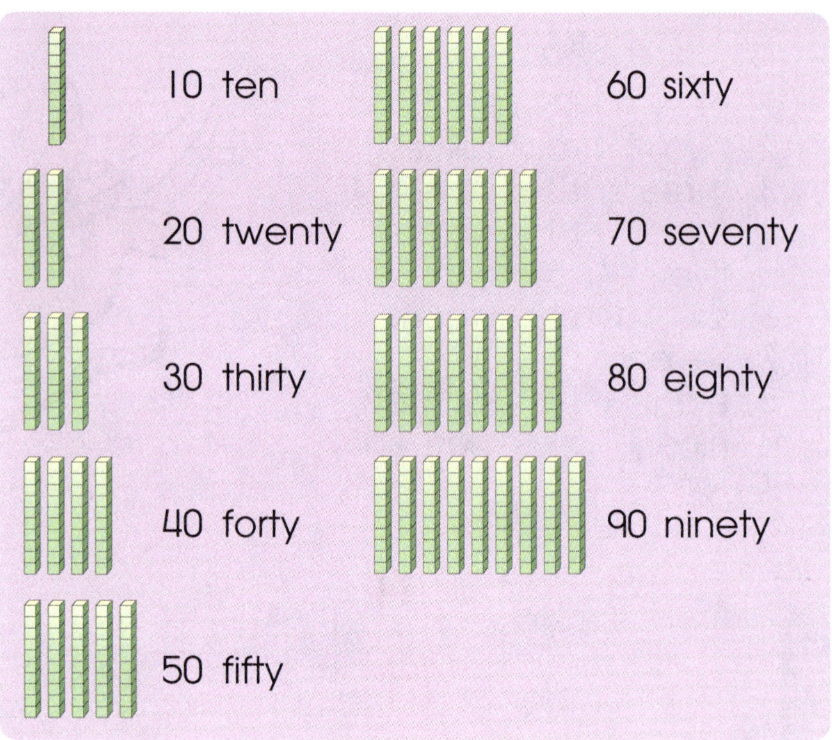

Write how many tens and ones there are.
Then write the number and number name.

1.

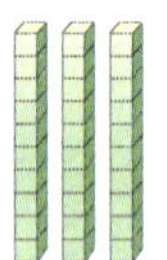

_____ tens _____ ones = _____

____

2.

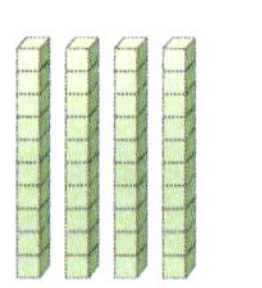

_____ tens _____ ones = _____

____

3.

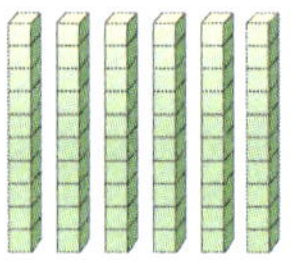

_____ tens _____ ones = _____

____

4.

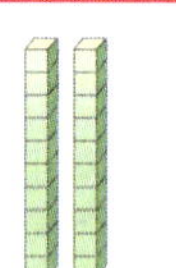

_____ tens _____ ones = _____

____

5.

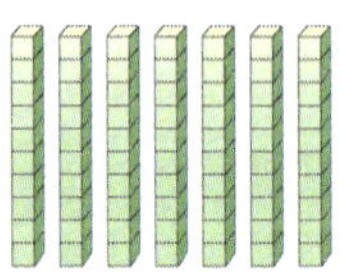

_____ tens _____ ones = _____

____

6.

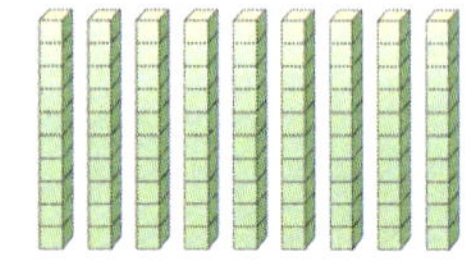

_____ tens _____ ones = _____

____

Complete the chart. Count to 100.

1	11	21			51			81	
2			32				72		
3	13			43				83	
			34			64			94
5					55				
	16			46			76		
		27				67			
8			38				78		98
	19				59			89	
10		30		50		70			100

Count by tens.
Circle the tens.

tens 

Count by fives
Circle the fives.

fives 

Connect the dots.

Start at the ▲ and count by 2s to 50.

Start at the ● and count by 5s to 100.

Start at the ■ and count by 10s to 100.

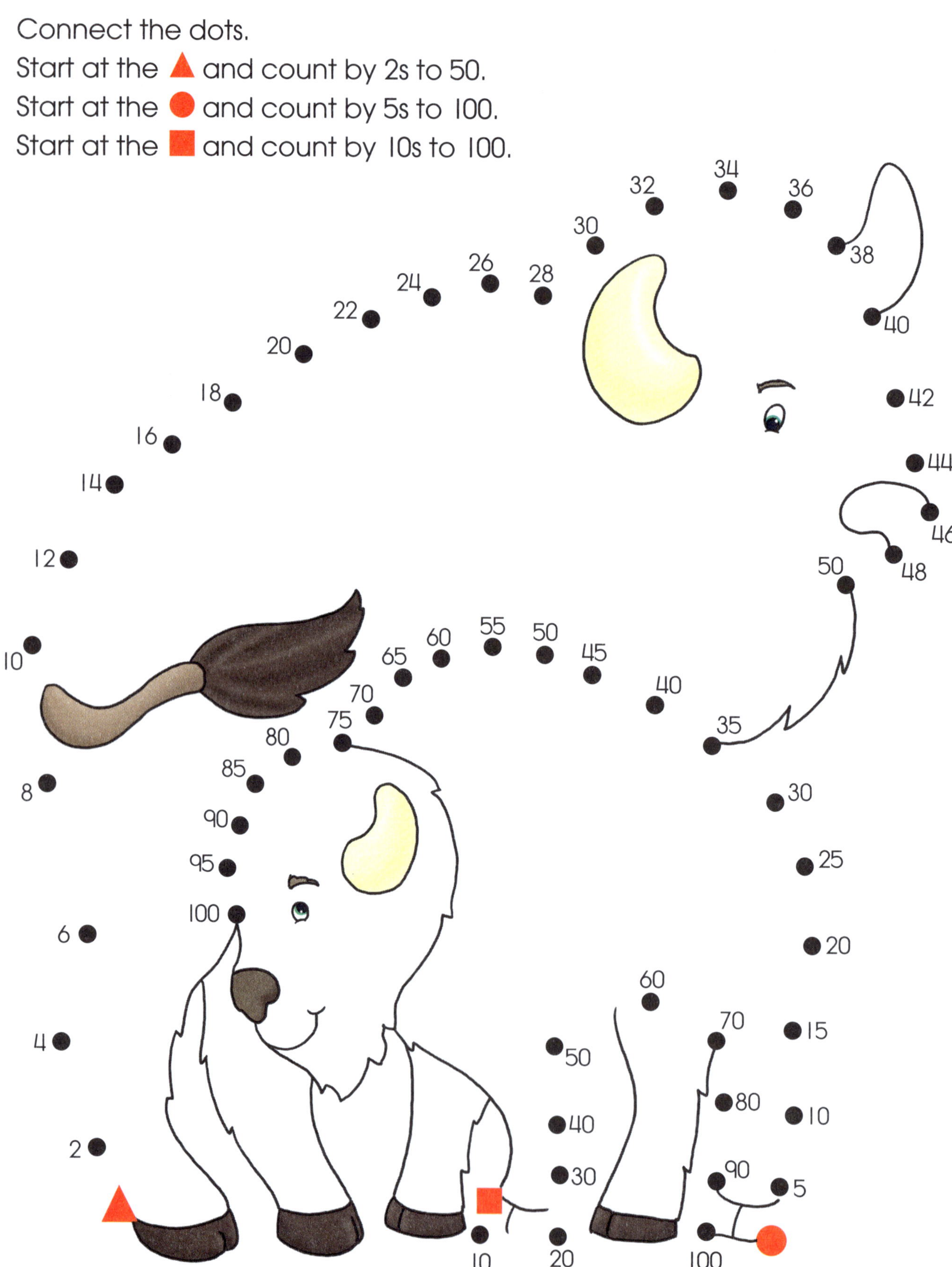

Write the missing numbers.

1. 21, 22, ____, 24, ____, 26, ____, 28, ____, 30

2. 61, ____, 63, ____, ____, 66, ____, ____, 69, ____

3. ____, 82, ____, 84, ____, 86, ____, 88, ____, 90

4. 35, 36, ____, 38, ____, 40, ____, ____, 43, ____

5. 56, ____, 58, 59, ____, 61, ____, ____, 64, ____

6. 87, ____, 89, ____, ____, 92, ____, ____, 95, ____

7. 44, 43, ____, 41, ____, 39, ____, ____, 36, ____

8. ____, 73, ____, 71, ____, ____, 68, ____, ____, 65

Which number comes **before**?

1. ____ 34 35	2. ____ 40 41	3. ____ 94 95
4. ____ 71 72	5. ____ 28 29	6. ____ 52 53

Which number belongs **between**?

7. 27 ____ 29	8. 61 ____ 63	9. 76 ____ 78
10. 40 ____ 42	11. 47 ____ 49	12. 69 ____ 71

Which number comes **after**?

13. 45 46 ____	14. 81 82 ____	15. 28 29 ____
16. 66 67 ____	17. 98 99 ____	18. 37 38 ____

Look at the tens digits in both numbers first and compare.
If the tens digits are the same, look at the ones digits.

Circle the number that is **greater**.

1. 65 68
2. 74 84
3. 39 93
4. 70 17
5. 25 62
6. 88 78
7. 40 39
8. 90 9
9. 55 62

Circle the number that is **less**.

10. 77 79
11. 18 80
12. 20 32
13. 65 71
14. 43 48
15. 70 63
16. 91 99
17. 77 69
18. 82 28

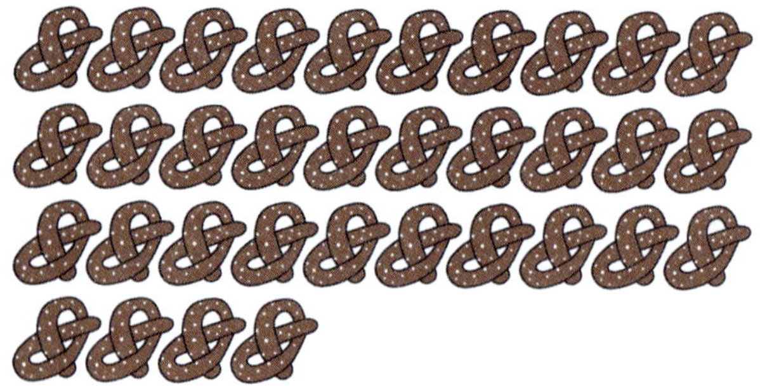

34   43

34 is **less** than 43.

$34 < 43$

The symbol points to the number that is **less**.

43 is **greater** than 34.

$43 > 34$

Write the numbers for each group. Circle $<$ or $>$ between the numbers.

1.

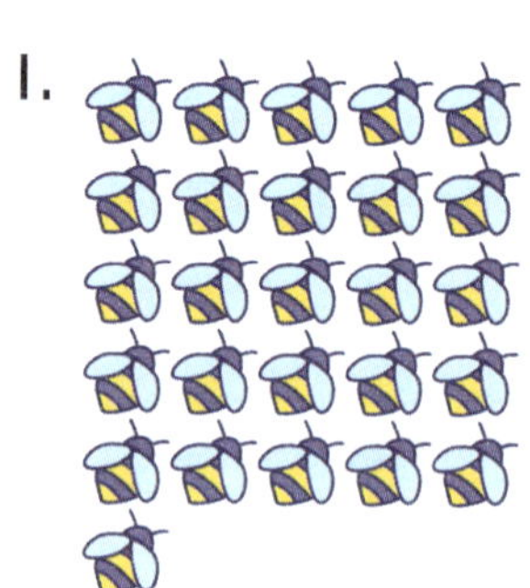

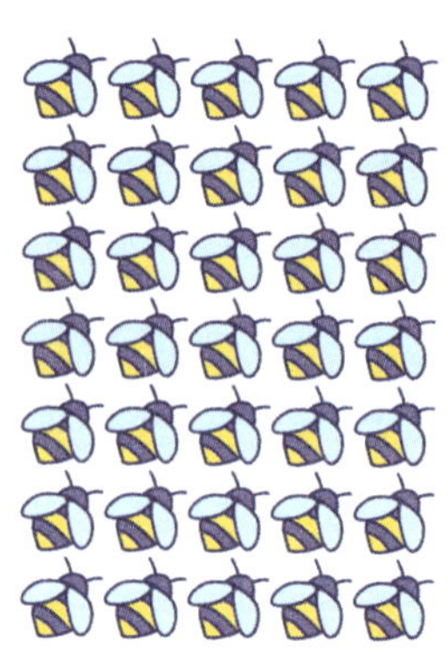

____ $<$ / $>$ ____

2.

____ $<$ / $>$ ____

Compare the numbers. Write $<$ or $>$ in the ◯.

3. 45 ◯ 48   4. 31 ◯ 13   5. 80 ◯ 18

6. 60 ◯ 6   7. 72 ◯ 27   8. 66 ◯ 76

9. 46 ◯ 64   10. 39 ◯ 41   11. 49 ◯ 42

Write the numbers in order from **least** to **greatest**.

1. 12 10 15

____ ____ ____

2. 45 49 36

____ ____ ____

3. 81 19 25

____ ____ ____

4. 36 24 18

____ ____ ____

5. 29 57 41

____ ____ ____

6. 30 72 55

____ ____ ____

7. 66 26 56

____ ____ ____

8. 87 78 72

____ ____ ____

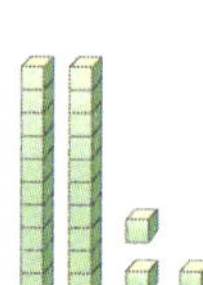

2 tens 3 ones = 23

Write the number of tens and ones. Then write the number.

1. 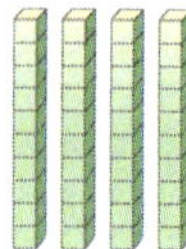

______ tens ______ ones = ______

2. 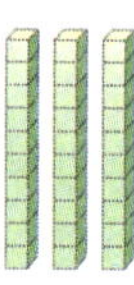

______ tens ______ ones = ______

3. 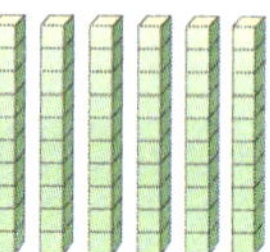

______ tens ______ ones = ______

4. 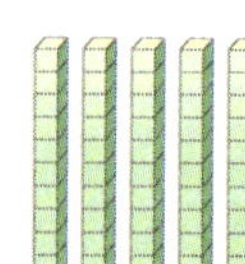

______ tens ______ ones = ______

5. 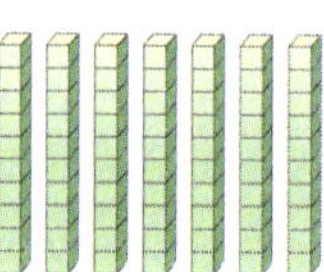

______ tens ______ ones = ______

6. 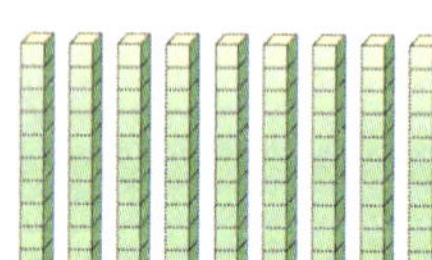

______ tens ______ ones = ______

COMPARE NUMBERS

25 is **less** than 32.

25  32

25 is **greater** than 23.

25  23

25 is **equal** than 25.

25  25

Write the numbers. Compare the numbers. Then write **<**, **>**, or **=** in the ◯.

1.

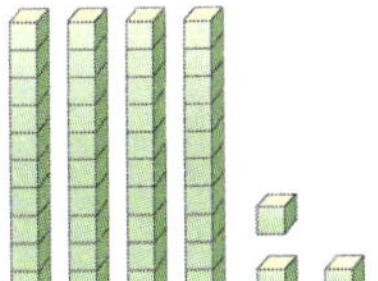

____ ◯ ____

2.

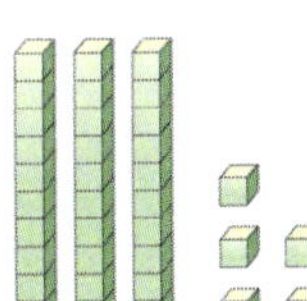

____ ◯ ____

3.

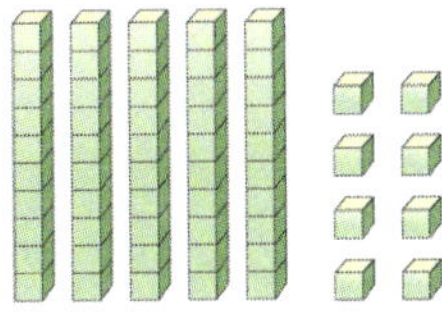

____ ◯ ____

4.

____ ◯ ____

$26 < 36$
more tens

$45 >$ 4 tens
$45 > 40$
more ones

twelve < 21
$12 < 21$
more tens

Remember: The symbol points to the number that is **less.**

Compare the numbers. Then write **<**, **>**, or **=** in the ◯.

1. 28 ◯ 25
2. 28 ◯ 82
3. 28 ◯ 30
4. 76 ◯ 76
5. 53 ◯ 35
6. 61 ◯ 6
7. 80 ◯ 8
8. 18 ◯ 80
9. 39 ◯ 35
10. 3 tens ◯ 13
11. forty-six ◯ 61
12. 64 ◯ sixty
13. eighty-three ◯ eighteen
14. 5 tens 6 ones ◯ 56
15. ninety-four ◯ 4 tens 9 ones
16. 19 ◯ nineteen
17. **Challenge:**

    I am less than 50. I am greater than 39. My tens digit is 2 more than my ones digit. What number am I? ____________

An **even number** of things can be matched in pairs.

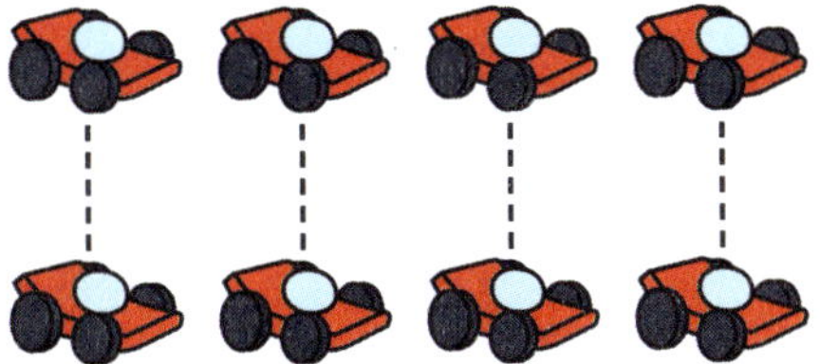

8 is an **even** number.

An **odd number** of things cannot be matched in pairs.

7 is an **odd** number.

Match up the objects in pairs if you can.
Count the objects, and write the number.
Tell whether the number is **even** or **odd**.

1.

______ is an ________________ number.

2.

______ is an ________________ number.

3.

______ is an ________________ number.

1. Count by 2s and circle the numbers.

2. You circled **even** numbers.
Look at the ones digit of the circled numbers.
The ones digit of an **even** number is:

_____, _____, _____, _____, or _____.

3. The numbers in the chart that are not circled are **odd** numbers. The ones digit of an **odd** number is:

_____, _____, _____, _____, or _____.

1	2	3	4	5
6	7	8	9	10
11	12	13	14	15
16	17	18	19	20
21	22	23	24	25
26	27	28	29	30
31	32	33	34	35
36	37	38	39	40

Write **even** or **odd**.

4. 27 __________ 5. 38 __________ 6. 50 __________

7. 62 __________ 8. 45 __________ 9. 79 __________

10. Circle the **even** numbers. 23 6 47 18 64 80 35 58 96

Write **even** or **odd**. Show an example for each problem.

11. The sum of two **even** numbers is an __________ number.

Example: ____________________

12. The sum of two **odd** numbers is an __________ number.

Example: ____________________

13. The sum of an **even** and an **odd** number is an __________ number.

Example: ____________________

An **ordinal number** tells the position of an object.

1. Write the **ordinal number** under each car.

2. Write the **ordinal number word** under each car.

Write the **ordinal number**, child's name, or number in the blank.

3. If Andy is first, then Chris is ______. If Ben is second, then Emma is ______.

4. If David is fourth, how many people are ahead of him? ______

5. If Andy is first, then __________ is the 7th person in line.

6. **Challenge:** If Ken is first, then who is 6th in line? __________

Use the **ordinal number** clues to solve each riddle.

1. It's a big smile.

READING

- 7th letter
- 1st letter
- 5th letter
- 6th letter

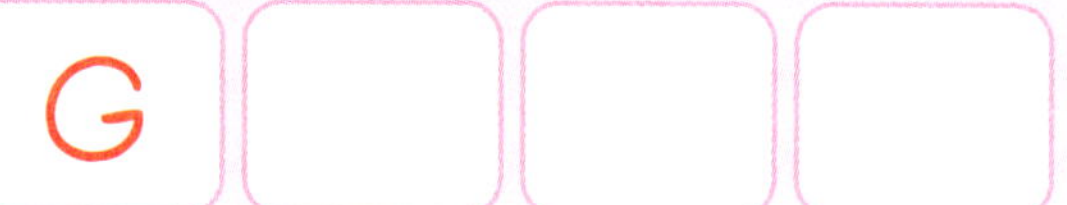

2. You use clocks to tell it.

ARITHMETIC

- 4th letter
- 3rd letter
- 6th letter
- 7th letter

3. You walk on it.

ORDINAL

- 7th letter
- 6th letter
- 5th letter
- 3rd letter

4. They are purr-fect animals.

SUBTRACT

- 7th letter
- 6th letter
- 4th letter
- 1st letter

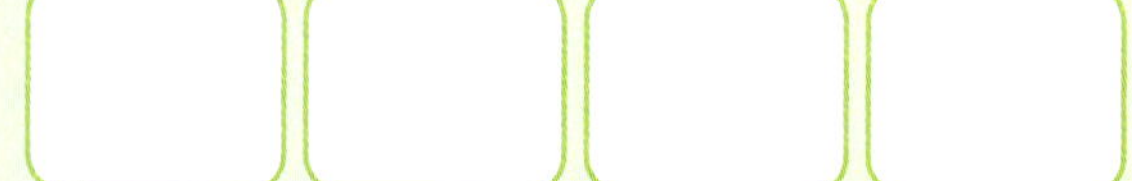

Solve the problems to fill in the puzzle.

	1. 1	2. 9		3.	4.	
5.		6.	7.		8.	9.
10.	11.		12.	13.		
	14.	15.		16.	17.	
18.		19.	20.		21.	22.
23.	24.		25.	26.		

Across

1. 18 + 1 = 19
3. 44 + 2
6. 38 + 0
8. 53 + 4
10. 31 + 8
12. 77 + 2
14. 45 + 4
16. 25 + 3
19. 20 + 9
21. 33 + 3
23. 85 + 3
25. 47 + 2

Down

2. 93 + 0
4. 63 + 2
5. 41 + 2
7. 84 + 3
9. 75 + 4
11. 92 + 2
13. 90 + 2
15. 91 + 1
17. 82 + 1
18. 55 + 3
20. 90 + 4
24. 86 + 3
26. 95 + 3

Add the **ones** first.
Then add the **tens**.

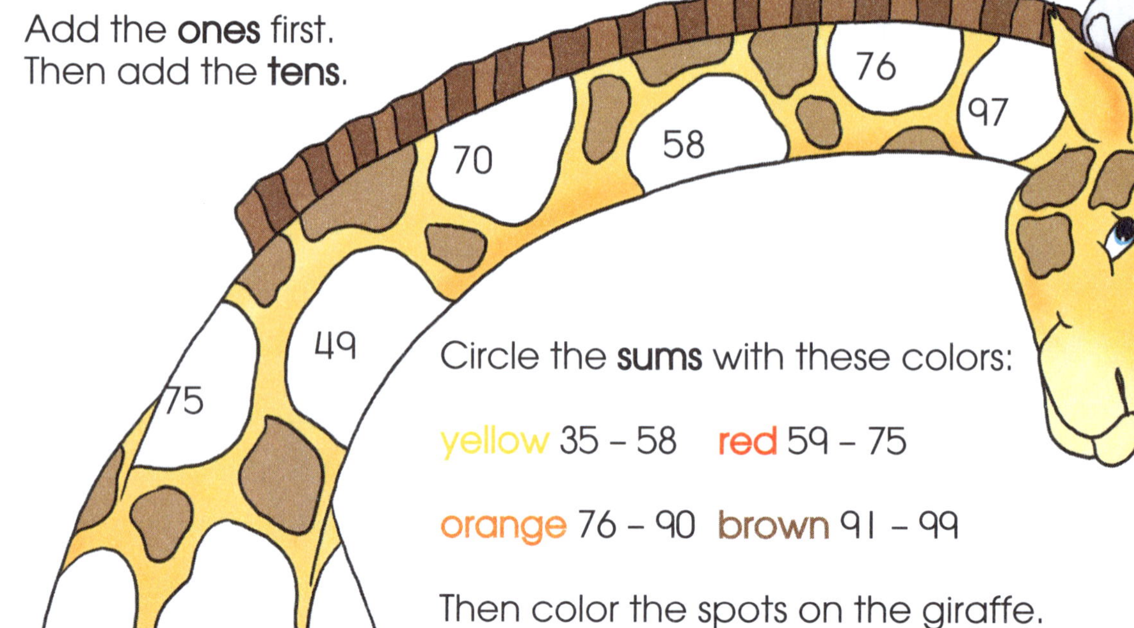

Circle the **sums** with these colors:

yellow 35 – 58 red 59 – 75

orange 76 – 90 brown 91 – 99

Then color the spots on the giraffe.

1. 14 + 23	2. 53 + 22	3. 38 + 11	4. 50 + 20
5. 45 + 13	6. 62 + 14	7. 77 + 21	8. 45 + 44
9. 20 + 20	10. 35 + 52	11. 88 + 10	12. 55 + 14
13. 56 + 32	14. 14 + 41	15. 12 + 47	16. 23 + 74

Clue:
There should be 5 yellow spots, 4 **red** spots, 4 orange spots, and 3 brown spots.

REGROUP FOR MORE TENS

2 tens 12 ones → 3 tens 2 ones

1 ten 2 ones

Trade 10 ones for 1 ten.

Regroup to have more tens.

1.  

_____ tens _____ ones

_____ tens _____ ten _____ ones → _____ tens _____ ones = _____

2. 5 tens 15 ones

_____ tens _____ ones = _____

3. 7 tens 11 ones

_____ tens _____ ones = _____

4. 3 tens 19 ones

_____ tens _____ ones = _____

5. 26 ones

_____ tens _____ ones = _____

6. 7 tens 10 ones

_____ tens _____ ones = _____

7. 3 tens 29 ones

_____ tens _____ ones = _____

Add the ones.	Regroup.	Add the tens.
36 + 26 = 12	1 (carried) 36 + 26 = 2	1 (carried) 36 + 26 = 62

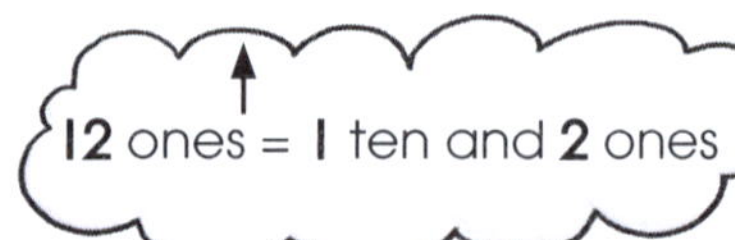

Move the 1 ten to the tens place on top.

Find the **sum**. Regroup if needed.

1. 29 + 23
2. 17 + 18
3. 58 + 24
4. 32 + 28
5. 17 + 43
6. 57 + 29
7. 44 + 17
8. 54 + 39
9. 24 + 26
10. 15 + 56
11. 78 + 13
12. 77 + 15

ADDITION PUZZLE

Solve the problems to fill in the puzzle.

Across

1. $47 + 17$
3. $39 + 39$
5. $48 + 49$
6. $66 + 18$
7. $45 + 14$
9. $56 + 17$
11. $23 + 18$
12. $19 + 19$

Down

1. $41 + 28$
2. $29 + 18$
3. $59 + 19$
4. $39 + 45$
7. $21 + 33$
8. $60 + 31$
9. $28 + 45$
10. $19 + 19$

Subtract the **ones**.

```
tens ones
   4 9
 -   5
 -----
     4
```

Subtract the **tens**.

```
tens ones
   4 9
 -   5
 -----
   4 4
```

Find the **difference**.

```
1.  37     2.  54     3.  62     4.  55
   - 5        - 3        - 1        - 5
   ---        ---        ---        ---

5.  46     6.  28     7.  97     8.  79
   - 3        - 2        - 4        - 6
   ---        ---        ---        ---

9.  88     10. 29     11. 69     12. 58
   - 4        - 7        - 2        - 5
   ---        ---        ---        ---
```

Subtract the **ones**.

$$\begin{array}{r} 75 \\ -\ 34 \\ \hline 1 \end{array}$$

Subtract the **tens**.

$$\begin{array}{r} 75 \\ -\ 34 \\ \hline 41 \end{array}$$

Check:

$$\begin{array}{r} 41 \\ +\ 34 \\ \hline 75 \end{array}$$

Find the **difference**. Check your answer.

1. $\begin{array}{r} 54 \\ -\ 21 \\ \hline 33 \end{array}$ Check: $\begin{array}{r} 33 \\ +\ 21 \\ \hline 54 \end{array}$

2. $\begin{array}{r} 74 \\ -\ 52 \\ \hline \end{array}$ Check: $\begin{array}{r} \\ +\ \\ \hline \end{array}$

3. $\begin{array}{r} 86 \\ -\ 36 \\ \hline \end{array}$ Check: $\begin{array}{r} \\ +\ \\ \hline \end{array}$

4. $\begin{array}{r} 39 \\ -\ 33 \\ \hline \end{array}$ Check: $\begin{array}{r} \\ +\ \\ \hline \end{array}$

5. $\begin{array}{r} 93 \\ -\ 42 \\ \hline \end{array}$ Check: $\begin{array}{r} \\ +\ \\ \hline \end{array}$

6. $\begin{array}{r} 81 \\ -\ 60 \\ \hline \end{array}$ Check: $\begin{array}{r} \\ +\ \\ \hline \end{array}$

Subtract to finish the number wheels.
Use mental math.

36 = 3 tens 6 ones → 2 tens and 1 ten 6 ones

2 tens 16 ones

Regroup to have more **ones**.
Trade 1 **ten** for 10 **ones**.

1.

_____ = _____ tens _____ ones → 4 tens _____ ones

2. 46 = 4 tens 6 ones
3 tens _____ ones

3. 81 = _____ tens 1 one
_____ tens 11 ones

4. 39 = 3 tens _____ ones
_____ tens _____ ones

5. 92 = _____ tens _____ ones
8 tens _____ ones

6. 13 = _____ ten _____ ones
_____ tens 13 ones

7. 60 = _____ tens
_____ tens _____ ones

Subtract the **ones**.	**Regroup**.	Subtract the **ones**.	Subtract the **tens**.
52 − 28	4 12 ~~5~~~~2~~ − 28	4 12 ~~5~~~~2~~ − 28 4	4 12 ~~5~~~~2~~ − 28 24
You cannot take 8 away from 2. So, regroup the 5 tens to have more ones.	52 = 5 tens 2 ones = 4 tens 12 ones	12 - 8 = 4	4 - 2 = 2

Find the **difference**. Regroup if needed.

1. 62 − 38
2. 80 − 24
3. 73 − 27
4. 56 − 45
5. 50 − 25
6. 93 − 65
7. 78 − 38
8. 88 − 49
9. 46 − 17
10. 85 − 21
11. 77 − 49
12. 84 − 66

Check your answers by adding.

Solve the problems to fill in the puzzle.

1.	2.		
3.			
		4.	5.
		6.	
7.	8.		
9.			
		10.	11.
		12.	

Across

1. $52 - 28$
3. $74 - 19$
4. $80 - 33$
6. $62 - 46$
7. $70 - 35$
9. $41 - 18$
10. $91 - 28$
12. $63 - 24$

Down

1. $50 - 25$
2. $73 - 28$
4. $70 - 29$
5. $92 - 16$
7. $71 - 39$
8. $92 - 39$
10. $81 - 18$
11. $50 - 11$

Watch out! Look for the + and – signs.

Find the **sum** or **difference**.

1. $56 - 25$	2. $29 + 18$	3. $43 + 31$	4. $40 - 12$
5. $45 - 26$	6. $65 + 20$	7. $78 - 28$	8. $73 + 17$
9. $87 - 37$	10. $53 - 35$	11. $66 + 15$	12. $54 - 44$
13. $39 + 48$	14. $80 - 50$	15. $35 + 27$	16. $49 - 47$
17. $46 + 33$	18. $84 - 15$	19. $39 + 29$	20. $53 + 16$

Solve this riddle:
Which land animal weighs the most?
Add and subtract to find the answer.

F	N	N	C
54 + 18	84 − 7	86 − 9	75 + 6

P	E	A	H
35 + 29	48 + 7	28 − 9	82 − 4

T	E	H	R
39 + 49	39 + 16	85 − 7	47 + 6

A	A	L	I
55 − 36	34 − 15	59 + 7	29 + 68

The ___ ___ ___ ___ ___ ___ ___
19 72 53 97 81 19 77

___ ___ ___ ___ ___ ___ ___ ___
55 66 55 64 78 19 77 88

A **chart** is a way to show a collection of data.

The data in this chart was recorded using **tally marks,** so this is called a tally chart.

/ = 1 𝍸 = 5

𝍸 /// = 8

Favorite Foods for Lunch

Food	Tally
Hamburger	𝍸 𝍸 𝍸 𝍸 //
Pizza	𝍸 𝍸 𝍸 ///
Taco	𝍸 𝍸 𝍸 𝍸

Use the **tally chart** to answer the questions.

1. Copy the tally marks for pizza. ____________________

   How many children like pizza for lunch? _______

2. How many children like tacos? _______

3. How many children like hamburgers? ____________________

4. Which food is the favorite? ____________________

5. How many children like tacos and pizza? ____________________

6. More children like hamburgers than pizza.

   How many more children like hamburgers? ____________________

7. How many children were in this survey? ____________________

Make a **tally chart** to record the colors of the birds in the picture. Then write the total for each.

Bird Color		
Color	Tally	Total
Blue		
Brown		
Red		

Use the **tally chart** to answer the questions.

1. There are the most of which color bird? _______
2. How many brown and red birds are there? _______
3. There are more blue birds than red birds. How many more blue birds are there? _______________
4. How many birds are there in all? _______________

Make a **tally chart** to record the number of flowers in the picture. Then write the total for each.

Number of Flowers		
Type of Flower	Tally	Total
Daisy		
Rose		
Tulip		
Sunflower		

Use the **tally chart** to answer the questions.

1. There are the fewest number of which type of flower? ___________
2. How many daisies and sunflowers are there? ___________
3. There are more roses than tulips. How many more roses are there? ___________
4. How many flowers are there in all? ___________

Baseball Card Collections		
Name	Tally	Total
	~~||||~~ ~~||||~~ ~~||||~~ ~~||||~~ ||	
	~~||||~~ ~~||||~~ ~~||||~~	
		25
Jason		19

Use these clues to complete the **tally chart**:

- John has 22 baseball cards.
- Nick collected more baseball cards than John.
- Alan collected fewer baseball cards than Jason.

Use the **tally chart** to fill in the blanks in the story.

Alan has _______ baseball cards, and Nick has _______ baseball cards. ___________________ has the most baseball cards. Nick and Alan have _______ baseball cards in all. Nick has _______ more baseball cards than Jason. Altogether, the boys have _______ baseball cards.

A **pictograph** is a way to show a collection of data.

The data in a pictograph can be recorded using pictures or symbols.

In this pictograph, each 😊 stands for 1 child's vote.

Favorite Type of TV Program	
Program Type	**Number of Votes**
Cartoons	😊😊😊😊😊😊😊😊😊😊😊😊
Animal Shows	😊😊😊😊😊😊
Movies	😊😊😊😊😊😊😊😊

Each 😊 = 1 child's vote

Use the **pictograph** to answer the questions.

1. How many children like animal shows? _______
2. How many children like cartoons? _______
3. How many children like movies? _______
4. Which is the favorite type of TV program? ____________
5. More children like cartoons than animal shows. How many more children like cartoons? ____________
6. How many children like cartoons and movies? ____________
7. How many children were asked about their favorite TV programs? ____________

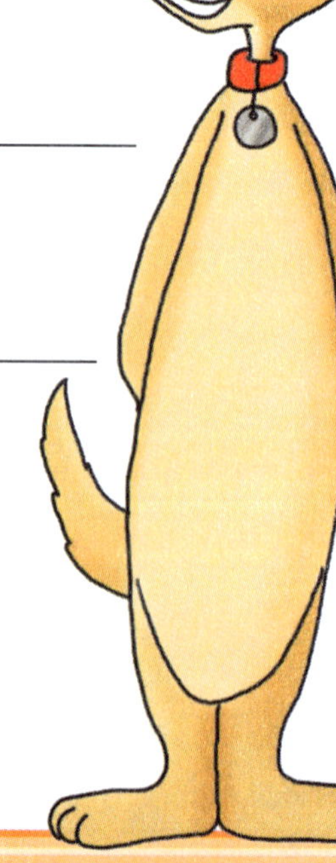

Sticker Collections	
Name	Number of Stickers
Daniel	☆☆☆☆☆☆☆☆☆☆☆☆
Amy	☆☆☆☆☆☆☆☆☆☆☆☆☆☆
Jim	☆☆☆☆☆☆☆☆☆☆☆
Megan	☆☆☆☆☆☆☆☆☆☆☆☆

Use the **pictograph** to answer the questions.

1. How many stickers does Jim have? _______
2. How many stickers does Daniel have? _______
3. How many stickers does Megan have? _______
4. How many stickers does Amy have? _______
5. Who has the fewest stickers? ____________
6. Which two children have the same number of stickers?

   ____________ and ____________
7. How many stickers do Amy and Megan have in all? ____________

As you've learned, a **pictograph** is a way to show a collection of data.

In some pictographs, a picture or symbol stands for more than 1 object. In this pictograph, each 🧦 stands for 2 socks.

Socks in the Lost & Found	
Day	Number of Socks
Monday	🧦🧦🧦🧦🧦
Tuesday	🧦🧦
Wednesday	🧦🧦🧦🧦🧦🧦
Thursday	🧦🧦🧦
Friday	🧦🧦🧦🧦

Each 🧦 = 2 socks

Use the **pictograph** to answer the questions.

1. If 1 🧦 stands for 2 socks, how many socks do 2 🧦 stand for? _______

   3 🧦? _______ 4 🧦? _______ 5 🧦? _______

2. How many socks were there in Lost & Found on Monday? _______
3. How many socks were lost on Friday? _______
4. How many socks were lost on Tuesday? _______
5. More socks were lost on Wednesday than Thursday. How many more socks were lost on Wednesday? ___________
6. How can you count the number of socks in the graph quickly?

   ____

Number of Library Books Read	
Name	Number of Books Read
Tom	📕📕📕
Rosa	📕📕📕📕📕
Justin	📕📕📕📕📕📕📕
Pam	📕📕📕📕

Each 📕 = 5 books

Use the **pictograph** to answer the questions.

1. What does each 📕 stand for? ______
2. How can you count the number of books in the graph quickly?

   ____

3. How many books did Pam read? ______
4. How many books did Rosa read? ______
5. Who read the most books? ________________
6. How many books did Tom and Justin read in all? __________
7. Justin read more books than Rosa.
   How many more books did Justin read? __________
8. How many books did the children read altogether? __________

Stamp Collections	
Name	Number of Stamps
Jenny	[stamp] [stamp] [stamp] [stamp] [stamp] [stamp] [stamp] [stamp]
Lisa	[stamp] [stamp] [stamp] [stamp] [stamp] [stamp] [stamp] [stamp] [stamp] [stamp]
Jose	[stamp] [stamp] [stamp] [stamp] [stamp] [stamp] [stamp] [stamp] [stamp]
Ray	[stamp] [stamp] [stamp] [stamp] [stamp] [stamp]

Use the **pictograph** to answer the questions.

1. What does each [stamp] stand for? ________________
2. How can you count the number of stamps in the graph quickly?

   ____
3. How many stamps does Jose have? _______
4. How many stamps does Jenny have? _______
5. Who has the most stamps? ________________
6. Who has fewer stamps than Jenny? ________________
7. Lisa has more stamps than Jenny.
   How many more stamps does Lisa have? ______________

A **bar graph** is a way to show a collection of data.

A bar graph uses bars to record data.

Read the number at the end of the bar to tell how many.

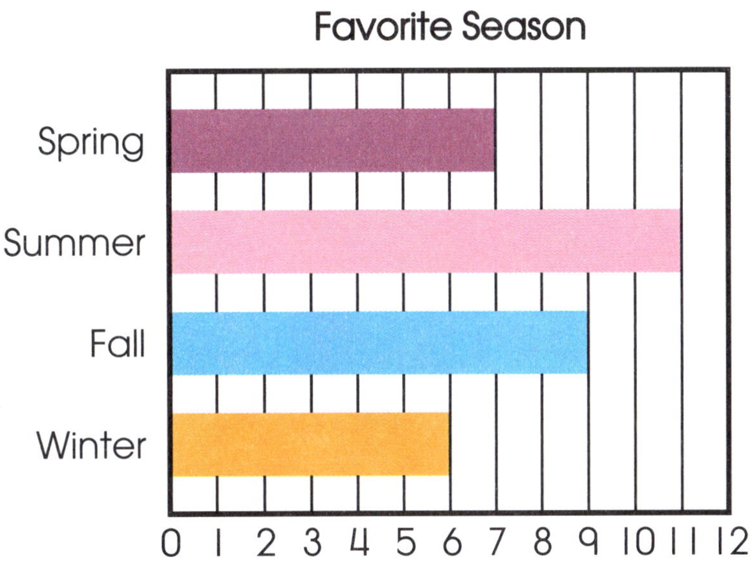

Use the **bar graph** to answer the questions.

1. How many children like winter best? _______
2. How many children like spring best? _______
3. How many children like fall best? _______
4. Which season is the favorite?
5. Which season is the least favorite? ________________
6. More children like summer than spring.
   How many more children like summer? _____________

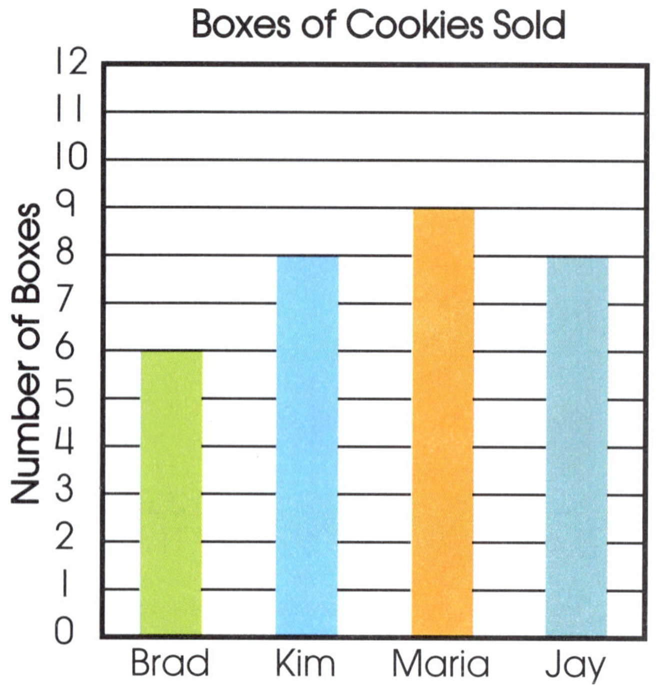

Read the number at the top of the bar to tell how many.

Use the **bar graph** to answer the questions.

1. How many boxes of cookies did Kim sell? _______

2. How many boxes of cookies did Maria sell? _______

3. How many boxes of cookies did Brad sell? _______

4. Who sold the most boxes? ______________

5. Who sold the fewest boxes? ______________

6. Which two children sold the same number of boxes?

   ______________ and ______________

7. How many boxes did the children sell in all? ______________

As you've learned, a **bar graph** is a way to show a collection of data.

To show larger amounts of things, the numbers on the side of a bar graph use greater numbers.

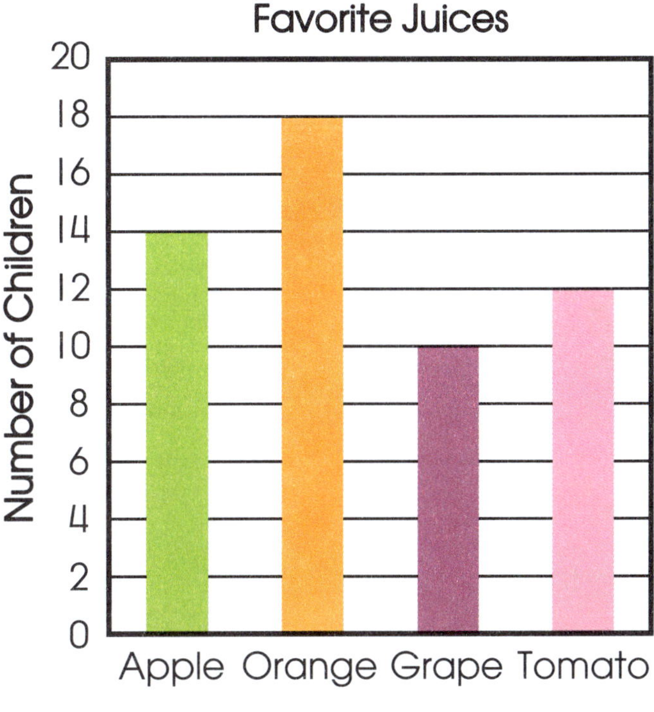

Use the **bar graph** to answer the questions.

1. How many children like tomato juice? _______

2. How many children like apple juice? _______

3. Which juice is the favorite? _____________
   How many children like it?

4. Which juice is the least favorite? _____________
   How many children like it? _______

5. More children like orange juice than tomato juice.
   How many more children like orange juice? _____________

6. How many children like apple juice and grape juice in all? _____________

7. Are there more than or less than 50 children in this survey? _____________

Use the **bar graph** to answer the questions.

1. How many children like cake for dessert? _______
2. How many children like fruit? _______
3. How many children like cookies? _______
4. What is the favorite dessert? ____________
   How many children like it? _______
5. More children like ice cream than cake.
   How many more children like ice cream? ____________
6. How many children like cake and ice cream in all? ____________

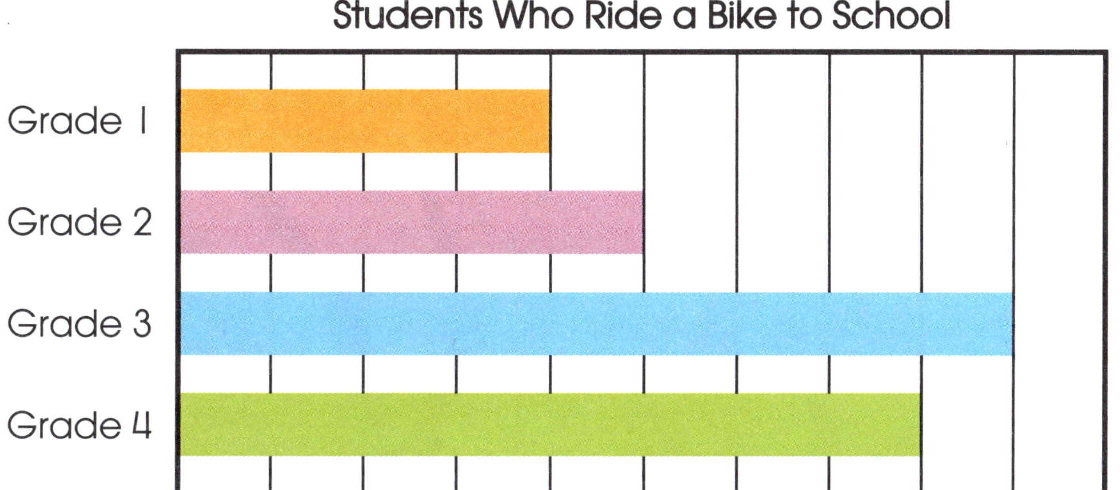

Use the **bar graph** to answer the questions.

1. How many children in grade 2 ride a bike to school? _______

2. How many children in grade 4 ride a bike to school? _______

3. Which grade has the most bike riders? _______
   How many bike riders are there? _______

4. How many children in grades
   1 and 2 ride a bike to school? _____________

5. How many more children in grade 3
   ride a bike to school than in grade 1? _____________

6. Are there more than or less than
   50 bike riders in grades 1 and 2? _____________

A **table** is a way to show a collection of data.

Favorite Color	
Color	Number of Votes
Red	17
Blue	20
Green	15
Purple	10

Use the **table** to answer the questions.

1. How many children like the color green? _______
2. How many children like the purple? _______
3. How many children like red? _______
4. Which color is the favorite? _____________
5. Which color is the least favorite? _____________
6. How many children like blue and green in all? _____________
7. More children like red than purple.
   How many more children like red? _____________

Favorite Season		
Season	Number of Votes in Grade 2	Number of Votes in Grade 3
Spring	28	34
Summer	40	38
Fall	32	29
Winter	17	22

Use the **table** to answer the questions.

1. How many children in grade 2 like summer best? _______

2. How many children in grade 3 like summer best? _______

3. How many children in grade 3 like winter best? _______

4. How many children in grade 2 like fall best? _______

5. Which season do children in grade 3 like best? _____________

6. Which season do children in grade 2 like least? _____________

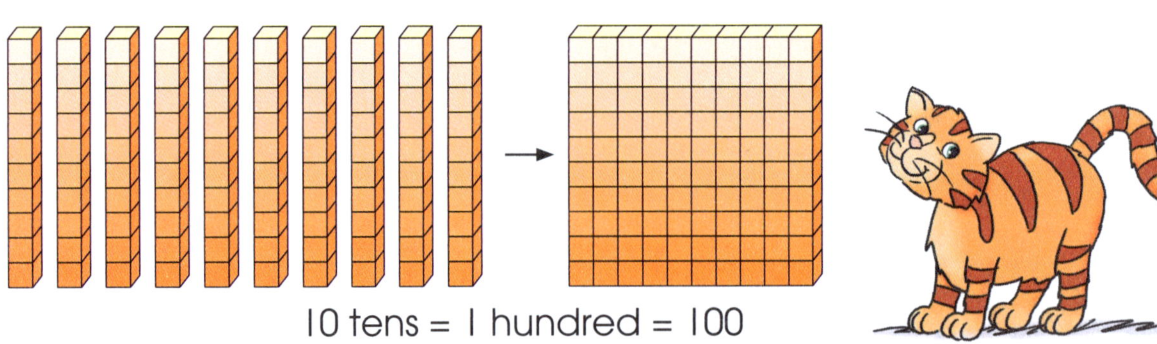

Write how many **hundreds** there are. Then write the number.

1. number

_____ hundreds = __________

2. number

_____ hundreds = __________

3. number

_____ hundreds = __________

4. number

_____ hundreds = __________

Write the number.

100 ____

200 ____

____

____

____

____

____

____

____

Connect the dots.
Count by 100s to 900.

200

300

500

100

600

700

400

800

900

Write the missing numbers.

100, 200, ______, 400, ______, 600, ______, 800, ______

100, ______, 300, ______, ______, 600, ______, ______, 900

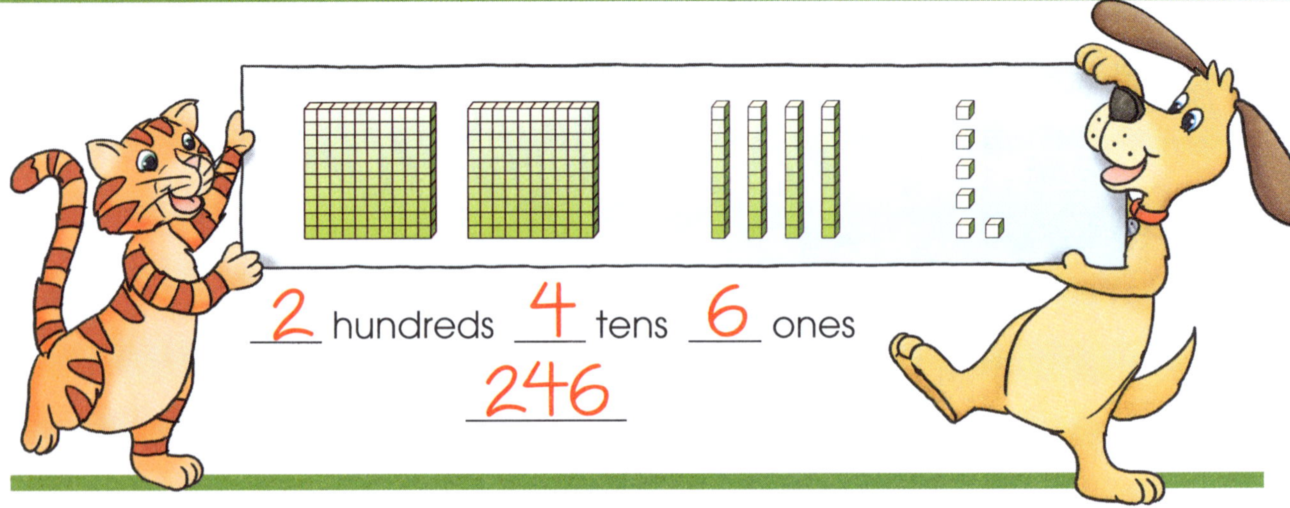

Write how many **hundreds**, **tens**, and **ones** there are.
Then write the number.

1.

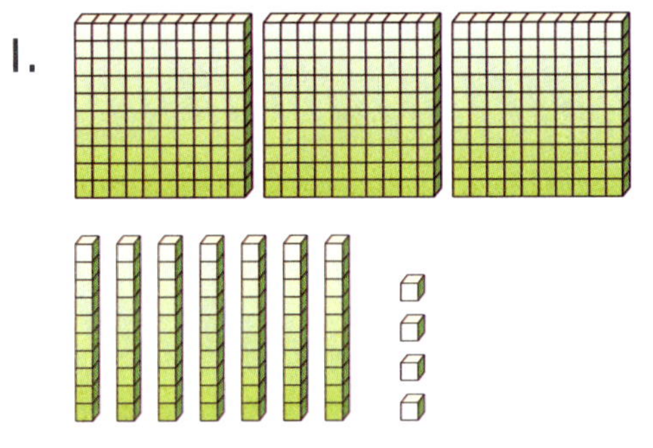

____ hundreds ____ tens ____ ones

____

2.

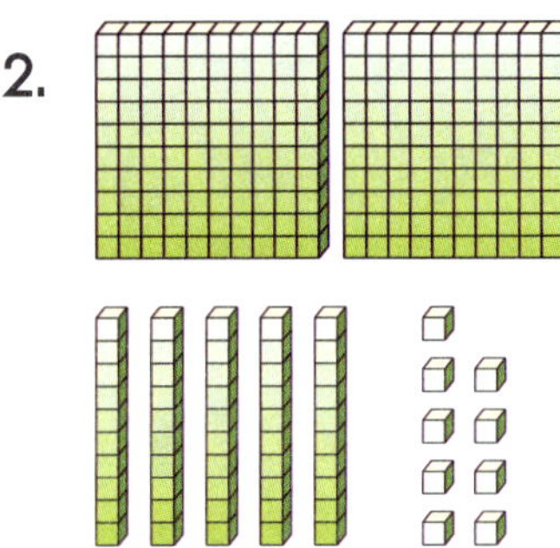

____ hundreds ____ tens ____ ones

____

3.

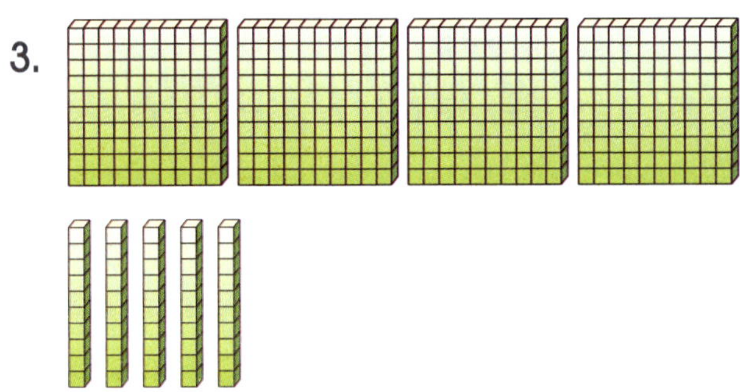

____ hundreds ____ tens ____ ones

____

4.

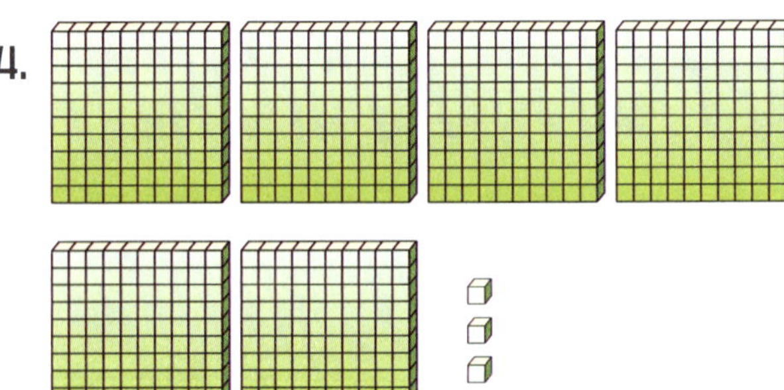

____ hundreds ____ tens ____ ones

____

FIND THE HUNDREDS

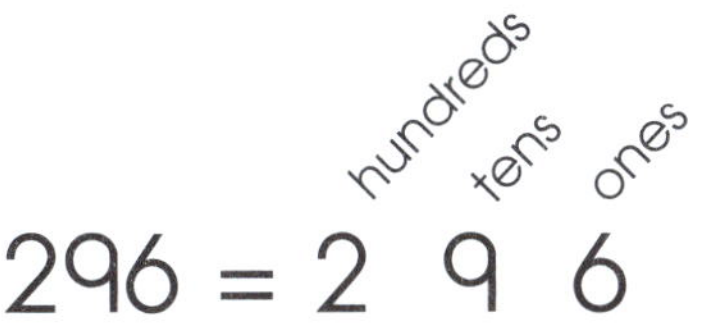

Read the question.
Circle the correct answer.

1.	Which number shows 4 hundreds?	324	422	243
2.	Which number shows 2 hundreds?	280	120	342
3.	Which number shows 8 hundreds?	618	580	800
4.	Which number shows 5 hundreds?	125	251	512
5.	Which number shows 1 hundred?	180	801	810
6.	Which number shows 9 hundreds?	490	966	489
7.	Which number shows 3 hundreds?	324	833	133
8.	Which number shows 6 hundreds?	465	678	396
9.	Which number shows 7 hundreds?	700	570	897
10.	Which number shows 5 hundreds?	205	355	555
11.	Which number shows 0 hundreds?	180	510	90
12.	Which number shows 9 hundreds?	192	944	899

13. **Challenge:** Make as many numbers as you can from these digits: 2, 5, and 8. Use one, two, or all three digits to make a number.

Making more than 10 numbers is great!

Read the problem.
Circle the correct digit in the number.

1. Circle the hundreds. 4 8 7
2. Circle the ones. 2 8 9
3. Circle the hundreds. 3 3 3
4. Circle the tens. 8 2 5
5. Circle the tens. 4 0 0
6. Circle the hundreds. 8 9 9
7. Circle the hundreds. 2 1 5
8. Circle the tens. 4 5 8
9. Circle the ones. 5 7 0
10. Circle the ones. 8 6 7
11. Circle the hundreds. 6 4 8
12. Circle the tens. 4 4 4

13. Circle Hanna's house number. It has 7 hundreds and 9 tens.

7 8 5 9 7 6 7 6 5 9 9 7 7 9 6

Connect the dots.
Start at the ▲ and count by 100s to 900.
Start at the ● and count by 10s to 290.
Start at the ■ and count by 1s from 451 to 470.

Which number comes **before**?

1. _____ 345 346
2. _____ 801 802
3. _____ 614 615
4. _____ 111 112
5. _____ 729 730
6. _____ 500 501

Which number belongs **between**?

7. 163 _____ 165
8. 411 _____ 413
9. 316 _____ 318
10. 240 _____ 242
11. 179 _____ 181
12. 299 _____ 301

Which number comes **after**?

13. 133 134 _____
14. 715 716 _____
15. 204 205 _____
16. 649 650 _____
17. 388 389 _____
18. 598 599 _____

Look at the hundreds digits in both numbers first and compare.
If the hundreds digits are the same, look at the tens digits.
If the hundreds and tens digits are the same, look at the ones digits.

Compare the hundreds.

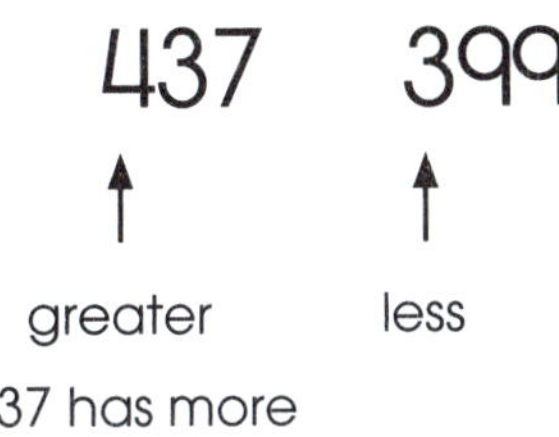

437 399

greater less

437 has more hundreds.

Compare the tens.

347 352

less greater

352 has more tens.

Compare the ones.

437 439

less greater

439 has more ones.

Circle the number that is **greater**.

1. 365 368
2. 574 584
3. 309 903
4. 700 170
5. 252 262
6. 878 788
7. 640 639
8. 901 910
9. 565 562

Circle the number that is **less**.

10. 770 790
11. 418 480
12. 620 532
13. 765 791
14. 943 948
15. 730 639
16. 391 399
17. 707 609
18. 828 728

Find the **sum**. Regroup if needed.

1. 65 + 52	2. 53 + 56	3. 47 + 85	4. 39 + 28
5. 95 + 12	6. 82 + 28	7. 63 + 37	8. 75 + 75
9. 90 + 46	10. 88 + 88	11. 91 + 19	12. 73 + 18
13. 49 + 49	14. 76 + 45	15. 57 + 75	16. 91 + 9

$$\begin{array}{r} \overset{1}{5}3 \\ 84 \\ +\ \ 9 \\ \hline 146 \end{array}$$

To check your answer, add the numbers in the opposite order.

$$\begin{array}{r} \overset{1}{\ }9 \\ 84 \\ +\ 53 \\ \hline 146 \end{array}$$

Find the **sum**. Regroup if needed.

1. $\begin{array}{r} 32 \\ 21 \\ +\ 15 \\ \hline \end{array}$

2. $\begin{array}{r} 63 \\ 12 \\ +\ 44 \\ \hline \end{array}$

3. $\begin{array}{r} 73 \\ 6 \\ +\ 25 \\ \hline \end{array}$

4. $\begin{array}{r} 97 \\ 98 \\ +\ 99 \\ \hline \end{array}$

5. $\begin{array}{r} 12 \\ 14 \\ 15 \\ +\ 18 \\ \hline \end{array}$

6. $\begin{array}{r} 45 \\ 21 \\ 30 \\ +\ 24 \\ \hline \end{array}$

7. $\begin{array}{r} 64 \\ 8 \\ 37 \\ +\ 40 \\ \hline \end{array}$

8. $\begin{array}{r} 56 \\ 55 \\ 4 \\ +\ \ 8 \\ \hline \end{array}$

9. 43 + 6 + 50 = ____

10. 78 + 31 + 88 = ____

11. 65 + 35 + 68 = ____

12. 37 + 8 + 39 = ____

13. 25 + 12 + 31 + 20 = ____

14. 40 + 50 + 60 = ____

15. 76 + 43 + 5 + 22 = ____

16. 25 + 35 + 45 = ____

ADDING WITH HUNDREDS

Add the **ones**. Regroup if needed.	Add the **tens**. Regroup if needed.	Add the **hundreds**.
$\begin{array}{r} \overset{1}{3}09 \\ +\ 473 \\ \hline 2 \end{array}$	$\begin{array}{r} \overset{1}{3}09 \\ +\ 473 \\ \hline 82 \end{array}$	$\begin{array}{r} \overset{1}{3}09 \\ +\ 473 \\ \hline 782 \end{array}$

Find the **sum**. Regroup if needed.

1. $\begin{array}{r} 462 \\ +\ 321 \\ \hline \end{array}$
2. $\begin{array}{r} 706 \\ +\ 132 \\ \hline \end{array}$
3. $\begin{array}{r} 450 \\ +\ 209 \\ \hline \end{array}$
4. $\begin{array}{r} 456 \\ +\ 123 \\ \hline \end{array}$
5. $\begin{array}{r} 366 \\ +\ 128 \\ \hline \end{array}$
6. $\begin{array}{r} 572 \\ +\ 309 \\ \hline \end{array}$
7. $\begin{array}{r} 278 \\ +\ 329 \\ \hline \end{array}$
8. $\begin{array}{r} 293 \\ +\ 275 \\ \hline \end{array}$
9. $\begin{array}{r} 435 \\ +\ 48 \\ \hline \end{array}$
10. $\begin{array}{r} 845 \\ +\ 17 \\ \hline \end{array}$
11. $\begin{array}{r} 670 \\ +\ 45 \\ \hline \end{array}$
12. $\begin{array}{r} 777 \\ +\ 19 \\ \hline \end{array}$

These are a challenge!

13. $\begin{array}{r} 352 \\ +\ 169 \\ \hline \end{array}$
14. $\begin{array}{r} 255 \\ +\ 355 \\ \hline \end{array}$
15. $\begin{array}{r} 675 \\ +\ 125 \\ \hline \end{array}$
16. $\begin{array}{r} 456 \\ +\ 345 \\ \hline \end{array}$

Find the **sum**. Regroup if needed.

1. $188 + 10$
2. $244 + 23$
3. $852 + 34$
4. $205 + 41$
5. $428 + 23$
6. $107 + 10$
7. $314 + 48$
8. $239 + 25$
9. $132 + 400$
10. $37 + 135$
11. $650 + 125$
12. $175 + 200$
13. $125 + 470$
14. $447 + 38$
15. $436 + 45$
16. $546 + 137$

Subtract the **ones**. Regroup if needed.	Subtract the **tens**. Regroup if needed.	Subtract the **hundreds**.	Check:
5 7̸ 3̸ (6 13) − 2 0 6 7	5 7̸ 3̸ (6 13) − 2 0 6 6 7	5 7̸ 3̸ (6 13) − 2 0 6 3 6 7	3 6 7 (1) + 2 0 6 5 7 3

Find the **difference**. Regroup if needed.
Check your answer.

1. $863 - 240$ Check: +

2. $478 - 435$ Check: +

3. $573 - 47$ Check: +

4. $350 - 38$ Check: +

5. $851 - 316$ Check: +

6. $617 - 395$ Check: +

SUBTRACTING THREE-DIGIT NUMBERS

Find the **difference**. Regroup if needed.

1. 146 − 22	2. 813 − 12	3. 486 − 74	4. 333 − 12
5. 750 − 400	6. 681 − 351	7. 175 − 114	8. 926 − 422
9. 487 − 29	10. 593 − 162	11. 296 − 89	12. 758 − 135
13. 832 − 109	14. 485 − 368	15. 398 − 250	16. 459 − 47

Solve this riddle:
Which bird is very sad?
Add and subtract to find the answer.

B	A	E
126 + 94	136 − 75	351 + 123

I	L	W
583 − 516	654 + 70	345 − 139

U	F	B
345 − 17	350 + 409	664 + 11

R	D	C
665 − 8	543 + 37	678 + 200

___ 61   ___ 220 ___ 724 ___ 328 ___ 474   ___ 675 ___ 67 ___ 657 ___ 580

Solve the problems to fill in the puzzle.

1.	2.	3.		4.	5.	6.
	7.				8.	
9.						
			10.	11.		
12.				13.		

Across

1. $\begin{array}{r} 65 \\ +\ 56 \\ \hline \end{array}$

4. $\begin{array}{r} 396 \\ -\ 125 \\ \hline \end{array}$

7. $\begin{array}{r} 634 \\ +\ 72 \\ \hline \end{array}$

8. $\begin{array}{r} 487 \\ -\ 444 \\ \hline \end{array}$

9. $\begin{array}{r} 560 \\ +\ 129 \\ \hline \end{array}$

10. $\begin{array}{r} 327 \\ -\ 253 \\ \hline \end{array}$

12. $\begin{array}{r} 695 \\ -\ 225 \\ \hline \end{array}$

13. $\begin{array}{r} 709 \\ +\ 204 \\ \hline \end{array}$

Down

2. $\begin{array}{r} 183 \\ +\ 95 \\ \hline \end{array}$

3. $\begin{array}{r} 578 \\ -\ 469 \\ \hline \end{array}$

5. $\begin{array}{r} 338 \\ +\ 406 \\ \hline \end{array}$

6. $\begin{array}{r} 765 \\ -\ 630 \\ \hline \end{array}$

9. $\begin{array}{r} 440 \\ +\ 214 \\ \hline \end{array}$

11. $\begin{array}{r} 360 \\ -\ 311 \\ \hline \end{array}$

Multiplication is a short way to add groups of equal size.

+ +

You can add: 2 + 2 + 2 = 6

Meaning: 3 groups of 2 = 6

You can multiply: 3 x 2 = 6

Fill in the blanks to finish the addition and multiplication sentences.

1.

_____ + _____ = _____

_____ groups of _____ = _____

_____ x _____ = _____

2.

_____ + _____ + _____ + _____ = _____

_____ groups of _____ = _____

_____ x _____ = _____

3.

_____ + _____ + _____ = _____

_____ groups of _____ = _____

_____ x _____ = _____

4.

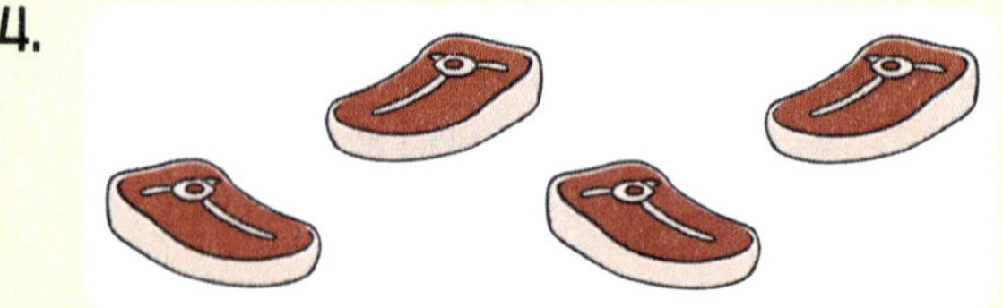

_____ + _____ + _____ + _____ = _____

_____ groups of _____ = _____

_____ x _____ = _____

4 + 4 + 4 = 12

How many 4s? 3

3 x 4 = 12

6 + 6 + 6 + 6 = 24

How many 6s? 4

4 x 6 = 24

Fill in the blanks to finish the addition and multiplication sentences.

1. 2 + 2 + 2 + 2 = ____

____ x ____ = ____

2. 3 + 3 + 3 + 3 = ____

____ x ____ = ____

3. 5 + 5 + 5 + 5 + 5 = ____

____ x ____ = ____

4. 4 + 4 + 4 = ____

____ x ____ = ____

5. 1 + 1 + 1 + 1 + 1 = ____

____ x ____ = ____

6. 5 + 5 + 5 = ____

____ x ____ = ____

7. 3 + 3 + 3 = ____

____ x ____ = ____

8. 4 + 4 + 4 + 4 = ____

____ x ____ = ____

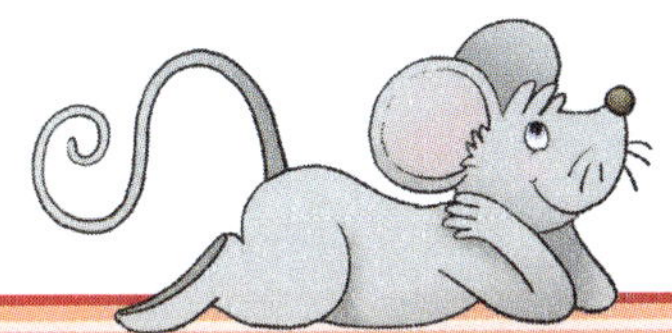

How many groups are there? 5

How many are in each group? 2

How many ? 10

5 x 2 = 10

Fill in the blanks.

1. How many groups are there? _____

How many  are in each group? _____

How many  ? _____

_____ x _____ = _____

2. How many groups are there? _____

How many  are in each group? _____

How many  ? _____

_____ x _____ = _____

3 groups of 

2 in each group

How many? 6

3 x 2 = 6

Fill in the blanks.

1.

____ groups of

____ in each group

How many? ____

____ x ____ = ____

2.

____ groups of

____ in each group

How many? ____

____ x ____ = ____

3.

____ groups of

____ in each group

How many? ____

____ x ____ = ____

4.

____ groups of

____ in each group

How many? ____

____ x ____ = ____

Fill in the blanks.

1.

_____ groups of

_____ in each group

How many ? _____

_____ x _____ = _____

2.

_____ groups of

_____ in each group

How many ? _____

_____ x _____ = _____

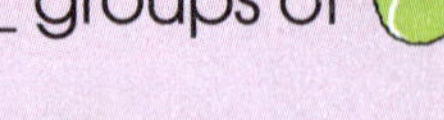

3.

_____ groups of

_____ in each group

How many ? _____

_____ x _____ = _____

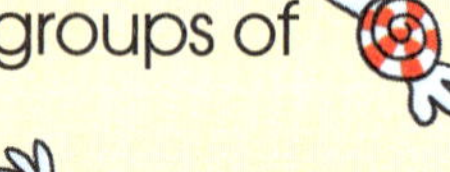

4.

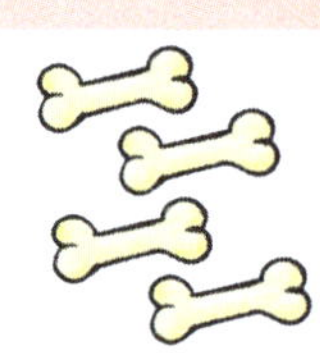

_____ groups of

_____ in each group

How many ? _____

_____ x _____ = _____

5. Draw **2** groups of **3** eggs.

_____ x _____ = _____

6. Draw **3** groups of **3** snakes.

_____ x _____ = _____

Fill in the blanks.

1.   

$3 \times 2 =$ ____

2.   

$2 \times$ ____ $=$ ____

3.  

$2 \times$ ____ $=$ ____

4.  

____ $\times$ ____ $=$ ____

5. Draw **2** groups of **5** circles.

____ $\times$ ____ $=$ ____

6. Draw **4** groups of **2** squares.

____ $\times$ ____ $=$ ____

The answer to a multiplication problem is called the **product**.
Find the **product**.

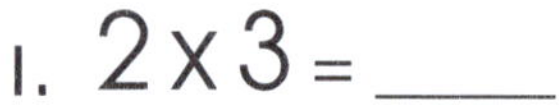

1. 2 x 3 = ____
2. 3 x 3 = ____
3. 3 x 5 = ____
4. 2 x 2 = ____
5. 2 x 4 = ____
6. 3 x 4 = ____
7. 3 x 1 = ____
8. 2 x 5 = ____
9. 3 x 0 = ____
10. 3 x 2 = ____
11. 2 x 1 = ____
12. 2 x 0 = ____

Fill in the chart.

x	0	1	2	3	4	5
2				6		
3	0				12	

Do you see any patterns?

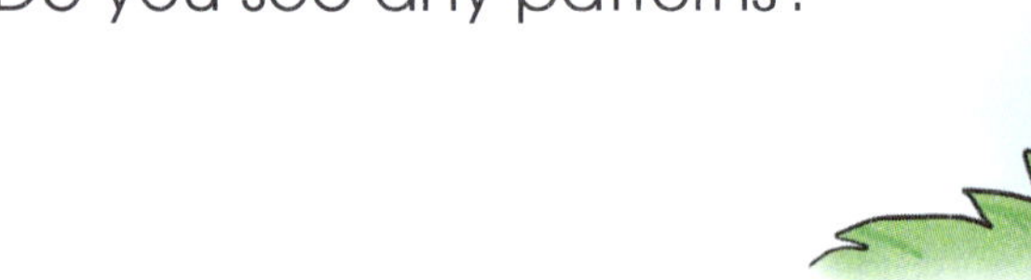

Find the **product**.

1. $4 \times 2 =$ ____
2. $5 \times 1 =$ ____
3. $5 \times 3 =$ ____
4. $4 \times 3 =$ ____
5. $4 \times 4 =$ ____
6. $5 \times 0 =$ ____
7. $4 \times 1 =$ ____
8. $5 \times 2 =$ ____
9. $5 \times 4 =$ ____
10. $4 \times 5 =$ ____
11. $4 \times 0 =$ ____
12. $5 \times 5 =$ ____

Fill in the chart.

x	0	1	2	3	4	5
2		2				
3						15
4	0			12		
5			10			

Do you see any patterns?

Write the missing numbers.

1. 8, ____, ____, 11, ____, ____, 14, ____, 16, ____

2. 43, ____, 45, ____, 47, ____, 49, ____, ____, 52

3. 175, ____, ____, 178, ____, ____, 181, ____, ____, 184

4. 604, ____, ____, 607, ____, 609, ____, ____, 612, ____

Which number comes **before**?

5. ____ 21 22
6. ____ 57 58
7. ____ 400 401
8. ____ 99 100
9. ____ 901 902
10. ____ 555 556

Which number belongs **between**?

11. 16 ____ 18
12. 39 ____ 41
13. 99 ____ 101
14. 138 ____ 140
15. 499 ____ 501
16. 888 ____ 890

Which number comes **after**?

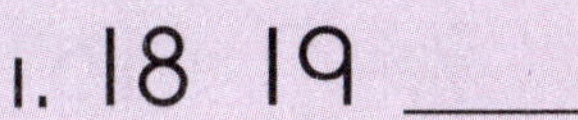

1. 18 19 ____
2. 65 66 ____
3. 47 48 ____
4. 98 99 ____
5. 308 309 ____
6. 798 799 ____

Circle the number that is **greater**.

7. 18 81
8. 60 16
9. 75 57
10. 183 138
11. 440 404
12. 693 637

Circle the number that is **less**.

13. 26 62
14. 70 79
15. 145 155
16. 372 327
17. 606 621
18. 565 556

19. Circle the number that shows 4 tens.

354 453 345 435 534

20. Circle the number that shows 5 hundreds.

354 453 345 453 534

Reviewing Numbers; Refers to Pages 208–211, 227–236, 270–277

Complete the **fact family**.

1. 4, 9, 13

____ + ____ = ____

____ + ____ = ____

____ − ____ = ____

____ − ____ = ____

2. 5, 7, 12

____ + ____ = ____

____ + ____ = ____

____ − ____ = ____

____ − ____ = ____

3. 7, 9, 16

____ + ____ = ____

____ + ____ = ____

____ − ____ = ____

____ − ____ = ____

Find the **sum**. Regroup if needed.

4. $\begin{array}{r} 45 \\ +\ 32 \\ \hline \end{array}$

5. $\begin{array}{r} 63 \\ +\ 18 \\ \hline \end{array}$

6. $\begin{array}{r} 59 \\ +\ 7 \\ \hline \end{array}$

7. $\begin{array}{r} 85 \\ +\ 69 \\ \hline \end{array}$

8. $\begin{array}{r} 37 \\ +\ 66 \\ \hline \end{array}$

9. $\begin{array}{r} 70 \\ +\ 59 \\ \hline \end{array}$

10. $\begin{array}{r} 345 \\ +\ 213 \\ \hline \end{array}$

11. $\begin{array}{r} 504 \\ +\ 235 \\ \hline \end{array}$

12. $\begin{array}{r} 342 \\ +\ 57 \\ \hline \end{array}$

13. $\begin{array}{r} 325 \\ +\ 145 \\ \hline \end{array}$

14. $\begin{array}{r} 670 \\ +\ 46 \\ \hline \end{array}$

15. $\begin{array}{r} 631 \\ +\ 59 \\ \hline \end{array}$

THINK CAP

Find the **difference**. Regroup if needed.

1. 78 − 35 = ____
2. 45 − 9 = ____
3. 82 − 37 = ____
4. 58 − 20 = ____
5. 94 − 54 = ____
6. 67 − 63 = ____
7. 256 − 32 = ____
8. 567 − 234 = ____
9. 678 − 245 = ____
10. 482 − 56 = ____
11. 516 − 352 = ____
12. 674 − 655 = ____

Find the **sum** or **difference**. Regroup if needed.

13. 73 + 26 = ____
14. 87 − 46 = ____
15. 81 − 18 = ____
16. 281 + 18 = ____
17. 64 + 53 = ____
18. 349 − 47 = ____
19. 333 + 409 = ____
20. 376 − 208 = ____

Find the **product**.

21. 3 x 4 = ____
22. 5 x 2 = ____
23. 4 x 1 = ____
24. 1 x 5 = ____
25. 4 x 5 = ____
26. 3 x 0 = ____

Use the pictograph to answer the question.

1. Which snack is the favorite? ______________

2. How many children like fruit as a snack? _______

3. More children like cookies than popcorn. How many more children like cookies?

    ____

Favorite Snacks	
Snack	Number of Votes
Popcorn	☺ ☺ ☺ ☺
Cookies	☺ ☺ ☺ ☺ ☺ ☺ ☺
Fruit	☺ ☺ ☺ ☺ ☺ ☺

Each ☺ = 1 child's vote

Use the bar graph to answer the question.

4. How many children like cheese pizza? __________

5. Which pizza was the least favorite?

    ____

6. How many children like pepperoni pizza? _______

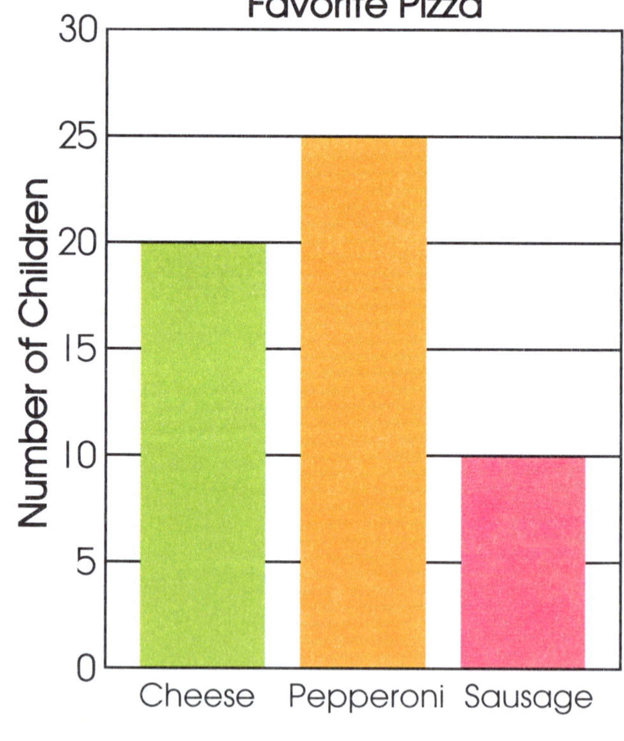

Use the groups of vegetables at the right to complete the tally chart.
Use the tally chart to answer the questions.

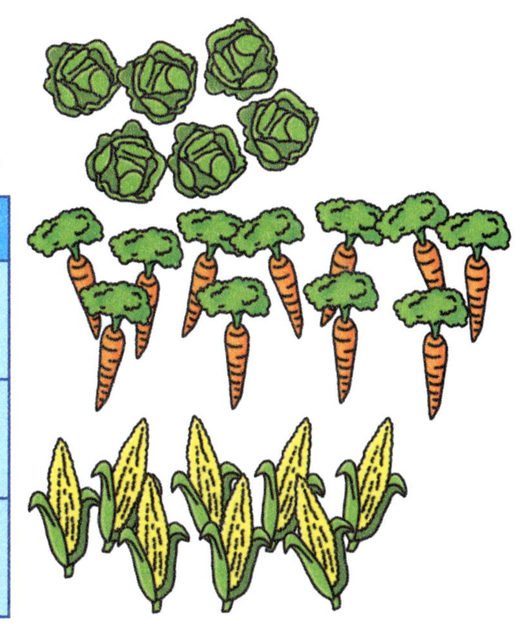

Vegetable	Tally	Total
Cabbages		
Carrots		
Ears of Corn		

1. How many carrots and ears of corn are there altogether? ____________

2. There are more carrots than cabbages. How many more carrots are there? ____________

Use the table to answer the questions.

Favorite Pet		
Pet	Girls' Votes	Boys' Votes
Cat	24	18
Dog	15	30
Bird	10	8

3. How many girls like cats? _______

4. How many boys like birds? _______

5. Which pet was the boys' favorite? _______

6. How many boys and girls like dogs? ____________

Page 1

3, 6
2, 4
5, 1
7, 9

Page 2

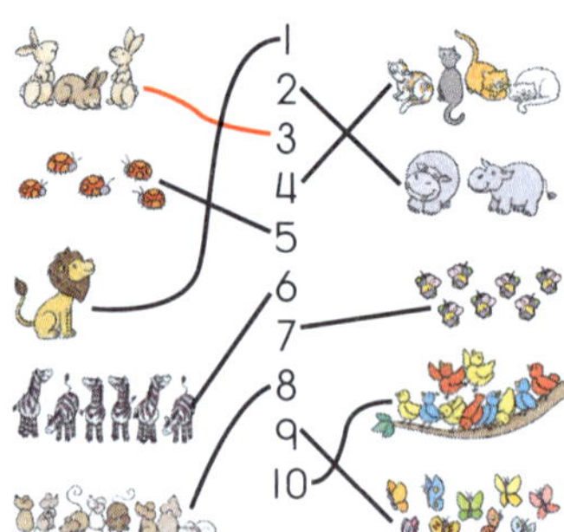

Page 3

2 7
6 5
3 9
10 8

Page 4

2, 4,
6, 8, 9
0, 1, 2, 3, 4,
5, 6, 7, 8, 9, 10

Page 5

1. 5 2. 7
3. 9 4. 3
5. 6 6. 10
7. 8 8. 4

Page 6

1. 5 frogs
2. 4 birds
3. 7 fish
4. 8 bees
5. 3 giraffes
6. 10 dolphins
7.  4

Page 7

1. 3, (4)
2. (6), 4
3. 5, (6)
4. 3, (5)
5. (7), 6
6. (3), 2

Page 8

1. 4 beavers
2. 2 dragonflies
3. 3 bats
4. 1 raccoon
5. 5 bees
6. 6 owls
7. 9

Page 9

1. 5, (3)
2. (4), 6
3. (6), 7
4. 9, (7)
5. 10, (8)
6. 6, (5)

Page 10

1. 2 2. 3
3. 4 4. 5
5. 3 6. 4
7. 5 8. 5

Page 11

1. 3 2. 5
3. 5 4. 4
5. 5 6. 2
7. 4 8. 5

Page 12

1. 2 2. 3
3. 2 4. 1
5. 1 6. 2
7. 1 8. 1

Page 13

1. 4 2. 3
3. 2 4. 2
5. 2 6. 1
7. 1 8. 3

Page 14

+	0	1	2	3	4	5
0	0	1	2	3	4	5
1	1	2	3	4	5	
2	2	3	4	5		
3	3	4	5			
4	4	5				
5	5					

Page 15

1. 4 2. 2 3. 2
4. 4 5. 5 6. 1
7. 2 8. 3 9. 5
10. 4 11. 1 12. 5 13. 3
14. 1 15. 3 16. 4 17. 3

Page 16

1. 7 2. 8
3. 9 4. 6
5. 10 6. 7
7. 10 8. 9

Page 17

1. 7 9 8 10
2. 7 9 10 8
3. 8 9 7 10
4. 9 7 8 10

Page 18

+	0	1	2	3	4	5	6	7	8	9
0	0	1	2	3	4	5	6	7	8	9
1	1	2	3	4	5	6	7	8	9	10
2	2	3	4	5	6	7	8	9	10	
3	3	4	5	6	7	8	9	10		
4	4	5	6	7	8	9	10			
5	5	6	7	8	9	10				
6	6	7	8	9	10					
7	7	8	9	10						
8	8	9	10							
9	9	10								

Each sum is 10.

Page 19

1. 9, 9 2. 7, 7 3. 10, 10
4. 10, 10 5. 8, 8 6. 8, 8

7. 9, 5 + 4 = 9 8. 7, 4 + 3 = 7
9. 6, 0 + 6 = 6 10. 10, 2 + 8 = 10
11. 9, 9 + 0 = 9 12. 8, 7 + 1 = 8

13. 2 + 7 = 9, 7 + 2 = 9
14. 4 + 6 = 10, 6 + 4 = 10
15. 0 + 8 = 8, 8 + 0 = 8

Page 20

1. 5 2. 5 3. 6
4. 8 5. 6 6. 4
7. 2 8. 6 9. 0 10. 5
11. 7 12. 3 13. 2 14. 2
15. 8 - 5 = 3

Page 21

1. 4, 3 2. 4, 5 3. 7, 0
4. 8, 1 5. 8, 2 6. 2, 6
7. 4, 9 - 4 = 5 8. 2, 7 - 2 = 5
9. 6, 6 - 6 = 0 10. 8, 10 - 8 = 2
11. 0, 8 - 0 = 8 12. 7, 8 - 7 = 1
13. 9 - 3 = 6, 9 - 6 = 3
14. 10 - 2 = 8, 10 - 8 = 2
15. 9 - 0 = 9, 9 - 9 = 0

Page 22

Page 23

1. 9 2. 5 3. 9
4. 9 5. 9 6. 5
7. 8 8. 9 9. 10
10. 10 11. 4 12. 7 13. 7
14. 3 15. 10 16. 10 17. 6

Page 24

1. 10 and 5, 15
2. 10 and 7, 17
3. 10 and 10, 20
4. 10 and 3, 13
5. 10 and 6, 16
6. 10 and 1, 11

Page 25

1. 13, 15, 17, 19
2. 12, 13, 14, 16, 17, 18
3. 6, 7, 9, 10, 12, 13
4. 11, 12, 14, 15, 16, 18, 19
5.

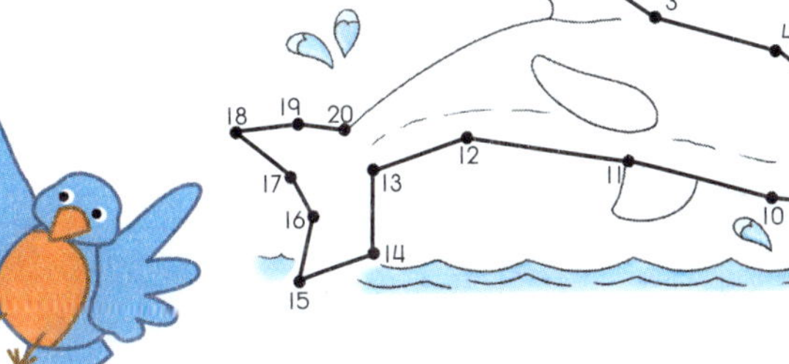

Page 26

1. 5 + 5 = 10 2. 6 + 4 = 10 3. 4 + 5 = 9
4. 6 + 3 = 9 5. 6 + 6 = 12 6. 6 + 5 = 11
7. 4 + 4 = 8 8. 2 + 6 = 8 9. 6 + 0 = 6

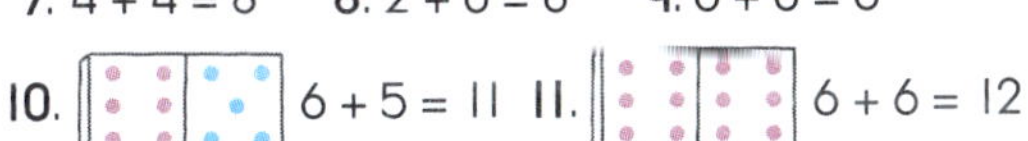

10. 6 + 5 = 11 11. 6 + 6 = 12
12. 4 + 6 = 10

Page 27

1. 11 2. 11 3. 10 4. 8
5. 12 6. 12 7. 9 8. 11
9. 12 10. 11 11. 10 12. 12

Page 28

1. 8, 2 2. 4, 8
3. 9, 3 4. 6
5. 7, 5 6. 8, 3
7. 7, 4 8. 6, 5

Page 29

1. 6 2. 6 3. 4
4. 6 5. 8 6. 8
7. 8 8. 9 9. 5
10. 7 11. 7 12. 4

Page 30

Page 31

Page 32

1. Answer given
2. 6 - 1, 5 + 0, 9 - 4
3. 10 - 2, 4 + 4, 2 + 6
4. 6 + 4, 7 + 3, 11 - 1
5. 12 - 0, 8 + 4, 7 + 5
6. 3 + 3, 12 - 6, 5 + 1
7. 9 + 2, 5 + 6, 8 + 3
8. 7 + 0, 11 - 4, 4 + 3

Page 33

3 Brown
1 Red
2 Yellow
4 Green
6 Blue
5 Black

Page 34

1. 2, 5; 25
2. 2, 6; 26
3. 3, 8; 38
4. 3, 4; 34
5. 2, 8; 28
6. 3, 0; 30

Page 35

1. 5, 6; 56
2. 3, 2; 32
3. 4, 7; 47
4. 6, 8; 68

Page 36

1. 2 tens 6 ones 26
2. 4 tens 1 one 41
3. 7 tens 0 ones 70
4. 5 tens 8 ones 58
5. 6 tens 2 ones 62
6. 8 tens 5 ones 85
7. 3 tens 7 ones 37

Page 37

1. 2 5
   4 3
   2 8
   3 0
   5 4
   6 5

2. 1 7
   7 1
   6 6
   1 9
   8 1
   4 0

Page 38

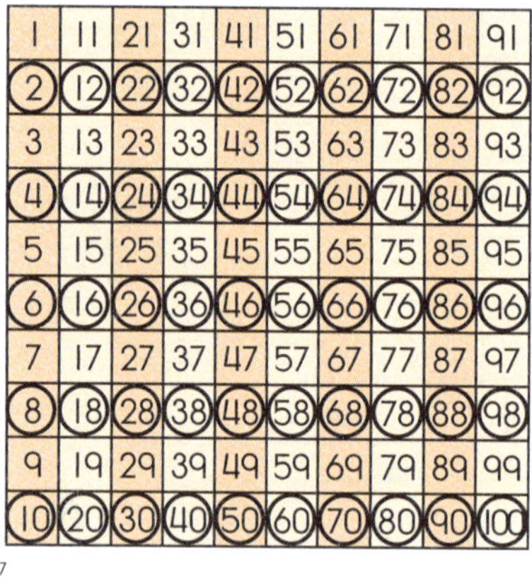

1	11	21	31	41	51	61	71	81	91
2	12	22	32	42	52	62	72	82	92
3	13	23	33	43	53	63	73	83	93
4	14	24	34	44	54	64	74	84	94
5	15	25	35	45	55	65	75	85	95
6	16	26	36	46	56	66	76	86	96
7	17	27	37	47	57	67	77	87	97
8	18	28	38	48	58	68	78	88	98
9	19	29	39	49	59	69	79	89	99
10	20	30	40	50	60	70	80	90	100

Page 39

1. 3, 6, 8, 9
2. 42, 43, 44, 47, 49
3. 71, 74, 76, 77, 79, 80
4. 32, 33, 34, 36, 38, 39, 40
5. 81, 82, 84, 85, 86, 87, 89
6. 62, 63, 64, 65, 66, 67, 68, 69
7. 92, 94, 95, 96, 97, 98, 100

Page 40

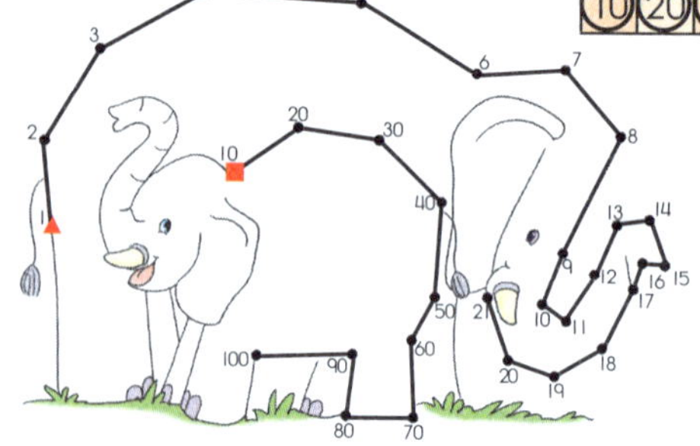

20, 40, 50
60, 80, 90, 100

Page 41

1. 17 2. 32
3. 23 4. 66
5. 80 6. 29
7. 44 8. 26
9. 23 10. 12
11. 19 12. 38
13. 28 14. 7
15. 39 16. 70

Page 42

1. 3 tens 2 ones — 32; 2 tens 3 ones — 23
2. 2 tens 4 ones — 24; 2 tens 7 ones — 27
3. 3 tens 5 ones — 35; 2 tens 9 ones — 29
4. 4 tens 3 ones — 43; 3 tens 4 ones — 34
5. 1 tens 5 ones — 15; 2 tens 5 ones — 25
6. 5 tens 0 ones — 50; 4 tens 1 ones — 41

Page 43

1. 23 2. 50 3. 31
4. 21 5. 35 6. 15
7. 18 8. 31 9. 43
10. 48 11. 25 12. 23
13. 59 14. 13 15. 25
16. 58 17. 44 18. 78

Page 44

1. 13 2. 14 3. 15 4. 12
5. 13 6. 14 7. 15 8. 12
9. 14 10. 12 11. 13 12. 11
13. 11 14. 9 15. 15 16. 10

Page 45

1. 13 2. 13 3. 12
4. 14 5. 12 6. 8
7. 15 8. 14 9. 14
10. 8 11. 6 12. 4
13. 6 14. 0 15. 7
16. 7 17. 8 18. 5

Page 46

1. 4 2. 4 3. 7
4. 6 5. 1 6. 7
7. 9 8. 7 9. 5
10. 9 11. 7 12. 7
13. 4 14. 0 15. 5
16. 8 17. 8 18. 9

Page 47

1. 12 2. 5 3. 15 4. 6
5. 3 6. 8 7. 13 8. 9
9. 15 10. 7 11. 6 12. 9
13. 9 14. 13 15. 0 16. 14

Page 48

1. 14 2. 15 3. 16
4. 14 5. 15 6. 16
7. 16 8. 17 9. 18
10. 13 11. 13 12. 15 13. 11
14. 17 15. 16 16. 14 17. 18

Page 49

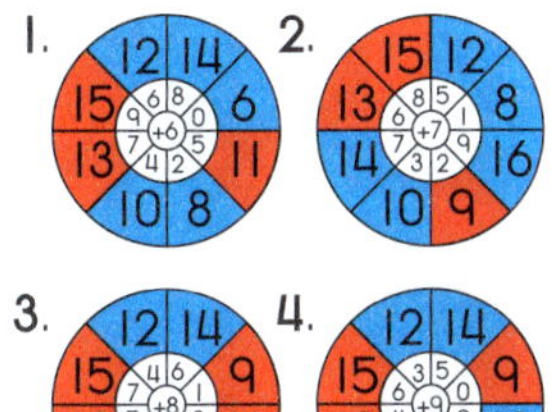

Page 50

+	0	1	2	3	4	5	6	7	8	9
0	0	1	2	3	4	5	6	7	8	9
1	1	2	3	4	5	6	7	8	9	10
2	2	3	4	5	6	7	8	9	10	11
3	3	4	5	6	7	8	9	10	11	12
4	4	5	6	7	8	9	10	11	12	13
5	5	6	7	8	9	10	11	12	13	14
6	6	7	8	9	10	11	12	13	14	15
7	7	8	9	10	11	12	13	14	15	16
8	8	9	10	11	12	13	14	15	16	17
9	9	10	11	12	13	14	15	16	17	18

1. 2 2. 4 3. 6
4. 8 5. 10 6. 12
7. 14 8. 16 9. 18

Page 51

1. 8, 9 2. 12, 13 3. 16, 17
4. 10, 11 5. 6, 7 6. 14, 15
7. 12, 13 8. 14, 15
9. 10, 11 10. 16, 17

Page 52

1. 9, 3 2. 9, 5 3. 8, 7
4. 8, 9 5. 8, 5 6. 5, 6
7. 8, 14 − 8 = 6
8. 9, 17 − 9 = 8
9. 3, 12 − 3 = 9
10. 8, 15 − 8 = 7
11. 9, 13 − 9 = 4
12. 6, 15 − 6 = 9

Page 53

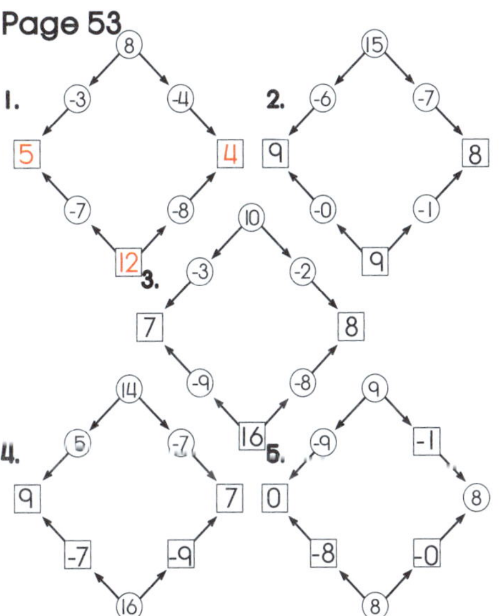

Page 54

1. 11, 11, 7, 4
2. 16, 16, 9, 7
3. 7, 7, 7, 0
4. 13, 8, 8, 5
5. 17, 17, 17, 17
6. 18, 9
7. 6 + 9 = 15 8. 9 + 0 = 9 9. 5 + 7 = 12
9 + 6 = 15 0 + 9 = 9 7 + 5 = 12
15 - 6 = 9 9 - 0 = 9 12 - 5 = 7
15 - 9 = 6 9 - 9 = 0 12 - 7 = 5

Page 55

1. 11 2. 13 3. 17 4. 13 5. 10
6. 15 7. 12 8. 14 9. 17 10. 16

Page 56

1. 14
2. 17
3. 8
4. 0
5. 16

Page 57

Page 58

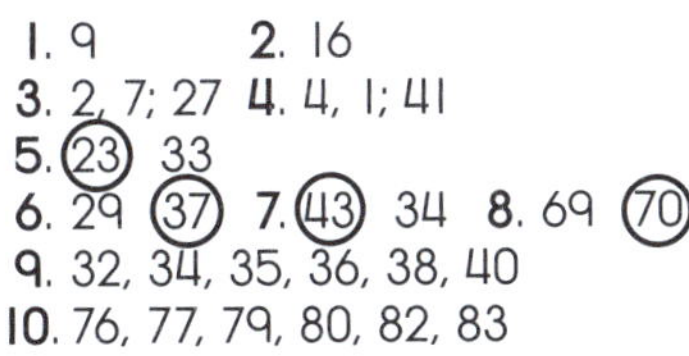

1. 9 2. 16
3. 2, 7; 27 4. 4, 1; 41
5. 23 33
6. 29 37 7. 43 34 8. 69 70
9. 32, 34, 35, 36, 38, 40
10. 76, 77, 79, 80, 82, 83

Page 59

1. 11 2. 12 3. 18
4. 7 5. 17 6. 14
7. 5 8. 0 9. 7
10. 7 11. 9 12. 7
13. 7 14. 13 15. 8 16. 9
17. 12 18. 8 19. 16 20. 18
21. 7 + 9 = 16
9 + 7 = 16
16 - 7 = 9
16 - 9 = 7

Page 60

1. 6 giraffes 2. 5 parrots
3. 8 elephants 4. 7 lions
5. 9 monkeys 6. 10 zebras

Page 61

1. 3 + 2 = 5, 5
2. 1 + 1 = 2, 2
3. 4 + 2 = 6, 6

Page 62

1. 3 + 4 = 7 fish, 7
2. 5 + 3 = 8 sea horses, 8
3. 3 + 3 = 6 jellyfish, 6
4. 4 + 5 = 9 fish, 9

Page 63

1. 2
+ 6
8 birds

2. 1
+ 5
6 turtles

3. 4
+ 3
7 dogs

Page 64

1. 3
+ 5
8 puppies

2. 2
+ 3
5 birds

3. 2
+ 6
8 kittens

Page 65

1. 3
+ 5
8 hats

2. 2
+ 3
5 bats

3. 2
+ 4
6 pennants

Page 66

1. 3 frogs
2. 2 cats
3. 4 rabbits
4. 5 dogs
5. 8 mice
6. 6 birds

Page 67

1. 5 − 2 = 3
2. 6 − 4 = 2
3. 8 − 3 = 5

Page 68

1. 7 − 2 = 5, 5
2. 8 − 4 = 4, 4
3. 7 − 4 = 3, 3
4. 9 − 3 = 6, 6

Page 69

1. 5
− 4
1 fish

2. 8
− 4
4 flowers

3. 7
− 5
2 turtles

Page 70

1. 5
− 3
2 bees

2. 6
− 4
2 bears

3. 6
− 2
4 jars

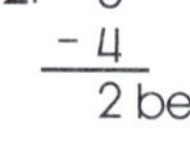
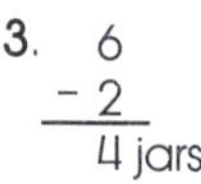
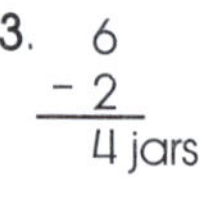
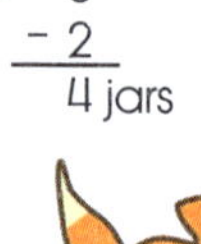

Page 71

1. 8
− 4
4 grasshoppers

2. 6
− 4
2 brown rabbits

3. 9
− 4
5 frogs

4. 7
− 3
4 purple spiders

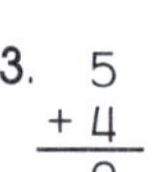

Page 72

1. 7 − 4 = 3
2. 5 − 3 = 2
3. 4 + 3 = 7
4. 6 − 2 = 4
5. 2 + 5 = 7

Page 73

1. 3
+ 6
9

2. 4
− 1
3

3. 5
+ 4
9

4. 6
− 2
4

Page 74

1. How many ladybugs were left?
10 − 5 = 5
2. How many beetles were there in all?
11 + 3 = 14
3. How many ants were there in all?
8 + 7 = 15
4. How many bees were left?
12 − 3 = 9

Page 75

1. 8
− 2
6 apples

2. 5
+ 4
9 pears

3. 7
− 4
3 bananas

Page 76

1. 7
+ 4
11 kites

2. 6
+ 6
12 squirrels

3. 8
− 2
6 swings

Page 77

1. 7
− 5
2 sheep

2. 8
+ 5
13 cows

3. 12
− 4
8 eggs

Page 78

1. 4¢
+ 5¢
9¢

2. 3¢
+ 5¢
8¢

3. 14¢
− 6¢
8¢

4. 17¢
− 3¢
14¢

Page 79

1. 10¢
− 6¢
4¢

2. 8¢
+ 4¢
12¢

3. 7¢
+ 3¢
10¢

4. 15¢
− 5¢
10¢

5. 6¢
+ 5¢
11¢

6. 12¢
− 7¢
5¢

Page 80

1. 4
2. 5
3. 3
4. 2
5. 6
6. 5
7. 3 + 5 = 8
8. 6 − 4 = 2

Page 81

1. 6
2. 7
3. 8
4. Bret
5. Zach
6. 9 + 4 = 13
7. 6 + 7 = 13
8. 8 − 6 = 2

Page 82

1. 7
2. 4
3. 4 + 2 = 6
4. 8 + 2 = 10
5. 8 − 4 = 4
6. 4 + 7 = 11

Page 83

1. 6
2. 10
3. 8
4. 8 − 6 = 2
5. 10 − 6 = 4
6. 6 + 8 = 14

Page 84

1. 3
2. 5
3. 6
4. dog
5. pony
6. 10 – 6 = 4
7. 5 + 6 = 11

Page 85

1. 8
2. 10
3. orange
4. banana
5. 8 + 6 = 14
6. 9 – 5 = 4
7. 6 + 6 + 9 = 21

Page 86

1.

June						
Sunday	Monday	Tuesday	Wednesday	Thursday	Friday	Saturday
		1	2	3	4	5
6	7	8	9	10	11	12
13	14	15	16	17	18	19
20	21	22	23	24	25	26
27	28	29	30			

2. Wednesday
3. Thursday
4. Tuesday
5. June 7
6. June 11
7. 7 days
8. 7 + 7 = 14 days
9. 30 days

Page 87

1. 4 : 30

2. 2 : 00

3. 3 : 30

4. 9 : 00

Page 88

1. "Her sister is 8 years old" should be crossed out.

   12
   – 5
   7 years

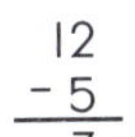

2. "Alex bought 7 gifts" should be crossed out.

   8
   + 5
   13 gifts

3. "Mark has 10 pizza slices" and "Jose has 9 pizza slices" should be crossed out.

   7
   – 5
   2 pizza slices

Page 89

1. 9, 8, 17
2. 8, 6, 5, 19
3. 5, 3, 8, 11

Page 90

1. 1¢, 2¢, 3¢, 4¢, 5¢, 6¢; 6¢
2. 5¢, 10¢, 15¢, 20¢, 25¢, 30¢; 30¢
3. 10¢, 20¢, 30¢, 40¢, 50¢; 50¢

Page 91

1. 10¢, 20¢, 30¢, 31¢, 32¢, 33¢; 33¢
2. 5¢, 10¢, 15¢, 20¢, 21¢, 22¢; 22¢
3. 10¢, 20¢, 30¢, 35¢, 40¢, 45¢; 45¢
4. 10¢, 20¢, 30¢, 40¢, 50¢, 51¢; 51¢

Page 92

1. 10¢, 20¢, 25¢, 26¢, 27¢, 28¢; 28¢
2. 10¢, 20¢, 30¢, 40¢, 50¢, 51¢, 52¢; 52¢
3. 10¢, 20¢, 30¢, 35¢, 40¢, 41¢; 41¢
4. 10¢, 15¢, 20¢, 21¢, 22¢, 23¢; 23¢
5. 10¢, 20¢, 25¢, 30¢, 31¢; 31¢

Page 93

1. 10¢
2. 33¢
3. 18¢
4. 25¢
5. 27¢
6. 36¢

Page 94

1. 36¢ glue
2. 33¢ paintbrush
3. 53¢ crayons
4. 30¢ pencils
5. 61¢ scissors
6. 46¢ notebook

Page 95

1. 25¢
2. 25¢
3. 28¢, crossed out
4. 25¢

Page 96

1. 36¢
2. 55¢
3. 76¢
4. 52¢
5. 87¢

Page 97

1. 25¢, 35¢, 45¢, 50¢, 51¢ - yes
2. 25¢, 50¢, 60¢, 65¢ - no
3. 10¢, 20¢, 25¢, 30¢ - yes
4. 10¢, 20¢, 30¢, 31¢, 32¢ - yes
5. 25¢, 50¢, 75¢, 76¢ - no

Page 98

1. 1 quarter, 1 dime, 3 pennies
2. 1 quarter, 2 dimes, 1 penny
3. 2 quarters, 1 dime, 2 nickels
4. 2 quarters, 2 nickels, 1 penny
5. 2 quarters, 2 pennies
6. 3 quarters, 1 dime, 2 pennies

Page 99

1. 1 quarter, 1 dime, 3 nickels
2. 3 dimes, 4 nickels
3. 1 quarter, 2 dimes, 1 nickel
4. 2 dimes, 4 nickels, 10 pennies

Page 100

1. 48¢
2. (50¢) circled
3. (50¢) circled
4. 60¢
5. 39¢
6. (50¢) circled

Page 101

1. 22¢, 31¢; eraser circled
2. 57¢, 52¢; scissors circled
3. 61¢, 60¢; whistle circled
4. 77¢, 82¢; notebook circled

Page 102

1. 25¢ (20¢)
2. 50¢ (40¢)
3. (35¢) 50¢
4. (50¢) 60¢
5. 75¢ (70¢)
6. 60¢ (50¢)
7. (70¢) 75¢
8. (75¢) 80¢

Page 103

1. D
2. D N
3. Q N P
4. Q D D P
5. Q P P

Page 104

1. Q N P P
2. Q P P P
3. Q D D
4. H N P
5. H D D
6. H Q D D P P P

Page 105

1. 32¢ + 50¢ = 82¢
2. 44¢ + 24¢ = 68¢
3. 44¢ + 15¢ = 59¢
4. 63¢ + 32¢ = 95¢
5. 63¢ + 24¢ = 87¢
6. 15¢ + 50¢ = 65¢

Page 106

1. P P — 35¢ − 33¢ = 2¢
2. P — 45¢ − 44¢ = 1¢
3. D — 75¢ − 65¢ = 10¢
4. P P P — 75¢ − 72¢ = 3¢
5. N — 95¢ − 90¢ = 5¢

Page 107

	Half Dollar	Quarter	Dime	Nickel	Penny
53¢	1				3
27¢		1			2
18¢			1	1	3
69¢	1		1	1	4
76¢	1	1			1
37¢		1	1		2
92¢	1	1	1	1	2

Answers can vary on the second table.

Page 108

Across	Down
a. 60	a. 62
b. 42	b. 45
c. 95	c. 90
d. 30	d. 35
e. 25	e. 25
f. 15	f. 10
g. 10	g. 10
h. 50	h. 55
i. 75	i. 74
j. 84	j. 89

Page 109

1. 3 o'clock
   3:00
2. 7 o'clock
   7:00
3. 9 o'clock
   9:00
4. 11 o'clock
   11:00
5. 8 o'clock
   8:00
6. 5 o'clock
   5:00

Page 110

1. 
   5 : 00
2. 
   10 : 00
3. 
   6 : 00
4. 
   12 : 00
5. 
   3 : 00
6. 
   8 : 00

Page 111

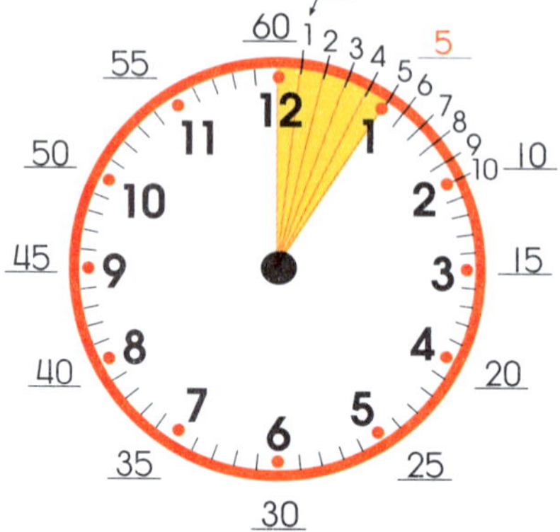

How many minutes are in an hour? 60

Page 112

1. 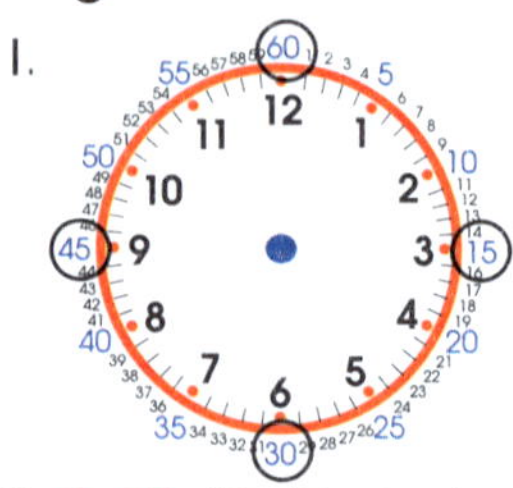

2. 5, 10, 15; 15 minutes
3. 5, 10, 15, 20, 25, 30; 30 minutes
4. 5, 10, 15, 20, 25, 30, 35, 40, 45; 45 minutes

Page 113

1. Half past 4
   4:30
2. Half past 10
   10:30
3. Half past 6
   6:30
4. Half past 8
   8:30
5. Half past 12
   12:30
6. Half past 3
   3:30

Page 114

1. 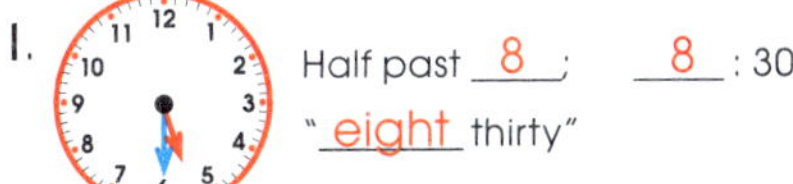 Half past 8; 8 : 30
   "eight thirty"
2.  Half past 6; 6 : 30
   "six thirty"
3.  Half past 12; 12 : 30
   "twelve thirty"
4.  Half past 5; 5 : 30
   "five thirty"

Page 115

1. 1:30 2. 6:00 3. 9:30
4. 10:30 5. 12:00 6. 5:30

7.  8.  9. 

10.  11.  12. 

Page 116

	One Hour Earlier	Now		One Hour Later
1.	8 : 30	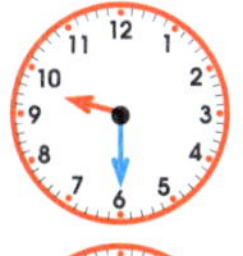	9:30	10 : 30
2.	2 : 00		3:00	4 : 00
3.	4 : 30		5:30	6 : 30
4.	1 : 30		2:30	3 : 30
5.	11 : 30		12:30	1 : 30

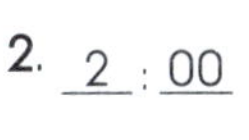

Page 117

1. Quarter past 6
   6:15
2. Quarter past 8
   8:15
3. Quarter past 1
   1:15
4. Quarter past 12
   12:15
5. Quarter past 10
   10:15
6. Quarter past 7
   7:15

Page 118

1.  Quarter past 7; 7 : 15
   "seven fifteen"
2.  Quarter past 10; 10 : 15
   "ten fifteen"
3.  Quarter past 9; 9 : 15
   "nine fifteen"
4.  Quarter past 3; 3 : 15
   "three fifteen"

Page 119

1. Quarter to 4
   3:45
2. Quarter to 9
   8:45
3. Quarter to 1
   12:45
4. Quarter to 7
   6:45
5. Quarter to 2
   1:45
6. Quarter to 10
   9:45

Page 120

1. 1:45 2. 2:15 3. 7:45
4. 11:15 5. 3:45 6. 8:15

7.  8.  9. 

10.  11.  12. 

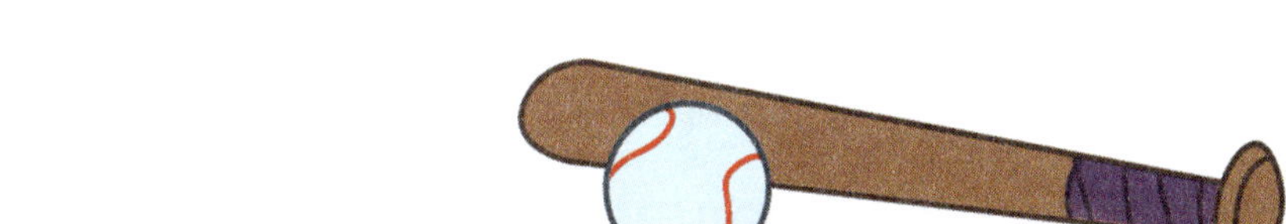

Page 121

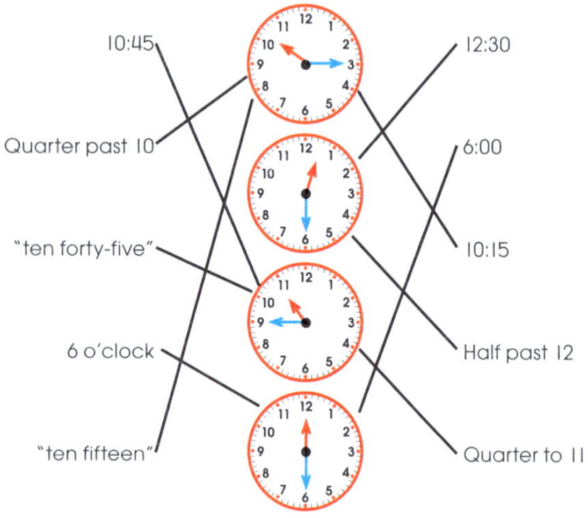

Page 122

1. 4:05
2. 5:15
3. 3:10
4. 6:35
5. 9:50
6. 2:20

Page 123

1. 9:15 2. 6:00 3. 5:20
4. 10:45 5. 4:40 6. 11:30

7. 
8.
9. 
10. 
11. 
12. 

Page 124

1.  7:00
2.  9:00
3.  12:00
4.  2:30
5.  4:45

Page 125

1. 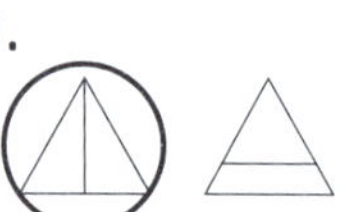
2. 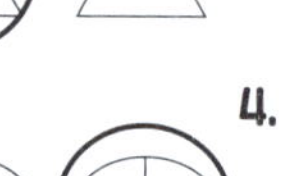
3. 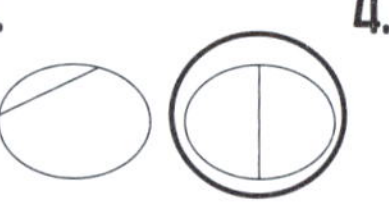
4.
5. 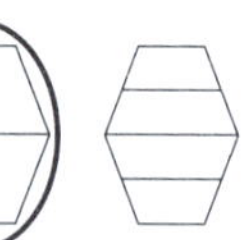
6. 

Page 126

1. 
2. 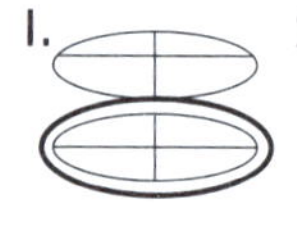
3. 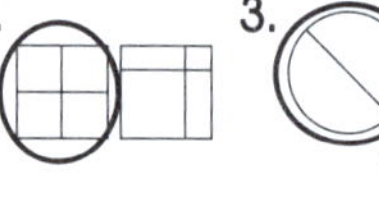
4. 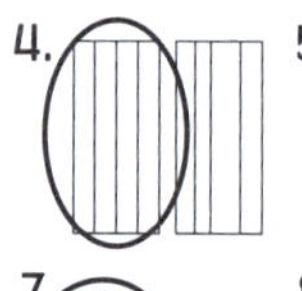
5.
6. 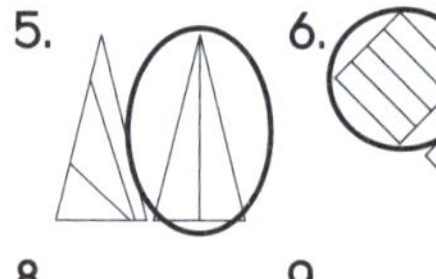
7. 
8. 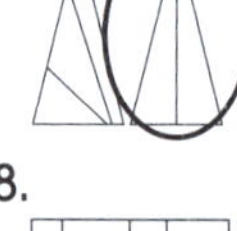 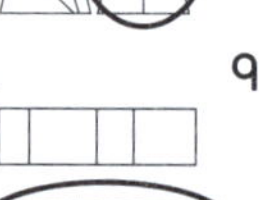 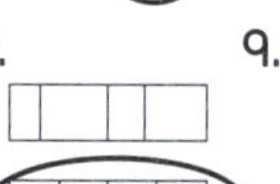
9. 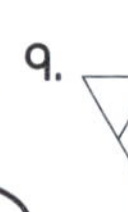 

Page 127

1. 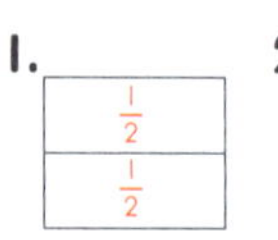
2. 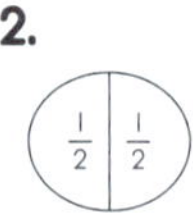
3. 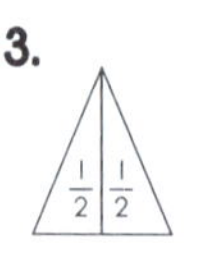
4. 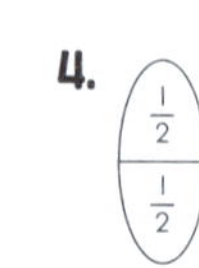
5. 
6. 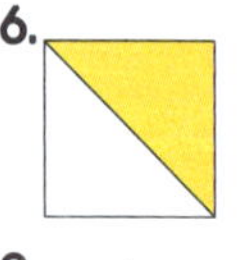
7. 
8. 
9. 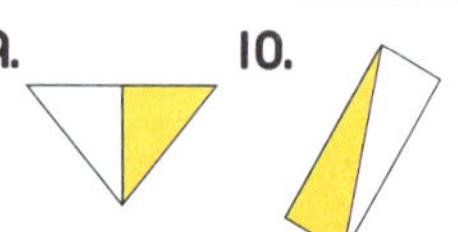
10.
11.
12. 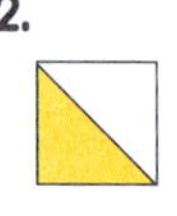

The $\frac{1}{2}$ section colored can vary.

Page 128

1. 
2. 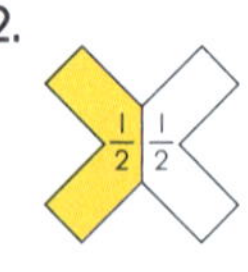
3. 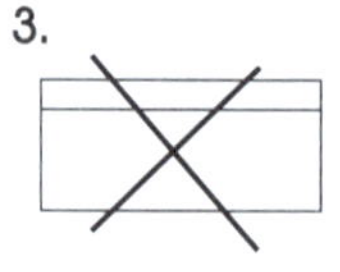
4. 
5. 
6. 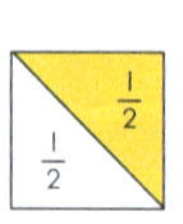
7. 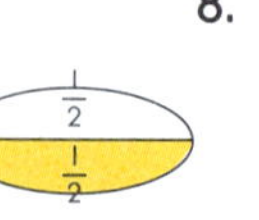
8. 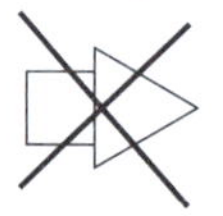
9.  

The $\frac{1}{2}$ section colored can vary.

Page 129

1. 2. 3. 4.

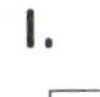
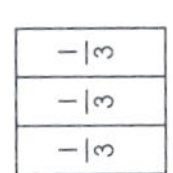
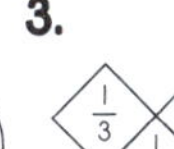

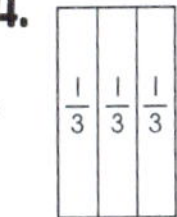
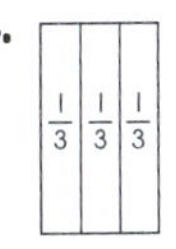

5. 6. 7. 8.

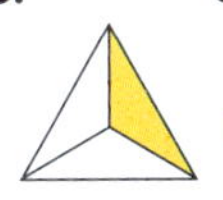
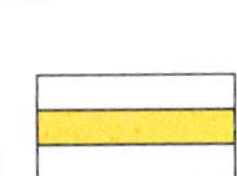
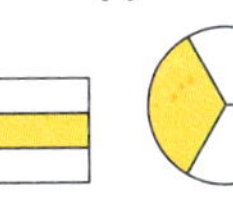
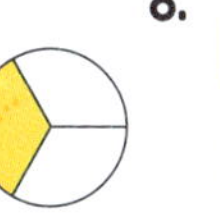
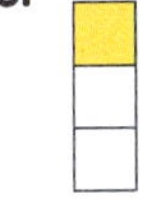
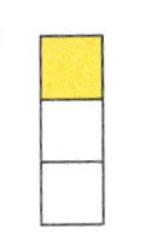
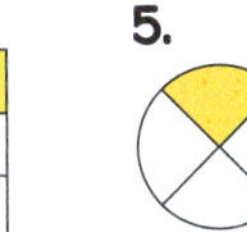

9. 10. 11. 12.

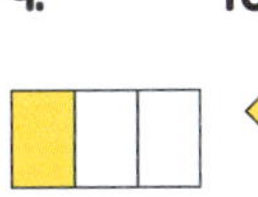
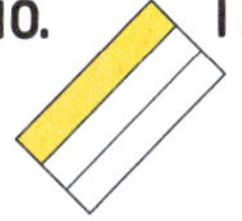
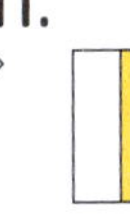
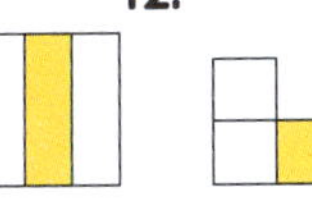

The $\frac{1}{3}$ section colored can vary.

Page 130

1. 2. 3. 4.

5. 6. 7. 8.

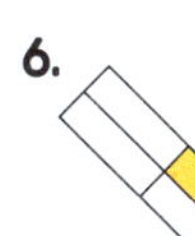
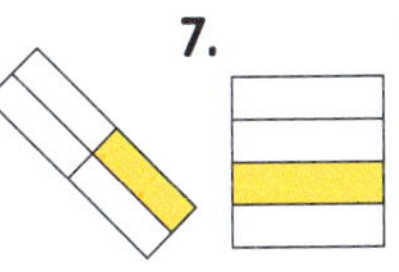
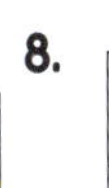
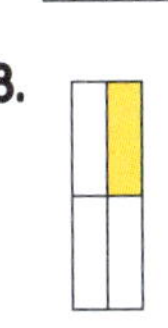

9. 10. 11. 12.

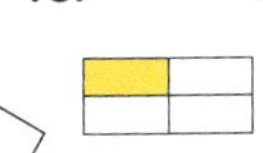

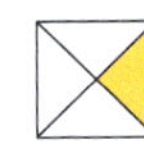

The $\frac{1}{4}$ section colored can vary.

Page 131

1. $\frac{1}{2}$
2. $\frac{1}{3}$
3. $\frac{1}{4}$
4. $\frac{1}{2}$
5. $\frac{1}{3}$
6. $\frac{1}{4}$

Page 132

1. $\frac{1}{2}$
2. $\frac{1}{4}$
3. $\frac{1}{3}$
4. $\frac{1}{4}$
5. $\frac{1}{3}$
6. $\frac{1}{4}$
7. $\frac{1}{3}$
8. $\frac{1}{3}$
9. $\frac{1}{4}$

Page 133

1. $\frac{2}{4}$
2. $\frac{3}{4}$
3. $\frac{1}{2}$
4. $\frac{4}{6}$
5. $\frac{3}{4}$
6. $\frac{1}{3}$

Page 134

1. $\frac{3}{4}$
2. $\frac{1}{3}$
3. $\frac{3}{8}$
4. $\frac{1}{4}$
5. $\frac{2}{6}$
6. $\frac{1}{3}$
7. $\frac{2}{3}$
8. $\frac{2}{4}$
9. $\frac{1}{2}$

Page 135

1. 2. 3.

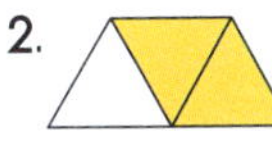
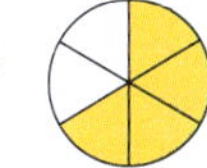

4. 5. 6.

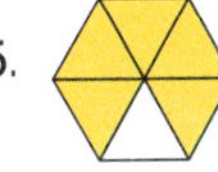
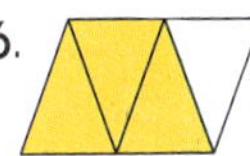

7. 8. 9.

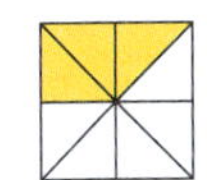

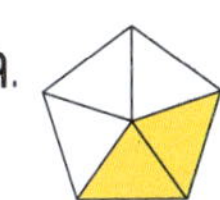

Sections colored can vary, please check your child's work.

Page 136

1. 2. 3.

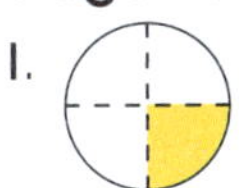
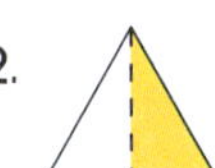
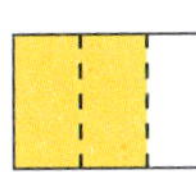

4. 5. 6.

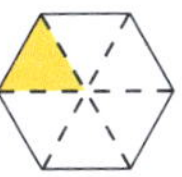
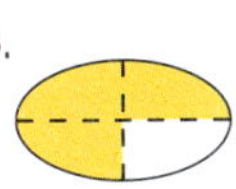
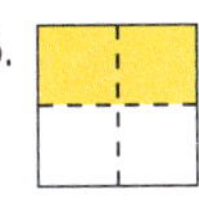

7. 8. 9.

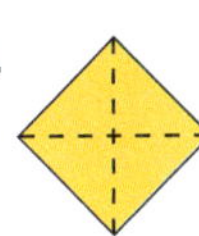

Sections colored can vary, please check your child's work.

Page 137

1. One is colored.
2. Three are colored.
3. Two are colored.
4. Seven are colored.
5. Two are colored.
6. One is colored.
7. One is colored.
8. Five are colored.

Page 138

1. $\frac{3}{4}$
2. $\frac{1}{3}$
3. $\frac{1}{2}$
4. $\frac{2}{6}$
5. $\frac{1}{4}$
6. $\frac{3}{5}$
7. $\frac{2}{4}$
8. $\frac{4}{8}$

Page 139

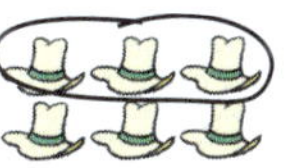

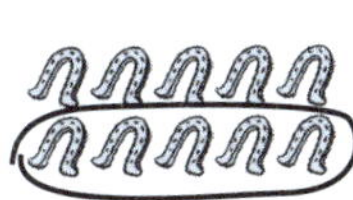

Objects circled can vary, please check your child's work.

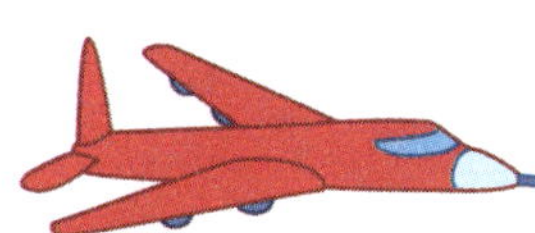

Page 140

1. 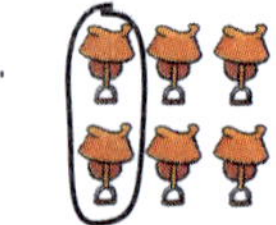
2. 
3. 
4. 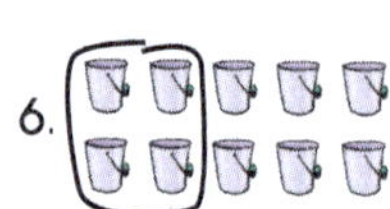
5.
6.

Objects circled can vary, please check your child's work.

Page 141

Objects colored can vary, please check your child's work.

Page 142

1. 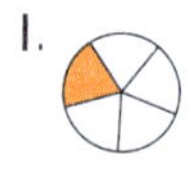 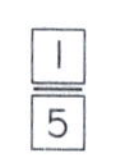

2.  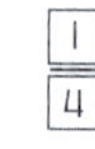

3. 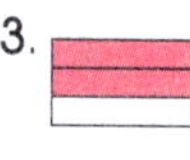 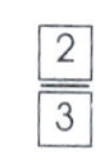

4. 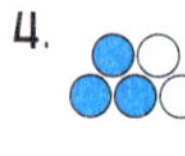 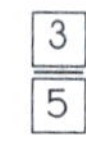

5. 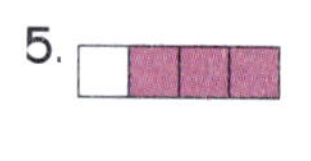 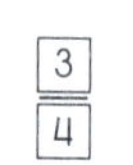

6.  

7. 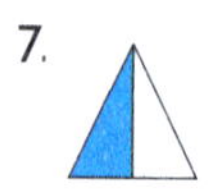 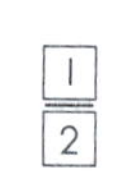

8. 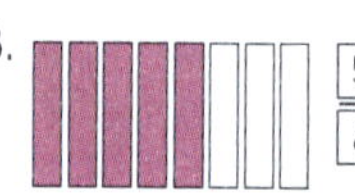

Sections colored can vary, please check your child's work.

Page 143

1. 10¢, 20¢, 25¢, 26¢, 27¢, 28¢; 28¢
2. 25¢, 50¢, 60¢, 65¢, 66¢; no
3. 92¢
4. 1 half dollar, 2 dimes, 2 pennies

Page 144

1. half dollar
2. 76¢
3. more
4. nickel
5. 59¢
6. 13¢

Page 145

1. 8 o'clock, 8:00
2. Half past 11, 11:30
3. Quarter to 2, 1:45

4. 
5. 
6. 
7.
8.
9.

Page 146

1. 5:00
2. 8:15
3. 12:30
4. 6:35
5. 10:30
6. 1:45
7. 5:30
8. 9:30

Page 147

1. 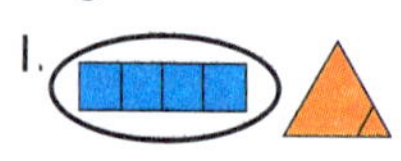  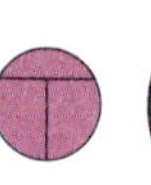 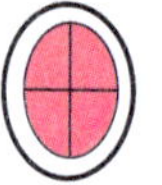
2. 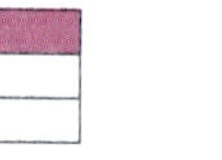
3. 
4. 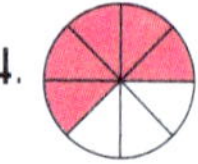
5. 
6. 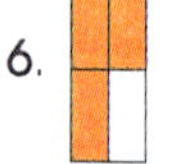
7. 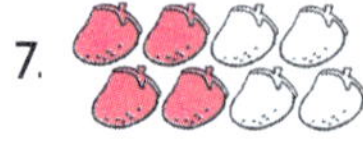
8. 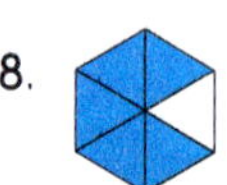
9. 
10. 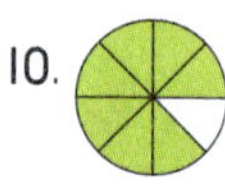

Sections colored can vary, please check your child's work.

Page 148

1. $\frac{1}{3}$
2. $\frac{1}{5}$
3. three-fourths
4. two-thirds
5. $\frac{1}{2}$
6. $\frac{3}{8}$
7. $\frac{1}{3}$
8. $\frac{3}{5}$
9. one-sixth

Page 149

1. 2 + 2 = 4
2. 3 + 3 = 6
3. 4 + 2 = 6
4. 1 + 3 = 4
5. 1 + 1 = 2
6. 5 + 1 = 6
7. 2 + 3 = 5

Page 150

1. 6
2. 5
3. 6
4. 6
5. 5
6. 4
7. 5
8. 6
9. 6
10. 2
11. 6
12. 4
13. 3
14. 6
15. 5
16. 4

Page 151

1. 4 - 3 = 1
2. 6 - 3 = 3
3. 2 - 1 = 1
4. 5 - 2 = 3
5. 4 - 2 = 2
6. 6 - 4 = 2
7. 6 - 1 = 5

Page 152

1. 3 2. 3 3. 2
4. 1 5. 2 6. 1
7. 4 8. 2 9. 2 10. 5
11. 1 12. 2 13. 3 14. 1
15. 3 16. 1 17. 1 18. 4

Page 153

1. 4 2. 3 3. 6 4. 5 5. 2
6. 2 7. 5 8. 1 9. 4 10. 6
11. 2 12. 1 13. 3 14. 3 15. 0
16. 5 17. 5 18. 0 19. 2 20. 4

Page 154

1. 4, 4, 3, 1
2. 6, 6, 1, 5
3. 4, 4, 0, 4
4. 6, 3
5. 2, 1
6. 4, 2

Page 155

1. Add 1: 5, 3, 1, 6
2. Add 3: 4, 6, 5, 3
3. Add 0: 6, 4, 1, 5

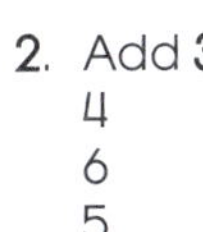

4. Subtract 1: 5, 2, 4, 1
5. Subtract 0: 5, 2, 6, 1
6. Subtract 2: 0, 1, 4, 3

7. 2 | +4 | 6 | -3 | 3 | -1 | 2 | +2 = 4

Page 156

1. 3 + 4 = 7
2. 5 + 2 = 7
3. 1 + 6 = 7
4. 5 + 3 = 8
5. 7 + 1 = 8
6. 2 + 6 = 8
7. 4 + 4 = 8

Page 157

1. 7 - 5 = 2
2. 7 - 4 = 3
3. 7 - 1 = 6
4. 7 - 3 = 4
5. 8 - 5 = 3
6. 7 - 0 = 7
7. 8 - 7 = 1

Page 158

1. 7 2. 8 3. 4
4. 5 5. 7 6. 3
7. 7 8. 8 9. 6
10. 8 11. 5 12. 7 13. 6 14. 3
15. 2 16. 5 17. 8 18. 4 19. 8

Page 159

1. 7, 7, 3, 4
2. 8, 4
3. 7, 7, 5, 2
4. 8, 8, 6, 2
5. 8, 8, 1, 7
6. 8, 0

Page 160

1. 4 + 5 = 9
2. 2 + 7 = 9
3. 3 + 7 = 10
4. 8 + 2 = 10
5. 3 + 6 = 9
6. 4 + 6 = 10
7. 5 + 5 = 10

Page 161

1. 9 - 4 = 5
2. 9 - 2 = 7
3. 9 - 6 = 3
4. 10 - 8 = 2
5. 10 - 4 = 6
6. 10 - 7 = 3
7. 10 - 5 = 5

Page 162

1. 9, 9, 3, 6
2. 9, 9, 4, 5
3. 10, 10, 4, 6
4. 10, 10, 3, 7
5. 10, 10, 8, 2
6. 5, 10

Page 163

1. 6 2. 9 3. 5
4. 10 5. 2 6. 8
7. 10 8. 6 9. 9
10. 10 11. 10 12. 9
13. 3 14. 7 15. 10
16. 10 17. 5 18. 8

Page 164

1. 6 2. 3
3. 10 4. 10
5. 8 6. 8
7. 3 8. 9
9. 4 10. 9 11. 3
12. 7 13. 6 14. 7
15. 7 16. 2 17. 8
18. 10 19. 6 20. 9

Page 165

1. + 2. - 3. - 4. +
5. - 6. + 7. - 8. -
9. + 10. - 11. - 12. +
13. + 14. - 15. - 16. +

Page 166

1. 3 + 8 = 11
2. 9 + 2 = 11
3. 3 + 9 = 12
4. 5 + 7 = 12
5. 6 + 6 = 12
6. 7 + 4 = 11

Page 167

1. 11 2. 12 3. 10
4. 11 5. 9 6. 9
7. 11 8. 9 9. 10
10. 12 11. 10 12. 11 13. 12
14. 12 15. 10 16. 9 17. 10
18. 10 19. 12 20. 9 21. 11

Page 171

9	4	12	0	7	5
+3	+7	-8	+9	-3	+2
12	11	4	9	4	7
-6	-6	-4	+2	+8	-4
6	5	0	11	12	3
-3	+5	+5	-7	-4	-2
=	=	=	=	=	=
3	10	5	4	8	1

Page 168

1. 12 - 3 = 9
2. 11 - 6 = 5
3. 12 - 6 = 6
4. 11 - 8 = 3
5. 11 - 2 = 9
6. 12 - 5 = 7

Page 169

1. 8 2. 3 3. 4
4. 8 5. 5 6. 9
7. 3 8. 4 9. 9
10. 3 11. 6 12. 2 13. 1
14. 7 15. 5 16. 3 17. 6
18. 3 19. 5 20. 7 21. 9

Page 170

1. 11, 11, 9, 2
2. 12, 6
3. 12, 12, 8, 4
4. 11, 11, 6, 5
5. 11, 11, 7, 4
6. 11, 11, 8, 3
7. 12, 12, 3, 9
8. 12, 12, 7, 5

ANSWER KEY

Page 172

1. 11 2. 12 3. 12 4. 11
5. 12 6. 10 7. 11 8. 12
9. 10 10. 12 11. 10 12. 11

Page 173

8	10	3	2	7
+2	-5	+8	+6	-4
10	5	11	8	3
-8	+2	-6	+3	+9
2	7	5	11	12
+7	+5	-5	-4	-8
=	=	=	=	=
9	12	0	7	4
L	I	O	N	S

Page 174

1. 4 + 9 = 13
2. 6 + 7 = 13
3. 7 + 7 = 14
4. 8 + 5 = 13
5. 8 + 6 = 14
6. 9 + 5 = 14

Page 175

1. 11, 11 2. 14, 14
3. 11, 11 4. 10, 10
5. 13, 13 6. 13, 13
7. 10, 10 8. 12, 12
9. 13, 13 10. 14, 14
11. 12, 12 12. 11, 11
13. 12, 12 14. 9, 9

Page 176

1. 14 - 8 = 6
2. 13 - 5 = 8
3. 14 - 7 = 7
4. 14 - 5 = 9
5. 13 - 7 = 6
6. 14 - 6 = 8

Page 177

1. 12 2. 7 3. 5
4. 6 5. 8 6. 14
7. 4 8. 13 9. 5
10. 11 11. 8 12. 12 13. 8 14. 4
15. 8 16. 6 17. 12 18. 8 19. 8

Page 178

1. 7 + 8 = 15
2. 9 + 9 = 18
3. 8 + 8 = 16
4. 9 + 8 = 17
5. 6 + 9 = 15

Page 179

1. 10
5 + 5
4 + 6

2. 11
5 + 6
8 + 3
4 + 7

3. 12
6 + 6

4. 13
6 + 7
4 + 9
10 + 3

5. 14
8 + 6
9 + 5
7 + 7
4 + 10

6. 15
9 + 6
7 + 8
10 + 5

7. 16
10 + 6
9 + 7
8 + 8

8. 17
9 + 8
10 + 7

9. 18
8 + 10
9 + 9

Page 180

+	0	1	2	3	4	5	6	7	8	9
0	0	1	2	3	4	5	6	7	8	9
1	1	2	3	4	5	6	7	8	9	10
2	2	3	4	5	6	7	8	9	10	11
3	3	4	5	6	7	8	9	10	11	12
4	4	5	6	7	8	9	10	11	12	13
5	5	6	7	8	9	10	11	12	13	14
6	6	7	8	9	10	11	12	13	14	15
7	7	8	9	10	11	12	13	14	15	16
8	8	9	10	11	12	13	14	15	16	17
9	9	10	11	12	13	14	15	16	17	18

Page 181

1. 6 2. 4 3. 10
4. 2 5. 12 6. 16
7. 8 8. 14 9. 18
10. 12 11. 6
12. 4 13. 8
14. 2 15. 14

Page 182

1. 9 2. 3 3. 7
4. 13 5. 5 6. 17
7. 15 8. 7 9. 13
10. 17 11. 9
12. 3 13. 13
14. 5 15. 17

Page 183

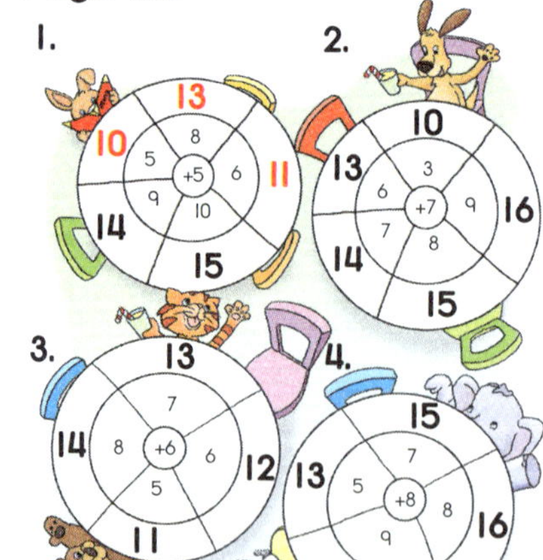

Page 184

1. 16 - 8 = 8
2. 17 - 8 = 9
3. 15 - 9 = 6
4. 18 - 9 = 9
5. 16 - 7 = 9

Page 185

1. 6 2. 8 3. 8 4. 6 5. 6
6. 9 7. 7 8. 7 9. 7 10. 9
11. 5 12. 8 13. 5
14. 3 15. 6
16. 8 17. 3
18. 9 19. 4

Page 186

1. 12
5 + 7 = 12
7 + 5 = 12
12 - 5 = 7
12 - 7 = 5

2. 13
4 + 9 = 13
9 + 4 = 13
13 - 4 = 9
13 - 9 = 4

3. 14
8 + 6 = 14
6 + 8 = 14
14 - 6 = 8
14 - 8 = 6

4. 15
8 + 7 = 15
7 + 8 = 15
15 - 8 = 7
15 - 7 = 8

5. 16
9 + 7 = 16
7 + 9 = 16
16 - 9 = 7
16 - 7 = 9

6. 17
8 + 9 = 17
9 + 8 = 17
17 - 8 = 9
17 - 9 = 8

Page 187

1. 7 2. 6 3. 5 4. 8 5. 9
6. 8 7. 7 8. 6 9. 9 10. 8
11. 7 12. 6 13. 5

Page 188

1. 7 + 3 = 10 2. 5 + 6 = 11 3. 8 + 9 = 17
4. 12 - 8 = 4 5. 18 - 9 = 9 6. 15 - 8 = 7
7. 8 + 1 = 9 8. 11 - 9 = 2 9. 5 + 9 = 14
10. 13 - 8 = 5 11. 14 - 8 = 6 12. 13 - 7 = 6

13. 5
8
6
9

14. 14
11
15
13

15. 7
8
4
2

16. 14
16
15
17

Page 189

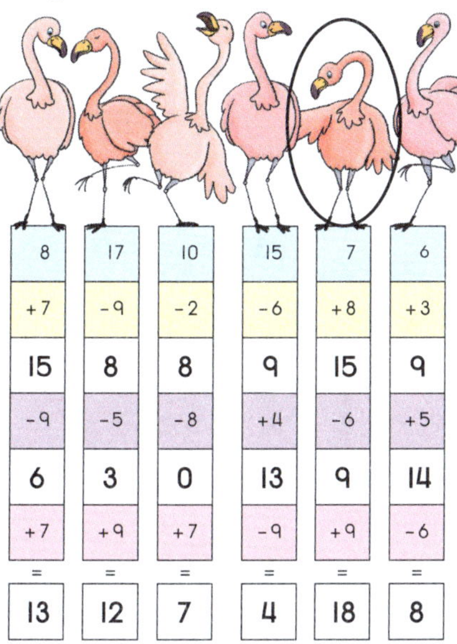

8	17	10	15	7	6
+7	−9	−2	−6	+8	+3
15	8	8	9	15	9
−9	−5	−8	+4	−6	+5
6	3	0	13	9	14
+7	+9	+7	−9	+9	−6
=	=	=	=	=	=
13	12	7	4	18	8

Page 190

1. 67 2. 99 3. 55
4. 79 5. 28 6. 89
7. 79 8. 97 9. 86
10. 98 11. 99 12. 69

Page 191

1. 86 2. 96 3. 78 4. 94
5. 95 6. 97 7. 99 8. 64
9. 81 10. 59 11. 66 12. 68
13. 77 14. 25 15. 70 16. 49
BLUE WHALE

Page 192

1. 55 2. 42 3. 62
4. 73 5. 21 6. 92
7. 25 8. 23 9. 63
10. 36 11. 42 12. 52

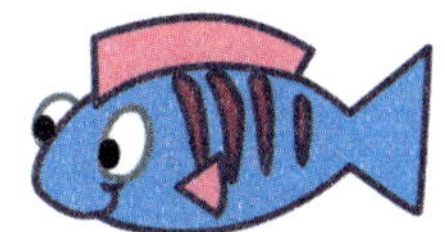

Page 193

1. 22 2. 47 3. 21 4. 21
5. 83 6. 21 7. 46 8. 23
9. 34 10. 40 11. 74 12. 7
13. 23 14. 29 15. 52 16. 84

Page 194

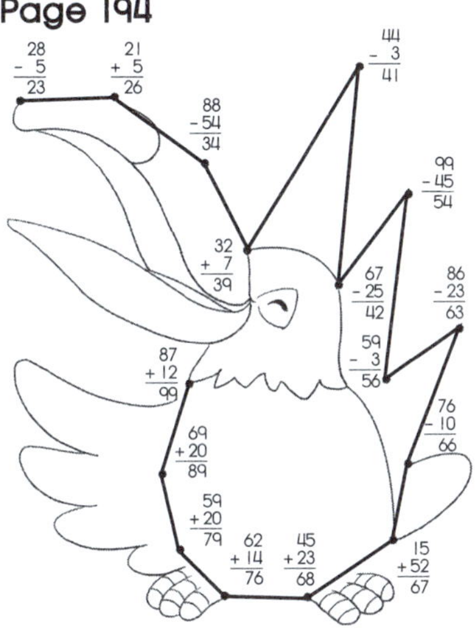

Page 195

Page 196

1. 62 2. 31 3. 40 4. 81
5. 82 6. 80 7. 85 8. 83
9. 85 10. 80 11. 87 12. 80
13. 94 14. 81 15. 92 16. 95

Page 197

1. 66 2. 89 3. 92 4. 88
5. 89 6. 89 7. 71 8. 35
9. 95 10. 68 11. 92 12. 94
13. 50 14. 25 15. 40 16. 65 17. 20

Page 198

1. 48 2. 14 3. 19 4. 16
5. 52 6. 25 7. 5 8. 13
9. 36 10. 29 11. 10 12. 28
13. 12 14. 27 15. 35 16. 20

Page 199

1. 47 2. 59 3. 77 4. 34
5. 18 6. 88 7. 65 8. 29
9. 19 10. 25 11. 9 12. 9
13. 40 14. 9 15. 1 16. 40 17. 18
GIANT SQUID

Page 200

1. 80 2. 27 3. 18 4. 90
5. 25 6. 93 7. 99 8. 50
9. 80 10. 86 11. 46 12. 2
13. 22 14. 72 15. 49 16. 72

Page 201

1. 2	7		2. 8	3. 4		4. 5
5		5. 3		6. 7		3
	7. 7	7			8. 4	
9. 9			10. 7	2		11. 6
12. 3	7		0		13. 3	3

Page 202

1. 892 2. 682 3. 690
4. 795 5. 994 6. 593
7. 893 8. 651 9. 871

Page 203

1. 956 2. 735 3. 912
4. 738 5. 521 6. 919
7. 932 8. 369 9. 851

Page 204

1. 116 2. 207 3. 618
4. 408 5. 315 6. 45
7. 356 8. 407 9. 218

Page 205

1. 316 2. 508 3. 652
4. 814 5. 691 6. 237
7. 833 8. 838 9. 594
10. 107 11. 909 12. 13

Page 206

Sally has the most correct answers
1. ~~97~~ (87) 2. 63 3. ~~493~~ (503)
4. ~~98~~ (48) 5. 46 6. ~~342~~ (331)
7. 64 8. 82 9. 530
10. ~~35~~ (45) 11. 47 12. 329
13. 66 14. ~~86~~ (82) 15. 511
16. 49 17. 33 18. ~~325~~ (315)

Page 207

1. 14 2. 6 3. 16 4. 11
5. 9 6. 8 7. 6 8. 6
9. 16 10. 8 11. 18 12. 9
13. 68 14. 80 15. 79 16. 78
17. 63 18. 66 19. 83 20. 60
21. 31 22. 53 23. 30 24. 20
25. 28 26. 25 27. 7 28. 36
29. 578 30. 661 31. 129 32. 616

ANSWER KEY

Page 208

1. 7, 8, 9, 10, 11, 12
2. 11, 12, 13, 14, 15, 16
3. 15, 16, 17, 18, 19, 20

Page 209

1. 5 2. 9 3. 13
4. 10 5. 17 6. 0
7. 5 8. 12 9. 17
10. 1 11. 18 12. 14
13. 5 14. 17 15. 20
16. 8 17. 19 18. 10

Page 210

1. 8 2. 14 3. 19
4. 10 5. 12 6. 18
7. 13 8. 15 9. 20
10. 7 11. 8 12. 2
13. 11 14. 13 15. 0
16. 9 17. 17 18. 12

Page 211

1. less 2. greater
3. greater 4. less
5. greater 6. greater
7. less 8. less
9. less 10. greater
11. 6
12. 9
13. Answers will vary; ≥ 8, 0–6

Page 212

1. 9 2. 7 3. 8
4. 8 5. 9 6. 10
7. 9 8. 10 9. 10
10. 10; 3 + 7 = 10

Page 213

1. 4 2. 6 3. 2
4. 5 5. 2 6. 6
7. 3 8. 5 9. 5
10. 6; 10 – 4 = 6

Page 214

1. 12, 12, 7, 5
2. 10, 5
3. 3, 9, 6, 6
4. 6, 12
5. 11, 5, 5, 6
6. 4, 11, 7, 11

Page 215

1. 5 + 9 = 14, 9 + 5 = 14, 14 - 5 = 9, 14 - 9 = 5
2. 9 + 6 = 15, 6 + 9 = 15, 15 - 6 = 9, 15 - 9 = 6
3. 7 + 6 = 13, 6 + 7 = 13, 13 - 6 = 7, 13 - 7 = 6
4. 8 + 9 = 17, 9 + 8 = 17, 17 - 8 = 9, 17 - 9 = 8
5. 8 + 6 = 14, 6 + 8 = 14, 14 - 6 = 8, 14 - 8 = 6
6. 7 + 9 = 16, 9 + 7 = 16, 16 - 7 = 9, 16 - 9 = 7

Page 216

1. 9 2. 3 3. 4 4. 4
5. 4 6. 7 7. 5 8. 7
9. 2 10. 8 11. 3 12. 6
13. 3 14. 3 15. 10 16. 10

Page 217

1. 4, 4 2. 6, 6 3. 9, 3
4. 6, 7 5. 7, 8 6. 9, 9
7. 7, 7 8. 7, 7 9. 9, 6
10. 6, 6 11. 9, 8 12. 5, 8

Page 218

13, 12, 7
8, 13, 9
12, 9, 9
8, 14, 15
16, 17, 5
SECRETARY BIRD

Page 219

Set A has more correct answers.

Set A	Set B
15, 12	13, ~~14~~, (16)
6, ~~8~~, (9)	~~6~~, (7), 8
~~14~~, (15), 13	12, ~~13~~, (14)
9, ~~8~~, (9)	~~7~~, (8), 9

Page 220

1. 13 2. 17 3. 16 4. 14
5. 11 6. 18 7. 14 8. 15
9. 17 10. 12 11. 18 12. 16
13. 17 14. 12
15. 15 16. 18
17. 18 18. 20

Page 221

Page 222

1. 1	2. 1		3. 6		4. 1	1
	6			5. 1	4	
6. 1		7. 9		3		8. 1
6			9. 6		10. 1	8
	11. 1	4		12. 1	6	
13. 1	7		14. 1	0		15. 7

Page 223

1. 3, 2; 32
2. 2, 9; 29
3. 8, 7; 87
4. 4, 0; 40
5. 9, 4; 94

Page 224

1. 3, 1; 31
2. 2, 9; 29
3. 1, 7; 17
4. 4, 0; 40
5. 7, 3; 73

ANSWER KEY

Page 225

1. 7 2. 10 3. 8
4. 15 5. 11 6. 18
7. thirteen 8. fourteen
9. nineteen 10. twelve
11. sixteen 12. seventeen

Page 226

1. 3, 5; 35; thirty-five
2. 4, 7; 47; forty-seven
3. 6, 0; 60; sixty
4. 2, 9; 29; twenty-nine
5. 7, 3; 73; seventy-three
6. 9, 2; 92; ninety-two

Page 227

1	11	21	31	41	51	61	71	81	91
2	12	22	32	42	52	62	72	82	92
3	13	23	33	43	53	63	73	83	93
4	14	24	34	44	54	64	74	84	94
5	15	25	35	45	55	65	75	85	95
6	16	26	36	46	56	66	76	86	96
7	17	27	37	47	57	67	77	87	97
8	18	28	38	48	58	68	78	88	98
9	19	29	39	49	59	69	79	89	99
10	20	30	40	50	60	70	80	90	100

Page 228

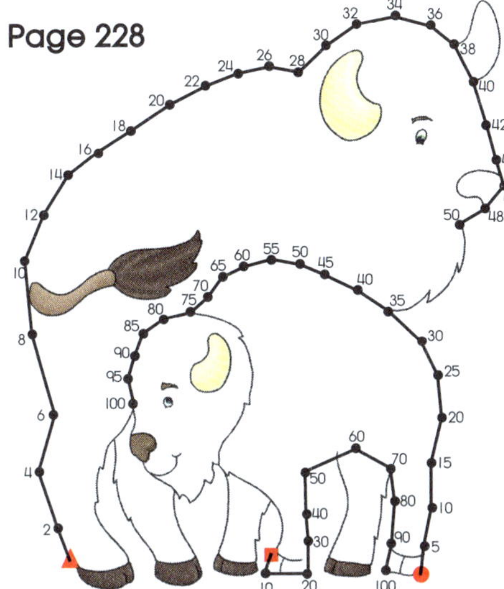

Page 229

1. 23, 25, 27, 29
2. 62, 64, 65, 67, 68, 70
3. 81, 83, 85, 87, 89
4. 37, 39, 41, 42, 44
5. 57, 60, 62, 63, 65
6. 88, 90, 91, 93, 94, 96
7. 42, 40, 38, 37, 35
8. 74, 72, 70, 69, 67, 66

Page 230

1. 33 2. 39 3. 93
4. 70 5. 27 6. 51
7. 28 8. 62 9. 77
10. 41 11. 48 12. 70
13. 47 14. 83 15. 30
16. 68 17. 100 18. 39

Page 231

1. 68 2. 84 3. 93
4. 70 5. 62 6. 88
7. 40 8. 90 9. 62
10. 77 11. 18 12. 20
13. 65 14. 43 15. 63
16. 91 17. 69 18. 28

Page 232

1. 26 < 35
2. 46 > 40
3. < 4. > 5. >
6. > 7. > 8. <
9. < 10. < 11. >

Page 233

1. 10, 12, 15
2. 36, 45, 49
3. 19, 25, 81
4. 18, 24, 36
5. 29, 41, 57
6. 30, 55, 72
7. 26, 56, 66
8. 72, 78, 87

Page 234

1. 4, 2; 42
2. 3, 9; 39
3. 6, 0; 60
4. 5, 3; 53
5. 7, 8, 70
6. 9, 4; 94

Page 235

1. 43 > 34
2. 35 < 37
3. 58 = 58
4. 63 < 90

Page 236

1. > 2. < 3. <
4. = 5. > 6. >
7. > 8. < 9. >
10. > 11. < 12. >
13. > 14. =
15. > 16. =
17. 42

Page 237

1. 11, odd
2. 24, even
3. 33, odd

Page 238

1. 2, 4, 6, 8, 10, 12, 14, 16, 18, 20, 22, 24, 26, 28, 30, 32, 34, 36, 38, 40
2. 0, 2, 4, 6, 8
3. 1, 3, 5, 7, 9
4. odd 5. even 6. even
7. even 8. odd 9. odd
10. 6, 18, 64, 80, 58, 96
11. even; example: 2 + 4 = 6
12. even; example: 3 + 7 = 10
13. odd; example: 3 + 2 = 5

Examples may vary for 11–13.

Page 239

1. 2nd, 4th, 5th, 6th
2. eighth, ninth
3. 3rd, 5th
4. 3
5. Mike
6. Emma

Page 241

	1. 1	2. 9		3. 4	4. 6	
5. 4		6. 3	7. 8		8. 5	9. 7
10. 3	11. 9		12. 7	13. 9		9
	14. 4	15. 9		16. 2	17. 8	
18. 5		19. 2	20. 9		21. 3	22. 6
23. 8	24. 8		25. 4	26. 9		
	9			8		

Page 240

1. GRIN
2. TIME
3. LAND
4. CATS

Page 242

1. 37 2. 75 3. 49 4. 70
5. 58 6. 76 7. 98 8. 89
9. 40 10. 87 11. 98 12. 69
13. 88 14. 55 15. 59 16. 97

Page 243

1. 2 tens 17 ones
   2 tens (1 ten 7 ones)
   → 3 tens 7 ones = 37
2. 6 tens 5 ones = 65
3. 8 tens 1 one = 81
4. 4 tens 9 ones = 49
5. 2 tens 6 ones = 26
6. 8 tens 0 ones = 80
7. 5 tens 9 ones = 59

Page 244

1. 52 2. 35 3. 82 4. 60
5. 60 6. 86 7. 61 8. 93
9. 50 10. 71 11. 91 12. 92

Page 245

1. 6	2. 4		3. 7	4. 8
5. 9	7		6. 8	4
7. 5	8. 9		9. 7	10. 3
11. 4	1		12. 3	8

Page 246

1. 32 2. 51 3. 61 4. 50
5. 43 6. 26 7. 93 8. 73
9. 84 10. 22 11. 67 12. 53

Page 247

1. 33 2. 22
3. 50 4. 6
5. 51 6. 21

Page 248

Page 249

1. 53 = 5 tens 3 ones
   4 tens 13 ones
2. 46 = 4 tens 6 ones
   3 tens 16 ones
3. 81 = 8 tens 1 one
   7 tens 11 ones
4. 39 = 3 tens 9 ones
   2 tens 19 ones
5. 92 = 9 tens 2 ones
   8 tens 12 ones
6. 13 = 1 ten 3 ones
   0 tens 13 ones
7. 60 = 6 tens
   5 tens 10 ones

Page 250

1. 24 2. 56 3. 46 4. 11
5. 25 6. 28 7. 40 8. 39
9. 29 10. 64 11. 28 12. 18

Page 251

1. 2	2. 4		
3. 5	5		
		4. 4	5. 7
		6. 1	6
7. 3	8. 5		
9. 2	3		
		10. 6	11. 3
		12. 3	9

Page 252

1. 31 2. 47 3. 74 4. 28
5. 19 6. 85 7. 50 8. 90
9. 50 10. 18 11. 81 12. 10
13. 87 14. 30 15. 62 16. 2
17. 79 18. 69 19. 68 20. 69

Page 253

72, 77, 77, 81
64, 55, 19, 78
88, 55, 78, 53
19, 19, 66, 97
AFRICAN ELEPHANT

Page 254

1. ### ### ### ///; 18
2. 20
3. 22
4. hamburgers
5. 20 + 18 = 38
6. 22 – 18 = 4
7. 22 + 18 + 20 = 60

Page 255

Bird Color		
Color	Tally	Total
Blue	### ### //	12
Brown	### ###	10
Red	### ////	9

1. blue
2. 10 + 9 = 19
3. 12 – 9 = 3
4. 12 + 10 + 9 = 31

Page 256

Number of Flowers		
Type of Flower	Tally	Total
Daisy	### ### ### ### ### /	26
Rose	### ### ### ### ### ### /	31
Tulip	### ///	8
Sunflower	### ### ###	15

1. tulips
2. 26 + 15 = 41
3. 31 – 8 = 23
4. 26 + 31 + 8 + 15 = 80

Page 257

Name	Tally	Total
John	|||| |||| |||| |||| ||	22
Alan	|||| |||| ||||	15
Nick	|||| |||| |||| |||| ||||	25
Jason	|||| |||| |||| ||||	19

Baseball Card Collections

15, 25, Nick, 40, 6, 81

Page 258

1. 6
2. 12
3. 8
4. cartoons
5. 12 – 6 = 6
6. 12 + 8 = 20
7. 12 + 6 + 8 = 26

Page 259

1. 11
2. 12
3. 12
4. 14
5. Jim
6. Daniel, Megan
7. 14 + 12 = 26

Page 260

1. 4, 6, 8, 10
2. 10
3. 8
4. 4
5. 12 – 6 = 6
6. Count by twos.

Page 261

1. 5 books
2. Count by fives.
3. 20
4. 25
5. Justin
6. 15 + 35 = 50
7. 35 – 25 = 10
8. 15 + 25 + 35 + 20 = 95

Page 262

1. 2 stamps
2. Count by twos.
3. 18
4. 16
5. Lisa
6. Ray
7. 20 – 16 = 4

Page 263

1. 6
2. 7
3. 9
4. summer
5. winter
6. 11 – 7 = 4

Page 264

1. 8
2. 9
3. 6
4. Maria
5. Brad
6. Kim, Jay
7. 6 + 8 + 9 + 8 = 31

Page 265

1. 12
2. 14
3. orange, 18
4. grape, 10
5. 18 – 12 = 6
6. 14 + 10 = 24
7. more than 50
   14 + 18 + 10 + 12 = 54

Page 266

1. 20
2. 25
3. 30
4. ice cream, 35
5. 35 – 20 = 15
6. 20 + 35 = 55

Page 267

1. 25
2. 40
3. grade 3, 45
4. 20 + 25 = 45
5. 45 – 20 = 25
6. less than 50
   20 + 25 = 45

Page 268

1. 15
2. 10
3. 17
4. blue
5. purple
6. 20 + 15 = 35
7. 17 – 10 = 7

Page 269

1. 40
2. 38
3. 22
4. 32
5. summer
6. winter

Page 270

1. 4 hundreds = 400
2. 6 hundreds = 600
3. 8 hundreds = 800
4. 5 hundreds = 500

Page 271

100
200
300
400
500
600
700
800
900
300, 500, 700, 900
200, 400, 600, 700, 800

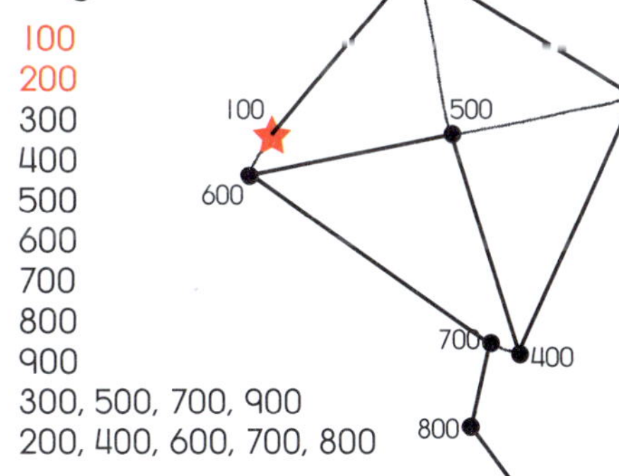

Page 272

1. 3 hundreds 7 tens 4 ones
   374
2. 2 hundreds 5 tens 9 ones
   259
3. 4 hundreds 5 tens 0 ones
   450
4. 6 hundreds 0 tens 4 ones
   604

Page 273

1. 422
2. 280
3. 800
4. 512
5. 180
6. 966
7. 324
8. 678
9. 700
10. 555
11. 90
12. 944
13. 2, 5, 8, 25, 28
    52, 58, 82, 85
    258, 285, 528
    582, 825, 852

Page 274

1. 478
2. 289
3. 333
4. 825
5. 400
6. 899
7. 215
8. 458
9. 570
10. 867
11. 648
12. 444
13. 796

Page 275

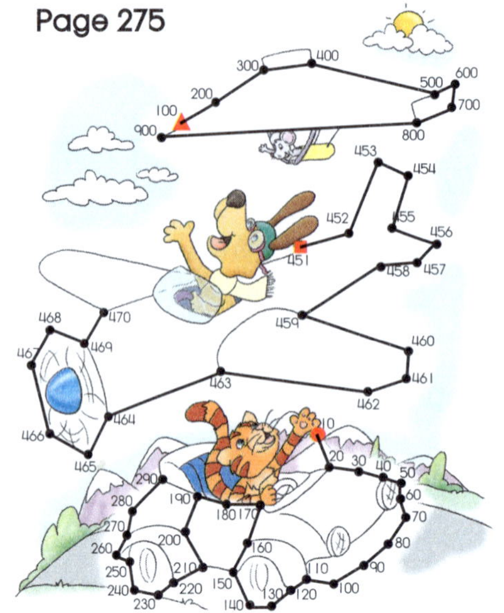

Page 276

1. 344 2. 800 3. 613
4. 110 5. 728 6. 499
7. 164 8. 412 9. 317
10. 241 11. 180 12. 300
13. 135 14. 717 15. 206
16. 651 17. 390 18. 600

Page 277

1. 368 2. 584 3. 903
4. 700 5. 262 6. 878
7. 640 8. 910 9. 565
10. 770 11. 418 12. 532
13. 765 14. 943 15. 639
16. 391 17. 609 18. 728

Page 278

1. 117 2. 109 3. 132 4. 67
5. 107 6. 110 7. 100 8. 150
9. 136 10. 176 11. 110 12. 91
13. 98 14. 121 15. 132 16. 100

Page 279

1. 68 2. 119 3. 104 4. 294
5. 59 6. 120 7. 149 8. 123
9. 99 10. 197
11. 168 12. 84
13. 88 14. 150
15. 146 16. 105

Page 280

1. 783 2. 838 3. 659 4. 579
5. 494 6. 881 7. 607 8. 568
9. 483 10. 862 11. 715 12. 796
13. 521 14. 610 15. 800 16. 801

Page 281

1. 198 2. 267 3. 886 4. 246
5. 451 6. 117 7. 362 8. 264
9. 532 10. 172 11. 775 12. 375
13. 595 14. 485 15. 481 16. 683

Page 282

1. 623 2. 43
3. 526 4. 312
5. 535 6. 222

Page 283

1. 124 2. 801 3. 412 4. 321
5. 350 6. 330 7. 61 8. 504
9. 458 10. 431 11. 207 12. 623
13. 723 14. 117 15. 148 16. 412

Page 284

220, 61, 474
67, 724, 206
328, 759, 675
657, 580, 878
A BLUE BIRD

Page 285

1. 1	2. 2	3. 1		4. 2	5. 7	6. 1
	7. 7	0	6		8. 4	3
9. 6	8	9			4	5
5			10. 7	11. 4		
12. 4	7	0		13. 9	1	3

Page 286

1. 4 + 4 = 8
   2 groups of 4 = 8
   2 x 4 = 8
2. 2 + 2 + 2 + 2 = 8
   4 groups of 2 = 8
   4 x 2 = 8
3. 5 + 5 + 5 = 15
   3 groups of 5 = 15
   3 x 5 = 15
4. 1 + 1 + 1 + 1 = 4
   4 groups of 1 = 4
   4 x 1 = 4

Page 287

1. 8, 4 x 2 = 8
2. 12, 4 x 3 = 12
3. 25, 5 x 5 = 25
4. 12, 3 x 4 = 12
5. 5, 5 x 1 = 5
6. 15, 3 x 5 = 15
7. 9, 3 x 3 = 9
8. 16, 4 x 4 = 16

Page 288

1. 4
   2
   8
   4 x 2 = 8
2. 3
   5
   15
   3 x 5 = 15

Page 289

1. 3 groups
   3 in each group
   9
   3 x 3 = 9
2. 1 group
   4 in the group
   4
   1 x 4 = 4
3. 2 groups
   2 in each group
   4
   2 x 2 = 4
4. 4 groups
   2 in each group
   8
   4 x 2 = 8

Page 290

1. 3 groups
   5 in each group
   15
   3 x 5 = 15
2. 4 groups
   4 in each group
   16
   4 x 4 = 16
3. 2 groups
   5 in each group
   10
   2 x 5 = 10
4. 2 groups
   4 in each group
   8
   2 x 4 = 8
5. 2 groups of 3 eggs

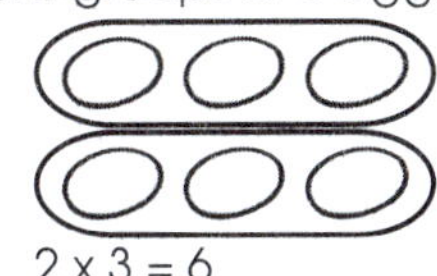

2 x 3 = 6

6. 3 groups of 3 snakes

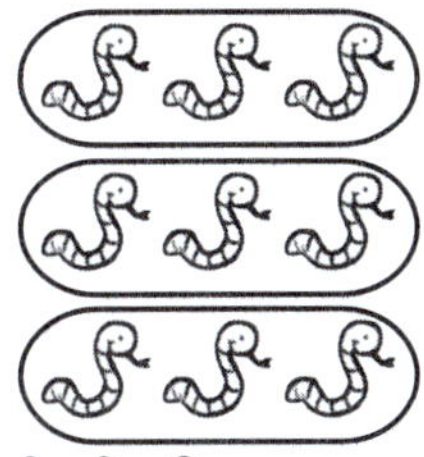

3 x 3 = 9

Page 291

1. 3 x 2 = 6
2. 2 x 2 = 4
3. 2 x 4 = 8
4. 2 x 5 = 10
5. 2 groups of 5 circles

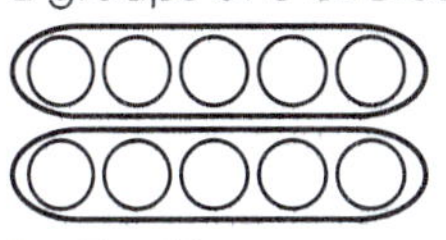

2 x 5 = 10

6. 4 groups of 2 squares

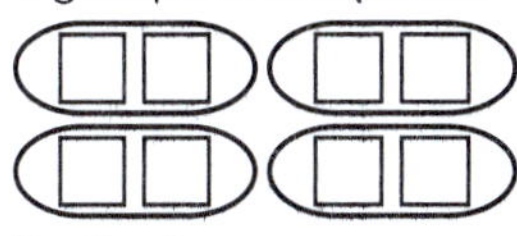

4 x 2 = 8

Page 292

1. 6 2. 9
3. 15 4. 4
5. 8 6. 12
7. 3 8. 10
9. 0 10. 6
11. 2 12. 0

x	0	1	2	3	4	5
2	0	2	4	6	8	10
3	0	3	6	9	12	15

Pattern: Each column goes up by the row number.

Page 293

1. 8 2. 5
3. 15 4. 12
5. 16 6. 0
7. 4 8. 10
9. 20 10. 20
11. 0 12. 25

x	0	1	2	3	4	5
2	0	2	4	6	8	10
3	0	3	6	9	12	15
4	0	4	8	12	16	20
5	0	5	10	15	20	25

Pattern: Each column goes up by the row number.

Page 294

1. 9, 10, 12, 13, 15, 17
2. 44, 46, 48, 50, 51
3. 176, 177, 179, 180, 182, 183
4. 605, 606, 608, 610, 611, 613
5. 20 6. 56 7. 399
8. 98 9. 900 10. 554
11. 17 12. 40 13. 100
14. 139 15. 500 16. 889

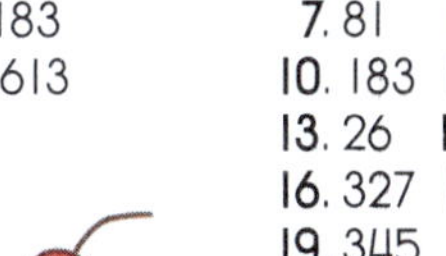

Page 295

1. 20 2. 67 3. 49
4. 100 5. 310 6. 800
7. 81 8. 60 9. 75
10. 183 11. 440 12. 693
13. 26 14. 70 15. 145
16. 327 17. 606 18. 556
19. 345
20. 534

Page 296

1. 4 + 9 = 13
   9 + 4 = 13
   13 − 9 = 4
   13 − 4 = 9
2. 5 + 7 = 12
   7 + 5 = 12
   12 − 5 = 7
   12 − 7 = 5
3. 7 + 9 = 16
   9 + 7 = 16
   16 − 7 = 9
   16 − 9 = 7

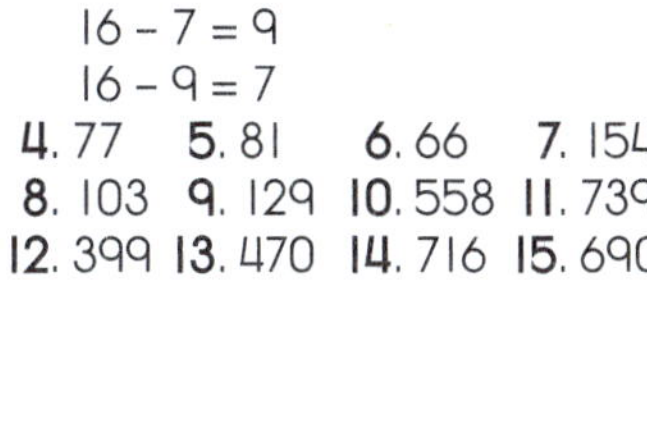

4. 77 5. 81 6. 66 7. 154
8. 103 9. 129 10. 558 11. 739
12. 399 13. 470 14. 716 15. 690

Page 297

1. 43 2. 36 3. 45 4. 38
5. 40 6. 4 7. 224 8. 333
9. 433 10. 426 11. 164 12. 19
13. 99 14. 41 15. 63 16. 299
17. 117 18. 302 19. 742 20. 168
21. 12 22. 10 23. 4
24. 5 25. 20 26. 0

Page 298

1. cookies
2. 6
3. 7 − 4 = 3
4. 20
5. sausage
6. 25

Page 299

Vegetable	Tally	Total
Cabbages	|||| |	6
Carrots	|||| |||| |	11
Ears of Corn	|||| |||	8

1. 11 + 8 = 19
2. 11 − 6 = 5
3. 24
4. 8
5. dog
6. 30 + 15 = 45

Award
Great Job!
Name
finished Big Math 1-2
from
School Zone Publishing Company.
WOOF!